Engaging Musical Practices

A Sourcebook for Middle School General Music

Edited by
Suzanne L. Burton

Published in partnership with
National Association for Music Education

ROWMAN & LITTLEFIELD EDUCATION
A division of
ROWMAN & LITTLEFIELD PUBLISHERS, INC.
Lanham • New York • Toronto • Plymouth, UK

KH

Published in partnership with National Association for Music Education

Published by Rowman & Littlefield Education
A division of Rowman & Littlefield Publishers, Inc.
A wholly owned subsidary of The Rowman & Littlefield Publishing Group, Inc.
4501 Forbes Boulevard, Suite 200, Lanham, Maryland 20706
http://www.rowmaneducation.com

10 Thornbury Road, Plymouth PL6 7PP, United Kingdom

British Library Cataloguing in Publication Information Available

Library of Congress Cataloging-in-Publication Data
Engaging musical practices : a sourcebook for middle school general music / edited by Suzanne L. Burton.
    p. cm.
"Published in partnership with NAFME: National Association for Music Education."
  ISBN 978-1-60709-437-1 (cloth : alk. paper) — ISBN 978-1-60709-438-8 (pbk. : alk. paper) — ISBN 978-1-60709-439-5 (electronic)
  1. School music—Instruction and study—United States. 2. Middle school education—United States. I. Burton, Suzanne L. (Suzanne Louise) II. National Association for Music Education (U.S.)
  MT1.E485 2012
  780.71'273—dc23   2011047816

∞™ The paper used in this publication meets the minimum requirements of American National Standard for Information Sciences—Permanence of Paper for Printed Library Materials, ANSI/NISO Z39.48-1992. Printed in the United States of America

5/1/13

Contents

Tables and Figures

TABLES

FIGURES

Foreword

This is a helpful book on a very important topic. Providing compelling music classes in the middle grades is more than simply important to students. Developing effective programs at this level is also essential to ensure a strong future for music education and music in our culture.

Middle school provides music educators with an opportunity to put the finishing touches on students' core music learning and link them into continuing paths of music making at the high school level. Effective paths (a.k.a. strands) also motivate and empower students to carry their music making beyond the school day and, eventually, beyond the end of their K–12 studies.

National opportunity-to-learn standards as well as best practice call for *every* student to study music at least through grade 8. Ideally, each student should take a core music class in middle school that addresses all of the national or state standards and, in addition, have the opportunity to elect a large ensemble experience such as band, orchestra, or choir. Unfortunately, too many middle grade schools across our country offer music only in the form of an elective large ensemble.

Almost all students are interested in music, and elective large ensembles can be powerful learning opportunities. Unfortunately, the fact that these classes are *elective* means that many students opt out of music instruction because they are simply not interested in making *that* kind of music in *that* type of group. When students do elect such ensembles, the classes are generally too *large* to provide the individual instruction and support necessary to adequately address basic student needs outlined in national and state standards, such as learning to harmonize, improvise, and compose music.

Whether or not music study is required, the best way to ensure that the largest possible number of students *learn* music is to provide engaging music classes in the middle grades that address all of the standards. Furthermore, the best way to ensure that students *maintain* their musical involvement is to engage them in compelling middle school strands that are available as a continuing elective sequence at the high school level.

Following the background chapter about the adolescent learner, and one on ways to reach students with special needs, each chapter of this book presents curriculum options or strands and instructional strategies that can attract, involve, and teach middle grade students. Each approach enables students to learn a wide range of standards. Some chapters focus on format (learning centers), others on media (singing, guitar, percussion, keyboard, steel pan, technology), and still others on content (composition, world music, film scores).

Any music educator interested in reaching and teaching the middle school learner should find many useful ideas in this book. Our profession owes a debt of gratitude to Suzanne Burton for recruiting a talented group of effective music educators willing to share what they have discovered about how we can help today's adolescents become tomorrow's music makers and audiences.

Scott C. Shuler
President, National Association for Music Education

Acknowledgments

For many students, middle school general music may be their last encounter with school music. Middle school general music has the potential reach of a school's entire student body. Therefore, practical and meaningful pedagogical resources are vital when it comes to inspiring these students toward a lifetime of musical endeavors. In this book, there are accessible ways to involve adolescents in active musicking that is relevant to their lives. With a collective passion for providing engaging musical experiences for middle school students, the authors have deftly threaded these concepts throughout the chapters in this book. I would like to thank each of them for saying "yes" to my invitation to contribute. I would also like to acknowledge Korren B. Knapp and Steve Soher for their adept work on the graphics presented in this book, and thank the staff at the National Association for Music Education and Rowman & Littlefield Education for their professionalism and support in seeing *Engaging Musical Practices: A Sourcebook for Middle School General Music* come to fruition.

SLB

Chapter One

Adolescent Development and the General Music Classroom

Krystal L. Rickard McCoy

The developmental phase of adolescence continues to be an intrigue to all who teach. During adolescence, students are often unpredictable in their behavior and eagerly seek to find their role in life. Music educators have a unique opportunity to connect with adolescents and gently guide them into the next phase of their lives. Educators who teach general music are especially important during adolescence, as they are often the only music teachers who sustain contact with all students during middle school. Because the most delicate stages of adolescence occur during middle school, general music teachers with the knowledge and willingness to adapt their music curriculum and teaching methods for the adolescents in their classroom will make a positive impact on the future of their students. This chapter focuses on five specific elements of adolescence: self-identification and self-concept, cognitive traits, social learning, transitioning between social realms, and adolescence in today's society. Each of these elements is followed by suggestions for practical application and curriculum planning in the general music classroom.

Adolescence (from the word *adolescere*, meaning "to grow to maturity") is a turbulent phase of life and a crucial developmental period for students between the ages of thirteen to nineteen (Erikson, 1968). During this time, young people face constant change through biological, psychological, and socially influenced disruptions (Adams, 2000). As early as 1904, Hall described adolescence as a rebirth, when humans become concerned with social responsibility and the welfare of others. With these aspects in mind, school is the perfect environment through which educators can address and cultivate students' positive growth during adolescence (Masia-Warner, Nangle, & Hansen, 2006). However, it is important for teachers who work with adolescents to understand the nature of this transitional period and how these young people learn and interact best.

Adolescents flourish in classrooms where they are able to take responsibility, control their conduct in the classroom, and assist with planning their own instruction. Moreover, adolescents succeed when they are able to achieve in a safe environment (Blair & Jones, 1964). When presented with opportunities to gain autonomy, achieve goals, and receive recognition, adolescents' development will progress in a successful manner.

SELF-IDENTIFICATION AND SELF-CONCEPT

During adolescence, students are constantly engaged in a complex process of self-identification. Positive self-identification occurs when students are surrounded by supportive learning opportunities. Adolescents observe adults in their lives when forming their identities, looking past the influence of their parents or caregivers. They focus on other adult role models such as a teacher or a friend of the family. The social environment of school provides many outlets for different types of exposure to adults and personal experiences. Erikson (1968) addressed adolescence in his stages of personality development. According to Erikson, the fifth stage of development, or adolescence, occurs when young people begin to collect and integrate their personal experiences to develop their own sense of personal identity. Erikson claimed that the process of personal identification is best facilitated when young people are willful, trusted by others, and have opportunities to be industrious and autonomous.

Adolescents' personal experiences, as first addressed by Erikson, have been further defined by self-concept theorists. Marcia (1966), whose research was based on Erikson, recognized that the most successful adolescents are those who have committed themselves to achieving goals. Marcia called these adolescents *identity achievers*. As O'Dea (2003) acknowledged, adolescents construct their concept of self through social acceptance, academic and athletic competence, and romantic appeal. Because young musicians in middle school are searching to find a place within the world's musical culture and desiring to establish a musical identity (Gembris, 2002), the general music classroom can provide a haven where students are able to achieve personal musical goals while developing their individual self-concepts. Programs that focus on the positive development of identity and self-esteem in adolescents have been noted to be successful, especially when students are provided with opportunities to thrive in non-competitive environments (O'Dea, 2003).

Adolescents search for ways to develop self-control when assuming their musical identities. As they become more autonomous, they require more freedom in the music classroom and less strict guidance from teachers (Grimmer, cited in Gembris, 2002). How can music teachers address these needs in adolescence? What types of activities will allow students to experience musical freedom within the "confines" of a teacher-facilitated classroom?

In order to further the musical learning of adolescents, the musical perspective that students bring to the classroom should be taken into consideration. Classroom activities that focus on individual experience and preference in music will open the doors to further musical identity development. Projects that address topics such as "My Musical Self" or "My Music Play List" allow students to contribute to the music classroom as individuals. Once music teachers recognize their students' personal musical identities and preferences, they can assist their students in further development and refinement of their musical preferences and identities. This process will help to establish an environment of musical respect, one in which music teachers honor the music that adolescents connect to, and one through which students can be guided in meaningful self-exploration and identification in music.

One example of assisting the formation of a meaningful self-identity is to develop a unit titled "Creating My Musical Identity." The objective of this unit is to guide students through an independent exploration of many varied and diverse types of music. Listening stations are an excellent way to foster independent exploration of music in the opening stages of such a unit and provide a means for adolescents to develop an expansive listening vocabulary. Adolescents should then be given many opportunities to make musical decisions throughout their general music experience.

COGNITIVE TRAITS

The evolving self-concept of an adolescent is influenced by the continuous development of the brain. The structures of the brain experience a major transition during adolescence. Traits such as the ability to remember and depth perception are fully developed by adolescence. However, intellectual development continues past adolescence and relies upon the motivation of each individual for advancement. Steinberg (1989) explained the specific differences between the brain of a child and that of an adolescent by declaring three differences. First, adolescents are able to consider that which is possible; they are able to see beyond reality. Second, adolescents are able to think through hypotheses with clarity in foresight. Finally, adolescents are better able to analyze abstract concepts.

Piaget (1928) classified adolescent cognitive development as formal operational thinking. Formal thought occurs when adolescents are able to think comprehensively and in an abstract manner. During this time, reality can become second to possibility with thoughts oriented toward the future. In fact, Piaget viewed adolescents as scientists, trying to construct their own understanding of the world. According to Piaget, adolescents use intellectual activity or cognition to adapt and survive on a daily basis. Disequilibrium occurs in the adolescent when he or she is unable to use existing cognitive structures to solve a problem. The disequilibrium caused by *cognitive conflict* instigates the modification of existent cognitive structures. Cognitive structures are continually being refined, improved, and revised during adolescence. The more differentiated and integrated cognitive structures are, the better they are able to aid in a student's adaptation to the environment or in development of problem-solving skills (Berzonsky, 2000).

Another important function of the adolescent brain is metacognition. Metacognition occurs when adolescents consider and revise their own thinking process. According to Elkind (1967), this may be a negative factor when considering the brain's development because adolescents focus on themselves and become engrossed with their own perspectives. However, these developments in the adolescent brain open a world of possibilities in the general music classroom. Self-reflection and self-assessment can be very effective in adolescents' musical development. Because adolescents crave opportunities where they can become experts of a situation, activities such as peer- and self-evaluation, creating concert evaluations, or writing performance reviews provide meaningful activities for reflection and evaluation that call upon the use of higher-order cognitive skills.

Audiation provides another compelling way for adolescents to harness their musical brainpower. Audiation (Gordon, 2007) occurs when the human mind gives syntactical meaning to music. By using the mind to consider musical expression, adolescents exercise their formal operational thinking. When presented with opportunities for improvising and composing music, young musicians use their audiation and become "musical scientists" as they play with different possibilities of musical outcomes. Such activities encourage adolescents to apply their already developed and newly formed cognitive abilities in the musical classroom.

SOCIAL LEARNING

Adolescents develop through a social sense of awareness as well. On a daily basis they move from one social setting to another. The school and community that surround adolescents provide much of their social life. Adolescents no longer accept the school environment, their teachers, or their parents in categorical terms, with adults in the school setting viewed as remote and out of touch. In some circumstances, adolescents will reject the values of parents or teachers just to assert their independence. Typically, a dichotomy exists in middle schools: these young people place a high value on their social connectivity, and yet they are often prohibited from communicating with one another in most school settings (Rathunde & Csikszentmihalyi, 2005). Structuring musical activities that foster intercommunication among adolescents (such as the use of cooperative learning techniques) may yield more positive results over the traditional, teacher-led classroom. Bandura (1986) noted the importance of social situations for learning and introduced the concept of observational learning. This type of learning occurs when students emulate the behavior they have learned by observing other students in social environments. When designing activities for students' musical engagement, the use of peer modeling as an instructional strategy should be kept in mind.

Montessori (1976) developed an educational philosophy based on the social learning of students. She claimed that adolescence is the development of self within the context of others. Even though most of her philosophy dominates early education, there are middle schools that implement her teaching philosophy. Montessori believed that many schools treat children poorly by not allowing them to explore their interests in a supportive and collaborative social environment. In a study conducted by Rathunde and Csikszentmihalyi (2005), middle schools applying the Montessori philosophy were compared with those using a traditional curriculum. Rathunde and Csikszentmihalyi (2005, p. 348) observed that the Montessori middle schools

1. had an explicit philosophy of intrinsic motivation that emphasized spontaneous concentration and freedom within discipline (i.e., the school was clearly based on Maria Montessori's extensive writings);
2. provided students with significant unstructured time for self-directed work (an average of approximately two hours per day) and did not use the typical block period organization (e.g., forty-five or fifty minutes per subject);
3. did not employ mandatory grading or standardized testing for comparative purposes and student placements;
4. had formalized opportunities for students to play a role in daily decisions that affected the school (e.g., curriculum choices, school purchases, destination of field trips, etc.); and
5. infrequently used whole-class lecture formats and instead encouraged students to work individually or collaboratively in smaller groups.

The Montessori students in this study spent more time with academic tasks and learning pursuits. Montessori students also tended to favor their schools and classmates more than the traditional middle school students.

Social learning in the music classroom is often taken for granted, especially when one is working with ensembles. The general music setting provides many important social opportunities for adolescents. Music teachers can integrate group work and student-led activities into their classroom approach. Incorporating group activities that involve students working together to solve a musical problem, invent a musical creation, or arrange a passage of music allow students to experience an interface of musical and social interaction. Furthering this concept, students should present their collaborative work for their peers in the spirit of sharing and positive critique. The possibilities of group work and presentation are endless and fulfill the adolescent need to be social and in control.

TRANSITIONING BETWEEN SOCIAL REALMS

A further look into social contexts leads one to consider the various social settings that adolescents find themselves in. Researchers have considered the transition adolescents must negotiate when moving from one social setting to another. According to Phelan, Davidson, and Cao (1991), little attempt has been made to explain how the multiple social worlds of an adolescent interact with one another. Moreover, little has also been done to assist adolescents with transitioning between social settings. One study was conducted to assess adolescents who act as mediators in these situations and how they function during social transitions (Phelan, Davidson, & Cao, 1991). The researchers concluded that by working to understand the multiple social worlds of adolescents, educators could facilitate each student's transition among the social worlds inside and outside of school more effectively. They determined that teachers should work to provide "boundary-crossing" opportunities for students in their classrooms. In crossing these boundaries or worlds, students learn to work in varying environments where differences are valued and respected, not feared.

Müler (cited in Gembris, 2002) addressed social settings in the world of music. He termed an adolescent's attempt to create individual meaning from multiple influences in an informal setting *self-socialization*. This development takes place outside of the typical school setting and within the culture of youth itself. Interestingly, research conducted by LeBlanc (1991) demonstrated a decrease in the willingness to listen to the music of others in the beginning of adolescence. With this knowledge, music teachers can facilitate the boundary-crossing activities that occur outside of the classroom. Along with relevant music related to the students' socio-cultural environment, music teachers can surround their students with unfamiliar music from a variety of cultures. Once an environment of communication and respect is created in the classroom, teachers should begin to establish safe routes for students to transition from one musical culture to another. Even more importantly, teachers can aid students in making musical connections between these cultures.

The surrounding community is ideal for providing a variety of musical cultures for students' self-socialization in the music classroom. General music teachers can create lessons or units that directly involve community members and musical groups of differing ages and cultures. Inviting musical guests into the classroom to discuss their musical journeys provides adolescents with important insight into the transition from classroom music to informal music making. Music teachers who acknowledge that music lives outside of their classroom will help students to negotiate between multiple musical worlds. A unit centered on the theme "The Music That Surrounds Me" could be incorporated into the classroom to further students' cultural awareness. During this unit, students keep a listening journal of music that they encounter outside of the classroom. In this journal they identify the style of music and its association with a specific event, culture, or generation. From this journal project, students select the music they would like to know more about and, in small groups, plan an event to host a community artist for a demonstration or a workshop. Assisting students in learning how to transition successfully between various musical worlds can be accomplished with a connection to the community.

ADOLESCENCE IN TODAY'S SOCIETY

With all previous information considered, we now view today's world through the eyes of the adolescent. With an apparent disconnect between adults and adolescents in our culture (Richardson, 2004), these young people face an inconceivable amount of outside influences that impact their developmental well-being on a daily basis. In current society, advertisers have realized the great economic power of adolescents in relationship to the consumer market on personal services, entertainment, educational training systems, and pop culture. Adolescents drive many consumer trends with their spending clout (Adams, 2000; Mintel, 2004).

In addition, adolescents' social worlds are much larger and often more important than their family life and school. The social world in which they live is primarily fulfilled through electronic means and surpasses face-to-face interaction. At one time, adults in the local community primarily influenced adolescents. With today's technology, adolescents can actively seek adult role models that could be located anywhere in the world. It is almost effortless for adolescents to make personal connections over the Internet through Skype, social networking sites, blogs, and cell phone technology.

The effects of these consumer and technological changes were predicted by the famous anthropologist Margaret Mead (1970), who suggested that adolescents were coming into power in the contemporary world. Mead (1970) declared three different types of societies in which humans exist. Today we are living in what Mead deemed the "prefigurative culture." This culture contains rapid technological and social changes. The parents and teachers in this type of culture claim to be interested in preparing their youth for the future but have no specific knowledge of what will be required in this future. Opportunities are constantly changing in a prefigurative culture. Effective education in a prefigurative culture succeeds when teachers focus on teaching students *how*: how to think, how to solve problems, how to evaluate, and how to adapt in an effective manner (Berzonzky, 2000). Teaching students *what* to think, believe, or value is simply ineffective during the present day because of the many available sociocultural and commercial influences on adolescents.

General music teachers should acknowledge that adolescents have exposure to many outlets of knowledge and communication through various aspects of technology. They have the ability to make a recording or create a video and instantaneously share it with the world. General music teachers should recognize this ability and make use of technology in the classroom through various creative projects and activities. For instance, students could easily record music for self-reflection or group evaluation. Class projects could be constructed in video format. Blogs or discussion questions could be posted by general music teachers on the school website to encourage students to consider concepts outside of the classroom, by way of an electronic format. There is much that can be done to guide the music education of our adolescents with the responsible educational use of technology and the Internet.

Every day, adolescents are faced with the influences of media, technology, and innumerable social situations. These students are often experiencing transitions from one social realm, with its specific modes of operating and coping, to another as they move throughout their days. The cognitive structures developed by these young people help them to survive and adapt to these changes. They are constantly challenged with the need to develop their identities amid a myriad of daily influences and distractions. Music teachers have an important window of opportunity through which to guide adolescents successfully into the next phase of their lives. All of the practical application suggestions in this chapter are provided as starting points for personal exploration of each general music teacher within his or her classroom. In the end, adolescent music students will benefit greatly from teachers who provide meaningful musical opportunities at a crucial point in the personal and social development of their students.

REFERENCES

Adams, G. (Ed.). (2000). *Adolescent development: The essential readings.* Malden, MA: Blackwell.

Bandura, A. (1986). *Social foundations of thought and action: A social cognitive theory.* Englewood Cliffs, NJ: Prentice-Hall.

Berzonsky, M. D. (2000). Theories of adolescence. In G. Adams (Ed.), *Adolescent development: The essential readings* (pp. 11–27). Malden, MA: Blackwell.

Blair, L. M., & Jones, S. (1964). *Psychology of adolescence for teachers.* New York, NY: Macmillan.

Elkind, D. (1967). Egocentrism in adolescence. *Child Development, 38,* 1025–38.

Erikson, E. H. (1968). *Identity, youth and crisis.* New York, NY: W. W. Norton.

Gembris, H. (2002). The development of musical abilities. In R. Colwell & C. Richardson (Eds.), *The new handbook of research on music teaching and learning* (pp. 487–508). New York, NY: Oxford University Press.

Gordon, E. E. (2007). *Learning sequences in music: A contemporary music learning theory.* Chicago, IL: GIA.

Hall, G. S. (1904). *Adolescence* (Vol. 1–2). New York, NY: Appleton.

LeBlanc, A. (1991). *Effect of maturation/age on music listening preference: A review of literature.* Paper presented at the Ninth National Symposium on Research in Music Behavior, Cannon Beach, OR.

Marcia, J. E. (1966). Development and validation of ego identity status. *Journal of Personality and Social Psychology, 3,* 551–58.

Masia-Warner, C., Nangle, D. W., & Hansen, D. J. (2006). Bringing evidence-based child mental health services to the schools: General issues and specific populations. *Education & Treatment of Children, 29,* 165–72.

Mead, M. (1970). *Culture and commitment.* New York, NY: Doubleday.

Mintel. (2004). Teen spending estimated to top $190 billion by 2006. *Market Research World.* Retrieved from www.marketresearchworld.net/index,php?option=com_content&task=view&id=615

Montessori, M. (1976). *From childhood to adolescence* (2nd ed.). New York, NY: Schocken.

O'Dea, J. A. (2003). Self-concept, weight issues and body image in children and adolescents. In T. Prester (Ed.), *Psychology of adolescents* (pp. 87–119). New York, NY: Nova Science.

Phelan, P., Davidson, A. L., & Cao, H. T. (1991). Students' multiple worlds: Negotiating the boundaries of family, peer, and school cultures. *Anthropology & Education Quarterly, 22*(3), 224–50.

Piaget, J. (1928). *Judgment and reasoning in the child.* New York, NY: Harcourt Brace Jovanovich.

Rathunde, K., & Csikszentmihalyi, M. (2005). The social context of middle school: Teachers, friends, and activities in Montessori and traditional school environments. *Elementary School Journal, 106*(1), 60–79.

Richardson, R. A. (2004). Early adolescence talking points: Questions that middle school students want to ask their parents. *Family Relations, 53*(1), 87–94.

Steinberg, L. (1989). *Adolescence* (2nd ed.). New York, NY: Alfred A. Knopf.

Chapter Two

Making It Happen: Creative Pedagogy for Learners with Special Needs

Deborah V. Blair

When a learner has a special need, it can become a barrier to her full inclusion in the music classroom (Jellison, 2006), or it can become a non-issue. When learners are in school settings, it is the responsibility of the teacher to creatively find a way to make the music room a place where music can be fully experienced by *everyone*—not just the students who really like music or are intuitively *good at it*, nor just those students who are well behaved, have good eye-hand coordination, a good ear, or can quickly decode musical notation. Everyone. How every student is enabled to engage in relevant and meaningful music experiences is the responsibility of the teacher—you!

This is an overwhelming responsibility, yet it is part of our role as teachers. Many of us are unprepared for creating fully inclusive learning environments or for accommodating the wide range of strengths and challenges that our students may have. This chapter will not attempt to address every type of challenge that you may face. Instead, we will look at some examples of music classrooms where student challenges have been met with some success. With these examples, you will be encouraged to creatively consider new ways to meet the needs of your students, to find ways to remove barriers that restrict musical and social interaction, and to see the music room through the eyes of your learners—as a place where they can be valued for their individual and collective musicianship and for their contributions to the music learning community of which each is a special part.

JUST GET ME THROUGH THE DAY

While we may have specific educational goals for our music students, some students use every ounce of their energy to get through the school day without incident. Their Individualized Education Plans (IEPs) include goals such as *improve social interaction, understand nonverbal communication,* or *learn to express emotions,* and meeting these goals is certainly possible within the realm of arts education. Accommodations in the IEP may include using visual rather than written instructional support or providing a structured class setting. The creative and seemingly free-flowing nature of a musical classroom may create considerable stress for students who need structured, predictable settings in order to thrive.

The goals and accommodations described here may also be appropriate for students on the autism spectrum. Students with autism may have curricular goals that seem to have little connection to the national standards for music. This is not to suggest that students with autism cannot grow musically in skill or understanding. Nor does it suggest that you are not pedagogically bound to find ways to include students on the autism spectrum in musical experiences. On the contrary, information found in an IEP (or information shared by the student's teacher or parent) will help you to better understand the barriers that may prevent middle school students from successful inclusion—barriers that you can now work to remove while proactively finding ways to provide children with autism with additional appropriate support.

It is a sultry day in early September. Paul's class is coming to music, but he feels assured that he knows what to expect. Yesterday he met with the teacher, Ms. Anders, and together they walked down the hallway from his new classroom, around the corner by the gym, to the music room. Ms. Anders allowed him to walk around the room, to touch the instruments that intrigued him, and to decide where in the music room he would like to sit. It would be his place every time he comes to music. Paul chose an area where he can see the music schedule and the clock. He likes knowing what will come next and how much time remains until music is over. After Paul visited the classroom, he practiced walking back to his classroom. It had seemed very far away when coming to the classroom, but now he realizes that it is just around the corner. Knowing where the music class is and that he will always return to his own classroom is important to Paul. The stress of "not knowing what will happen next" can sometimes be unbearable.

Now, entering the music room with his classmates, he settles into his seat and looks at the music schedule. There are pictures next to each item that let him know what to expect within the fifty minutes of class time. Paul's reading skills are below grade level, and in order to help Paul quickly make sense of the schedule, Ms. Anders has included teen-friendly pictures that provide Paul and his classmates with cues about the upcoming lesson.

Paul sees that they will be doing some drumming today and that they will be singing "Take Time in Life."[1] Paul is relieved because he knows this song even though it is new for his classmates. Ms. Anders provided Paul and his family with recordings of several songs that the sixth graders would be learning this year so that he could listen to them at home. The familiarity enabled him to enjoy the music and to not worry about new sounds, about not being able to read the lyrics, and about not knowing what might happen musically. Paul loves music, and making music with his peers is an important part of feeling—of being—included.

Paul's music teacher, Ms. Anders, also felt much less worried about Paul coming to music class. Last year, she sensed a breakthrough after several consultations with Paul's classroom teacher and the district's exceptionalities specialist. Instead of regular outbursts, Paul seems comfortable in his class and with his peers. His level of musical engagement had improved dramatically, and while not everything was perfect, it was now a joy to have Paul come to music. To see him included musically and socially made it worth the extra effort to accommodate Paul's needs. After visiting Paul in his own classroom, Ms. Anders's efforts seemed small compared to the extraordinary effort Paul made every day to *just get through the day*.

GETTING THE HELP YOU NEED

Sometimes students like Paul can be so disruptive that teachers begin to dislike or become annoyed by them. Teachers may feel as though the student continually undermines *their* lesson. With well over two hundred students in her middle school music classes, Ms. Anders could very easily have decided she *didn't have time* to worry about Paul. In actuality, Ms. Anders was beginning to feel that she was at her own breaking point with Paul. How did this change?

A very important first step was realizing that she could be doing more with and for Paul but that *she needed help* to figure out what that might be. She consulted[2] with Paul's other teachers and with specialists who had a better understanding of Paul's strengths and challenges. They provided her with a copy[3] of Paul's IEP and explained the technical terminology. Ms. Anders learned about the strategies that Paul's classroom teacher used in her classroom and found ways to include the same strategies in the music classroom, both for consistency and for enabling Paul to be successful. These support professionals seemed to genuinely appreciate her interest in Paul's success and Ms. Anders left the meeting feeling like she was part of a team.

Most importantly, Ms. Anders used her preparation time to visit Paul's classroom, to see what barriers existed for him before school, during class, at lunch, and other points in the day. She also saw that Paul had strengths that she was not aware of but now were visible as she created extra opportunities for interaction with him. In her class, there were thirty other students for whom she also provided music instruction. Of course, the large number of students limited her ability to focus on Paul and how she might better serve his musical needs. Yet the extra time spent with Paul outside of music class provided her with information that enabled a deeper sense of trust between her and Paul. Their one-on-one time became the key to his sense of security when in music with his peers.

What did Ms. Anders learn? The autism spectrum covers a wide range of characteristics, and no child has the same range or combination of strengths and challenges. Paul did not have significant cognitive challenges. Written words were a challenge, but he understood ideas conceptually. Thus, his classroom teacher relied on pictures and iconic representation for helping Paul in his schoolwork. Ms. Anders realized that the graphic representation she sometimes used for melodic contour was a good strategy, but perhaps she could now be more intentional in her use of it, or use it more often. Because written words were a challenge, she realized decoding musical notation might be an unnecessary barrier for him, so she began to offer both musical notation and iconic representation for songs or pieces of music. By providing this option for everyone, Ms. Anders was incorporating *universal design*; that is, she designed this aspect of her instruction to seamlessly provide support for all of her students without singling out a student and his special need.

The need for predictability and structure was important for Paul's social success. When visiting his classroom, Ms. Anders noticed that his classroom teacher wrote the schedule on the board for the entire class—more evidence of universal design. Not all of her students needed this support to cope with a long school day, but they all seemed to appreciate knowing the schedule. Conversely, Paul did require this extra support, and it helped alleviate his fear of not knowing what would happen next. While the teacher cannot predict everything, this small accommodation did much to improve Paul's school day. *I can do that!* Miss Anders thought. She went back to her computer, found music activity icons online,[4] and created a music schedule for Paul. Knowing that something new might be unsettling, she visited his classroom before the next music class to show him the chart, explained the activities the pictures represented, and took time to answer his questions.

Ms. Anders remembered that Paul had never had a successful concert experience. To enable future success, she wrote a teen-friendly social story[5] for what might happen at a concert (see figure 2.1).

Applause and flashing cameras are the epitome of unpredictability, startling the senses, which can be a particular struggle for some children with autism. Standing on risers in close social contact was a stretch for Paul's coping skills. Practicing this ahead of time and reading about it in the social story

Performing in a Concert

I will go to school for the concert.	school	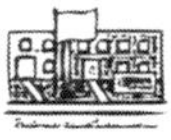
I will go to my classroom at 6:45 p.m.	classroom	
The teacher will line us up in concert order.	line up	
We'll walk down to the gym and get on the risers.	risers	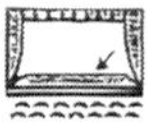
We will sing our songs for our parents and guests.	sing	
The audience will clap when we are finished.	clap	
People will take our picture.	take pictures	
I will go home with my parents after the concert.	home	

Figure 2.1. Performing in a Concert

did much to alleviate his fears (he had a copy of this custom concert story at home and a copy at school).

Not to be overlooked is the love and respect that you, the teacher, can model in your classroom for your student on the autism spectrum. While the inability to read social cues and body language may lead to amusing situations for very young children, it can lead to painful experiences, including bullying, for older students as peers begin to notice that somehow, this student is different. Your efforts to find ways to remove the barriers that prevent successful social inclusion will do much to connect the learner to his peers.

The strategies that Ms. Anders put into place may work for your students, or you may need to find additional strategies because each child is unique. *Don't give up.* As Hourigan and Hourigan (2009) share, finding and implementing strategies takes "time, patience, and practice" (p. 41). Not only will the student improve, but you will, too, as you develop your own teaching practice. Learn about your students' strengths and challenges, talk to specialists and other teachers, and, most importantly, talk to your student and find out what he thinks would help.

BEYOND *SIT STILL AND BE QUIET!*

Students with attention deficit hyperactivity disorder (ADHD) struggle with appropriate school behavior—where *sit still and be quiet* is still the norm. Unfortunately, many teachers equate quiet classrooms with successful classroom management. Many middle school students with ADHD are bright and creative students, yet the inability to focus or sustain attention, to organize work, or, if completed, to turn it in to the teacher, may hamper the students' success in academic settings. Impulsivity, both verbal and kinesthetic, may become bothersome to teachers and eventually frustrate peers.

Unless a student has additional challenges, most students with ADHD are fully included in schools; it is common for a single classroom to have multiple students with ADHD. By middle school, many of these students may have been diagnosed with ADHD and careful monitoring of appropriate medication may be in progress. Students with ADHD benefit from structured environments where teachers and parents support the learner in focusing strategies and organizational skills. All students have to learn how to organize their lives, and middle school is often the first environment where they are personally accountable for planners, assignments, and schedules (not to mention multiple classroom settings with different rules and expectations in each room). This can be overwhelming for students with ADHD. It may seem as though the student does not care, but do not let this fool you. Like other students, they want to be successful: he or she may put up a front of not caring in order to save face with self or peers after years of unsuccessful classroom experiences.

Explore ways to unobtrusively help your student find strategies to be successful. A website for your program is an example of universal design. It can help your students (and parents/caregivers) remember performance dates, assignments, and other important class-related information. Collaborate with classroom teachers to bookmark your webpage on their classroom computers and send the URL link home to parents. Make positive professional connections with your students' parents so that you can work together to support their child's success. *Don't give up.* Do what you know is in the child's best musical interests. It will take extra time, extra energy, and creative planning, just like everything else in life that is worth doing.

In the classroom, you will need to help students with ADHD learn how to self-regulate their behavior. This is a collaborative process, and your students need the entire school community to support them in their efforts. Going through a school day knowing that you annoy everyone around you is not a happy way for a middle school student to live. Students with ADHD can become immune to external behavior plans and no number of checks on the board next to their name will improve their behavior, but it will deepen the descent into poor self-esteem and feelings of being intrinsically *bad*.

Consider Sonja's story of Tyler.[6] Sonja is an elementary general music teacher who confided that she was *so frustrated* with Tyler that she did not know what to do. Indeed, she seemed to be at the end of her rope. But after spending time with Tyler in his classroom, at lunch, and during his gym class (her preparation time), Sonja began to *see school* through Tyler's eyes. Although Tyler is a second grade student, learning from Sonja's experience will be helpful for music teachers of students of any age. Here, she describes her changing perspective of Tyler.

> *Tyler doesn't like school very much. He says he gets in trouble a lot. Tyler is in second grade and has ADHD. He is not on medication. I had the opportunity to spend some time observing Tyler in his regular classroom and in gym class. What I witnessed truly opened my eyes to what life at school is like for Tyler. It gave me a renewed empathy and understanding towards all children dealing with ADHD.*
>
> *My perspective of Tyler before shadowing him was that he is very bright, very talkative, very needy, and always interrupts. He does, however, always volunteer to answer questions or to be a helper. He never sits still; he stands when others are sitting and walks around the room. He is easily distracted and is, himself, a distraction to others. He seems to be easily bored.*
>
> *What a difference a day makes! I decided to shadow Tyler and I'm now in his classroom at the beginning of the day. The time is 9:05 and Tyler sits at his table busily doing his board work. He works at a very fast pace, almost scribbling the words on paper, as if he is on fast forward. He is clearly concentrating on his work.*

The teacher calls to Tyler, "Go give yourself a check. You didn't put your name by your lunch choice." (Evidently, this is a classroom rule.) Tyler is engrossed in his work and does not hear the teacher who calls his name again. "Tyler, why didn't you put your name next to a lunch choice?" Tyler looks up from his work: "What? Oh, I forgot."

Tyler receives his first check of the day.

Ten minutes later, after the announcements came on the classroom television, the TV makes an abrupt noise, to which Tyler blurts out, "The TV farted!"

Tyler receives a second check. The time is 9:15 a.m. and Tyler already has two checks by his name. One more check and he will receive a pink slip.

Tyler is in gym class, with a substitute teacher. The gym is loud and it is time to line up. Tyler gets to the front of the line first but Eric goes to open the door. Tyler yells, "No, Eric, you're not first!" Eric goes and sits by the wall and begins to cry. Tyler hurt his feelings by yelling. Eric tells on Tyler, and the substitute teacher, seeing that Eric has been crying, gives Tyler a check.

This is his third check of the day. Tyler will be given a pink slip.

As the class walks to music, their next class, I accompany Eric and Tyler. Tyler gives me his side of the story: Eric wasn't following the rules. If you are first in line, then you get to hold the door. That is the rule. Eric wasn't following directions, while Tyler was, and he wanted to be the one to hold the door. After all, he had reached the front of the line first. Tyler had done it the right way. Eric didn't like being yelled at.

Tyler was completely frustrated by this. He did not think he had "yelled" at Eric. Tyler said, "You know why I always talk loud? It's because it sounds like there are 10 or 17 TVs on at max volume." "Eric is sensitive," I told Tyler. "Maybe you can be more careful when you talk to him."

"I already have two pink slips from when Eric has told on me!" Tyler clearly has no patience for Eric. "I have nine pink slips this year and I haven't been to a single assembly[7] in my whole life!"

Nine pink slips? My heart broke in the instant Tyler spoke those words. It wasn't just the words he spoke but the hurt and frustration in his eyes and voice. It wasn't fair. Here, Tyler is following the rules like he is supposed to, but instead of being rewarded for it, he gets a check for yelling at Eric (who is not following the rules). Eric gets the attention from the teacher because he is the one who is crying, while Tyler retreats back into a state of resentment. Resentful because, for him, he wasn't even yelling; he was trying to be heard over the roar of "10 or 17 TVs on at max volume."

My perspective of Tyler changed. I now see him as a bright, sensitive, active, caring boy who really wants to do well in school. He loves to do the "right" thing. He thrives on praise and tries so hard to follow the rules. He just wants to be understood.

There is a sadness in Tyler's eyes, a sadness that should not belong to a little boy just eight years old. A sadness and frustration that school has let him down.

Rewarding kids for their good choices is important and sounds like a great idea, but excluding students from this reward is wrong. Tyler makes good

choices all day long, but he has ADHD. He is impulsive, talkative, forgetful,
easily distracted, and hyper. He walks around the room instead of sitting. He is
very smart and very sweet. He longs to be just like everybody else. He longs to
belong—included fully in his school community.

Looking at school through his eyes, I find I don't like it. Looking at school
through his eyes, I feel misunderstood.

After this experience with Tyler, Sonja became motivated to rethink her music lesson plans. She found techniques to use movement in ways that were musically appropriate, yet provided all of her learners with the opportunity to move and to use their movements to express musical ideas. Sonja reconsidered the pacing of her lessons and increased the level of student engagement. She used more opportunities for students to work together rather than in isolation, allowing them to share ideas, encouraging meaningful *talking* rather than insisting on *being quiet*. She became empathetic to Tyler's experience of school, and this fundamental change in her own attitude allowed her to enjoy Tyler rather than find him a source of irritation. This alone made a difference in Tyler's experience of music at school. Because every student is unique, special needs or not, your students' success depends on your willingness to learn about your students' strengths and challenges and find ways to build on those strengths while simultaneously removing barriers that restrict success.

FOCUSING ON STRENGTHS, SUPPORTING CHALLENGES

A wide range of learning disabilities[8] may challenge some of the students with special needs who may be in your music classes. Too numerous to itemize or to consider every pedagogical strategy, be advised that most disabilities come in combinations and that every student will have a unique amalgamation of strengths and challenges. Again, the key to success is focusing on strengths so that students can build both confidence and competence, while removing barriers that impede successful inclusion.

Reading may be a challenge for some of your students. If you are using songs (with the need to read lyrics) or any kind of reading activity, be advised that students may need additional support. If you can identify this problem ahead of time (through an IEP or in consultation with other teachers), you can minimize this obstacle by providing reading materials or lyrics for practice at home, in the regular classroom, or perhaps with a reading specialist if the student receives extra reading support. If the text is within a song, you might provide or make an audio recording for the student. Lack of fluency in reading can impede success and removing this barrier will enable student success as well as seamlessly enable her inclusion in singing experiences. Reading musical notation presents an additional challenge with the need to decode multiple layers of information: pitch, rhythm, text, and score reading all while transferring the information to singing or playing an instrument, often simultaneously in time with others! We frequently take this skill for granted. As suggested earlier, providing musical notation graphically[9] and in standard musical notation to all students can enable musical success while not singling out any student.

Processing delays are a common learning disability and, in music, present a challenge to the simultaneity needed in ensemble settings. When students cannot decode notation quickly and transfer notated musical ideas to instrument or voice, they may repeatedly be *the cause* of musical mistakes, such as being late for entrances or cut-offs, dragging tempos, or simply being in the wrong place in the music. A student may hear the directions, "let's start at measure 24," but by the time the student locates measure 24 in the music, decodes the starting note, and finds it on his instrument, the rest of the group may have started and be well into the piece of music.

"Frustration, Anxiety, and Tension"[10] are the descriptors for a teacher professional development program by Rick Lavoie in which teachers experience the ways that students with learning disabilities encounter school every day. The teachers role-play a classroom setting where the pace is too fast, the material confusing, and the teacher demanding. Students with learning disabilities may live out their school day, every day, feeling frustrated and anxious. Living out every school day with musical material or musical performance just out of reach must be frustrating and, in the long run, debilitating for middle school students.

How can you find ways to enable your students' success? *Talk to the student.* Find out what the child would like to do in music, what his musical interests are, and find ways to incorporate them into your curriculum. Ask students which peers they feel comfortable with (they know who will not pick on them) and make sure they can work with accepting peers when doing collaborative projects. Talk to the students' teachers and parents. Find out what strategies are working at home and in other classrooms. *Don't give up.* Being fair does not mean that you treat all students the same. Being fair means giving each child, special needs or not, the tools and strategies for success. Every student is unique; you can expect that what you will provide as pedagogical support may vary widely among your students.

MUSIC IN THE SELF-CONTAINED CLASSROOM

As a middle school music teacher, you may be asked to teach students who are in self-contained music classrooms, which typically have a small number of students and a teacher whose expertise is teaching students with special needs. Teaching students with more extreme needs is especially challenging: collaboration with the teacher will be essential. Again, this collaboration will help you determine student strengths and challenges so that you can best design appropriate musical experiences. Additional time spent in students' classrooms should be considered part of your *preparation* for lesson planning. This extra time will allow you to find out about their musical interests, a great starting point for the lessons you will create. Spending additional time with your students with special needs will enable you to begin to build trust, which is very important as these students typically have not felt successful in school and may have had limited success in prior music classrooms. Here, I share my experience of spending time with high school students in their self-contained classroom, early in the school year, as I explored ways to connect their school and non-school experiences to their musical experiences.

> *I have arrived at lunchtime to the self-contained classroom where students have finished their lunches and are enjoying "leisure time." The students in this classroom have special needs that are fairly extreme and prevent successful inclusion in other classrooms. All of the students have a combination of special needs including autism, low cognition, processing delays, and emotional impairments. Low tolerance for frustration and a lack of understanding for the consequences of one's actions have resulted in juvenile incarceration for a few of the students. Some of the students have supportive home situations, but some have been in abusive settings or are now in foster care. Many of these students are considered at-risk socioeconomically and/or have parents with disabilities as well.*
>
> *As I enter the classroom, I notice that three of the girls are listening to music—one is listening to R & B with a CD and headphones and rocks rhythmically to the music. Two girls, best friends, sing along to country and western music. Like their teenaged peers, they know all the words by heart. Mrs. Miller's warm greeting as I am introduced to the class seems to let the students know that I am a "friend," and a group of students playing UNO invite me to join them. Later, I join the two girls listening to the country music and ask them about their favorite singers. I am hoping to start my music lessons with songs that they know and love, enabling musical connections to the music of their personal lives.*
>
> *Thinking that I was off to a good start, I return to their classroom the next week with a selection of popular songs, including some country music, for the class to analyze. With a brief introduction and scaffolding throughout our group listening experience, the students figure out the form and have an opportunity to describe everything else they hear and know about the music.*

On the surface, it would seem that I was off to a good start. Because I know these students do not manage transitions well, I decided to begin music classes in their own classroom. Moving from room to room is difficult, and I mini-mized a *trigger* to negative behaviors by coming to the familiar surroundings of their own classroom. I had arranged for music class to occur immediately after their leisure time so that I could arrive early and spend time in the classroom building relationships that might foster trust. Not only is my once-a-week visit announced by my early arrival, allowing for an easier transition to music, but our time together has enabled me to better learn about the ways I can support these students. For example, I have learned that the biggest obstacle these students face in school is learning how to interact socially (such as students learning how to take turns in a card game) or learning to make other appropri-ate social choices during leisure time. Another successful strategy I used was to begin our structured music time with songs that they know. Here, we listened to the songs together, figuring out the "A" section (verse, or *story*) and the "B" section (chorus, or *part that repeats a lot*). After a few listenings, the students would continue to describe the music as I wrote their ideas on the board.

Mrs. Miller told me that these students were functioning cognitively at a K–2 grade level. During my transition time the following week, I observed Mrs. Miller as she gave a reading assessment to one of the more advanced students. The student struggled to read words (at a grade 1 level) on sight, and her fluency was halting. Yet the previous week I had diligently written all the students' ideas on the board and had constructed a complicated form chart for two of the country songs to which we had listened. *What was I thinking? They couldn't begin to read these words!* They did, however, *describe* the music very well. I quickly discarded the worksheets I had brought for the next lesson (form charts to complete with partners) and created cards with visual cues for the musical ideas we would be exploring this week. This technique was much more appropriate for the students.

After the music class, I was able to observe a math lesson and was amazed to learn that some students were able to find patterns in numbers while others could not count to twenty. The visual frame the teacher had constructed to enable the understanding of patterns in numbers was a good reminder of the visual support that some music software can provide—for example, Garage-Band or Super Duper Music Looper (SDML).

Creating music with SDML[11] became a highly successful musical experi-ence for these students for a variety of reasons, and we spent much of the school year composing music together using the school's portable laptop lab. Because social interaction was extremely challenging, the students found mu-sical success working individually; as an added bonus, the use of headphones provided a buffer for noise or other distractions. Students could choose to work with a partner but were not required to do so, eliminating the require-ment of whole group musical interaction (such as those found in ensemble settings), which the students found almost impossible to handle. Processing delays became a non-issue as students were able to work at their own pace, a common recommendation in their IEPs. Using technology is culturally relevant for teens, and the software enabled them to be successful in ways that they typically had not before experienced—creating music that sounded *cool* and using technology with some level of expertise.

This scenario was not without its problems, and I offer these suggestions to avoid student frustration and the possibility of meltdowns, which are demoralizing for the student and, frankly, scary for the teacher and for the student's peers. Nothing will alienate a student from his peers or create *difference* like a public meltdown. Removing the *trigger* of technology-driven (or non-technology-driven) obstacles is well worth the time and effort. If you are new to the technology or software, practice ahead of time. If you are using a laptop lab, make sure you have reserved the time and that the laptops are fully charged. Find out the requirements for the process of student login. My students had difficulty with numbers but the login included an alpha-numeric code. Find a way to get around this—my students did! They would work around this obstacle by signing in as *guest.* However, as a result, none of their work could be saved, often resulting in a meltdown or aggressive outburst when a newly created song could not be retrieved. Some school districts limit the size of student server space on school computers. Find out how to create room for the large media files your students will be creating (thus again removing the frustration of not being able to save work). If you are in multiple buildings, make sure you are included on technology email alerts. My students' passwords were changed, but because the students did not value reading, they did not notice the school email informing them of the change; even if they had, they could not have easily constructed new passwords. *Don't give up.* Working creatively with students with special needs will require you to be proactive in both lesson design and administrative or technology-driven tasks that may be new to you or may require extra time and effort.

FOSTERING INCLUSION

All human beings have basic needs. When basic survival needs are met, we turn to meeting our needs of belonging (Blair, 2009b; Noddings, 1984; van Manen, 1991), human interaction, and personal expression. When students have difficulty expressing emotion personally or through the arts, it is not because they do not have emotions—it is because *they have difficulty expressing them*, which may become something that impedes learning and full interaction with others.

In the media, you will find many examples of people who have removed barriers to inclusion. Two favorites come to mind. The first is a dance teacher who found a way to allow children with disabilities to experience ballet. In the book *Ballerina Dreams*, Lauren Thompson describes Joann, a dance teacher/physical therapist, and group of five girls who, with able-bodied helpers, dance and jump and move artfully to music in ways that their physical bodies had previously prevented. The girls have a dream to be the best ballerinas they can be. Joann *finds a way* to help them realize their dreams. The book focuses on the girls' accomplishments and how they achieved their full potential through sheer determination. Another favorite story is that of Patrick Henry Hughes,[12] a young man with multiple disabilities who participates in his college marching band, with his wheelchair being pushed throughout marching routines by his father. At first, Patrick did not imagine that he could ever be in the marching band. Dr. Byrne, University of Louisville band director, simply replied, "The next step was working out what we needed to make happen in order for Patrick to be involved in the marching band—other than just parking on the sidelines and playing his instrument."[13] In other words, obstacles become barriers when we allow them to be barriers. Find a way around the obstacle. Do not allow obstacles to limit your students' quality of life, to limit human interaction and musical expression. *Don't give up.*

It takes a special teacher to take the time to learn about her learners, to creatively develop new strategies, and to implement them with a goal toward inclusion and the development of musicianship. It takes a special teacher to decide *"I'm going to find a way to make it happen."*

TERMINOLOGY

Inclusion is a term used to describe the ideology that each child, to the maximum extent appropriate, should be educated in the school and classroom he or she would otherwise attend. It involves bringing support services to the child (rather than moving the child to the services) and requires only that the child will benefit from being in the class (rather than having to keep up with the other students) (from Council for Exceptional Children, www.cec.sped.org).

An *Individualized Education Program* (IEP) is an educational plan designed by a team of professionals who work with a student. It may include the parent, school principal and school/district psychologist, the student's teacher, a special education specialist, and any others who can provide information and support for the student. Specific curricular goals and assessment objectives are designed for the students with suggestions for appropriate accommodations and modifications in instructional support. Guidelines on an IEP should be followed by all of the student's instructors, including music, art, and so forth.

Adaptations in the classroom, accommodation and modification: "An accommodation is used when the teacher believes that the student can achieve the same level of participation or accomplishment as the rest of the class, but just needs some additional support. An accommodation allows a student to complete the same assignment or activity as the other students in the class, but the student is offered a change in such things as formatting, setting, amount of time needed, or type of response that is required . . . a modification to help the student participate and learn at the highest possible level for his or her individual abilities. A modification is used when the student is not able to complete the same assignment or participate in the same way due to the nature of his or her disabilities. A modification changes the standard of participation or the extent of what an assignment or test measures" (Adamek & Darrow, 2005, pp. 62–63).

Autism (or Autism Spectrum Disorders) is a general term used to describe a group of complex developmental brain disorders known as Pervasive Developmental Disorders (PDD). The other pervasive developmental disorders are PDD-NOS (Pervasive Developmental Disorder—Not Otherwise Specified), Asperger's Syndrome, Rett Syndrome, and Childhood Disintegrative Disorder. Autism affects the way a child perceives the world and makes communication and social interaction difficult. The child may also have repetitive behaviors or intense interests. Symptoms, and their severity, are different for each of the affected areas—communication, social interaction, and repetitive behaviors. A child may not have the same symptoms and may seem very different from another child with the same diagnosis. It is sometimes said that if you know one person with autism, you know one person with autism (www .autismspeaks.org).

Universal design is a term first used in architecture for the principle of providing seamless access in physical environments. In learning environments, principles of universal design would require *seamless access* to classrooms, classroom technology, information, skill building, and social interaction with teacher and peers. In short, the teacher must consider the classroom from her learners' eyes—not just the room itself, but also opportunities for barrier-free, appropriately supported active engagement during musical experiences in ways that enhance learning for *all* students (Hitchcock, et al., 2002; McCord & Watts, 2006; Woodward & Ferretti, 2007).

A *social story* is a story that explains, in simple and temporal and/or sequential ways, a social situation. Because children on the autism spectrum
thrive in predictable situations, knowing what to expect in social situations
can alleviate stress and enable a child to better cope in new social contexts.
In addition, children with autism have difficulty understanding social norms
and nonverbal communication. These stories may include examples of "what
to expect" so that students may improve their social skills and their ability
to respond to others appropriately, thus enabling interaction and acceptance
among peers.

The core characteristics of *ADHD* are developmentally inappropriate levels of
inattention, hyperactivity, and impulsivity. These problems are persistent and
usually cause difficulties in one or more major life areas: home, school, work,
or social relationships. Clinicians base their diagnosis on the presence of the
core characteristics and the problems they cause. Children with ADHD are
often blamed for their behavior. However, it's not a matter of their choosing
not to behave. It's a matter of "can't behave *without the right help*." ADHD
interferes with a person's ability to behave appropriately (www.ldonline.org).

A *learning disability* is a neurological disorder. In simple terms, a learning disability results from a difference in the way a person's brain is *wired*.
Children with learning disabilities are as smart or smarter than their peers.
However, they may have difficulty reading, writing, spelling, reasoning,
and recalling and/or organizing information if left to figure things out by
themselves or if taught in conventional ways. Common learning disabilities
include the following:

- Dyslexia—a language-based disability in which a person has trouble understanding written words. It may also be referred to as a reading disability
  or reading disorder.
- Dyscalculia—a mathematical disability in which a person has a difficult
  time solving arithmetic problems and grasping math concepts.
- Dysgraphia—a writing disability in which a person finds it hard to form
  letters or write within a defined space.
- Auditory and Visual Processing Disorders—sensory disabilities in which
  a person has difficulty understanding language despite normal hearing
  and vision.
- Nonverbal Learning Disabilities—a neurological disorder, which originates
  in the right hemisphere of the brain, causing problems with visual-spatial,
  intuitive, organizational, evaluative and holistic processing functions
  (www.ldonline.org/ldbasics).

These disabilities may prevent success in the music classroom as students attempt to read lyrics, decode musical notation (or write musical notation, if required), understand spatial/temporal relationships in music, or have difficulty organizing musical sound if there is an auditory disorder.

REFERENCES

Adamek, M., & Darrow, A. (2005). *Music in special education*. Silver Spring, MD: American Music Therapy Association.

Blair, D. V. (2009a). Fostering wakefulness: Narrative as a curricular tool in teacher education. *International Journal of Education and the Arts, 10*(9). www.ijea.org/v10n19/index.html

Blair, D. V. (2009b). Learner agency: To understand and to be understood. *British Journal of Music Education, 26*(2), 173–87.

Florian, L. (Ed.). (2007). *The SAGE handbook of special education*. Thousand Oaks, CA: Sage.

Hitchcock, C., Meyer, A., Rose, D., & Jackson, R. (2002). Providing new access to the general curriculum: Universal design for learning. *Teaching Exceptional Children, 35*(2), 8–17.

Hourigan, R., & Hourigan, A. (2009). Teaching music to children with autism: Understanding and perspectives. *Music Educators Journal, 96*(1), 40–45.

Hughes, P. H. (2008). *I am potential: Eight lessons on living, loving, and reaching your dreams*. Philadelphia, PA: Da Capo Press.

Jellison, J. (2006). Including everyone. In G. McPherson (Ed.), *The child as musician: A handbook of musical development* (pp. 257–72). New York, NY: Oxford University Press.

McCord, K., & Watts, E. (2006). Collaboration and access for our children: Music educators and special educators together. *Music Educators Journal, 92*(4), 26–33.

Noddings, N. (1984). *Caring: A feminine approach to ethics and moral education*. Berkeley and Los Angeles: California University Press.

Thompson, L. (2007). *Ballerina dreams*. New York, NY: Feiwel and Friends.

van Manen, M. (1991). *The tact of teaching: The meaning of pedagogical thoughtfulness*. London, Ontario, CA: Althouse Press.

Woodward, J., & Ferreti, R. (2007). New machines and new agendas: The changing nature of special education technology research. In L. Florian (Ed.), *The SAGE handbook of special education* (pp. 440–49). Thousand Oaks, CA: Sage.

ADDITIONAL RESOURCES

Online Resources

ADHD: http://ldonline.org/adhdbasics

Americans with Disabilities Act: www.usdoj.gov/crt/ada/adahom1.htm
Assistive Technology: www.abledata.com
Autism Society of America: www.autism-society.org
Autism Speaks: www.autismspeaks.org
(The) Center for Applied Special Technology: www.cast.org
Center for Music Learning, University of Texas at Austin (Dr. Judith Jellison): http://
  cml.music.utexas.edu/DisabilitiesArchive/DisabilitiesOpener.htm
Children and Adults with ADD/ADHD: http://chadd.org
Closing the Gap: Changing Lives with Assistive Technology: www.closingthegap
  .com
Council for Exceptional Children: www.cdc.sped.org
IDEA and Section 504: www.ed.gov/policy/speced/guid/idea/idea2004.html
Learning Disabilities: http://ldonline.org
Music Educators, Special Educators and Families Website: www.coe.ilstu.edu/mese
  (Illinois State University, Dr. Kim McCord and Dr. Emily Watts)
Universal Design for Learning: www.cast.org/research/udl/index.html

Learning about Life with a Disability

Temple Grandin: www.templegrandin.com
Dame Evelyn Glennie: www.evelyn.co.uk
Patrick Henry Hughes: www.patrickhenryhughes.com

Books

Hammel, A. M., & Hourigan, R. M. (2011). *Teaching music to students with special needs: A label-free approach.* New York, NY: Oxford University Press.
Notbohm, E. (2005). *Ten things every child with autism wishes you knew.* Arlington, TX: Future Horizons, Inc.
Notbohm, E. (2006). *Ten things your student with autism wishes you knew.* Arlington, TX: Future Horizons, Inc.

Joey Pigza Books

(The leading character in these books for youth is a boy experiencing life with
  ADHD.)
Gantos, J. (2000). *Joey Pigza swallowed the key.* New York, NY: Harper Trophy.
Gantos, J. (2002). *Joey Pigza loses control.* New York, NY: Harper Trophy.
Gantos, J. (2005). *What would Joey do?* New York, NY: Harper Trophy.

NOTES

1. Available in *World Music Drumming* by Will Schmid (Hal Leonard), www.worldmusicdrumming.com/publications.html, and available in the 2008 Pearson Silver Burdett Making Music, www.pearsonschool.com.

2. For more information on collaboration, see K. McCord and E. Watts (2006), Collaboration and access for our children: Music educators and special educators together, *Music Educators Journal, 92*(4), 26–33.

3. Every teacher is responsible for her students' progress. If you do not receive a copy of a student's IEP, you should request one. Be aware of current privacy laws, but in order for a student to thrive in your classroom, it is important to be aware of special needs and his/her individualized education program.

4. Your district exceptionalities specialist may have software to assist you—for example, Boardmaker Software (www.mayer-johnson.com).

5. See also C. Gray (2010), *The new social story book* (Arlington, TX: Future Horizons). This resource contains over 150 social stories that teach everyday social skills to children with autism or Asperger's syndrome, and their peers. It also includes a CD of printable, editable social stories.

6. For the full article, see D. V. Blair (2009a).

7. Pink-slip-free assemblies were used as a reward for students who had not been given a pink slip during a marking period. These were school-wide, community-building events, much anticipated by the student body.

8. For additional resources on learning disabilities, see www.ldonline.org. For legal information on education and learners with disabilities, see http://idea.ed.gov, as well as www.ldonline.org and www.cec.sped.org.

9. For ideas in using graphic (or "iconic") musical representation in the music classroom, I have provided this website for teacher use: http://web.me.com/deborahvblair/Musical_Mapping_for_the_Music_Classroom/Welcome.html.

10. Rick Lavoie website: www.ricklavoie.com/videos.html and http://teacher.scholastic.com/professional/specialneeds/howhard.htm.

11. Super Duper Music Looper: www.sonycreativesoftware.com. For these students, SDML was an appropriate choice due to the musical sound bank and the visual representation it offers. (GarageBand also has these characteristics, but the GarageBand screen was visually overwhelming and the actions required too many steps for this particular set of learners.)

12. See Hughes (2008), as well as www.patrickhenryhughes.com.

13. For the entire ESPN news story, see www.youtube.com/watch?v=-qTiYA1WiY8 (Dr. Byrne's quote at 3:15).

Chapter Three

Singing in Middle School General Music Classes

Frank Abrahams

Christina Macedo was sitting in her supervisor's office. It was October of her first year teaching general music and chorus at Horace Mann Middle School. Yesterday, her supervisor had observed a seventh grade general music class. The observation was a disaster. Christina could not get the students to sing. She had no trouble with the fifth and sixth graders, but by seventh and eighth grade, the boys thought that males who sang in class were gay, and the girls just giggled. She had tried everything she could think of, but nothing had worked. Fortunately, Ms. Macedo's supervisor had some ideas for her.

Research confirms what Ms. Macedo experienced in her general music classes. Both Svengalis (1978) and Green (1997) reported that students and their teachers consider singing to be a feminine activity. Hanley (1998) suggested that boys "don't sing because they are hung up on the image that boys don't sing, and those who do are gay or sissies or weak or whatever" (p. 51). Nonetheless, singing has been and still is at the heart of the general music curriculum. In fact, the first of the nine content standards for music education in the United States reads, "Singing alone, and with others, a varied repertoire of music" (Consortium of National Arts Education Associations, 1994).

While general music classes certainly teach music, good middle school general music programs also promote opportunities for students and their teachers to pose and solve problems together as they meet the challenges of the music they are learning. Good middle school general music programs broaden students' view of reality and change the way students see the world. Music as an art form is a catalyst for emotional response and is expressive in ways that go beyond the spoken word. Good middle school general music programs are student centered and engage students in active learning. Singing in general music classes engages students in making music. In the act of making music, they become part of the music, and the music becomes a part of them. They are not *talking about* music; they *are* the music. This means that students are changed because of their participation. They learn to understand themselves and to see themselves as part of the cultural past, present, and future.

The purpose of this chapter is to present ideas that help teachers engage with students in successful singing experiences in middle school general music classes. The ten ideas that follow could have been given to Chris Macedo by her supervisor. Because no two middle school teaching situations are alike, there is no quick fix, and you don't learn to be an outstanding teacher by reading a chapter in a book. Yes, the information in this chapter is important, the resources suggested are helpful, and the ideas are worth consideration, but it's still only a chapter in a book. What I hope to do is to provoke thinking by sharing ideas that I have found to be successful both in my own teaching and that of former students and colleagues.

USE SINGING TO HELP STUDENTS ATTAIN UNDERSTANDING OR MASTERY OF MUSICAL CONCEPTS

Use singing in general music class to help students attain understanding or mastery of a particular musical concept. Do not include singing just so the students have a fun activity or to meet some other outside goal. When planning your curriculum for the year, determine which goals might be met with singing activities. Provide opportunities for students to sing solos when appropriate; however, take care because students who feel they might be forced to sing by themselves may choose not to participate at all.

Connect singing in the classroom to singing in other aspects of the school music program. Often the school musical is an activity that engages students from general music classes. In some schools, a particular grade presents a musical. In that case, preparation of the musical is part of the general music curriculum. The same is true for choir. In some schools, all students in a particular grade are in the choir. In that case, preparing choral music often happens in general music classes. Singing in a large group is less threatening for timid singers, and they appreciate the safety that larger numbers of participants provide.

DO NOT USE GENERAL MUSIC AS A VOICE CLASS

Do not try to teach vocal technique in a general music class. Group vocal technique is best addressed in dedicated voice classes or in the choral rehearsal. But it is important that any teacher working with adolescents' changing voices understand what is happening to the vocal mechanism and have some strategies for dealing with it. The issues of the changing voice in both male and female adolescent singers are significant. Helping young men through the change is best accomplished individually or in small groups away from the entire class and especially away from the girls. Young men are very sensitive about the change and are embarrassed when their voices do not respond as they once did or as they wish they would. Respect and empathize with those feelings. They are profound and real. Find time before school, after school, or during a lunch or activity period to help your middle school students who are having difficulty navigating their changing voices.

Boys' Changing Voices

It's a fact of life that boys' voices change during the middle school years. Specifically, the vocal folds increase about 10 millimeters in length, causing boys' ranges to drop about an octave, sometimes more. At the same time, the folds increase in thickness. The voice becomes unpredictable, and the young man going through the change has little control over what happens. The larynx can adjust suddenly, causing the voice to crack, often at inopportune times. When this occurs, the young man feels embarrassed and uncomfortable. Freer (2009) suggested that when boys learn to mix their head and chest registers prior to the onset of the change, they are often more successful negotiating the mixing of registers during the change. Freer also recommended that music teachers talk to young men about the voice change—openly and frankly, but with sensitivity.

Since the mid-1970s, Cooksey has studied the changing voice. In the article "Male Adolescent Transforming Voices: Voice Classification, Voice Skill Development, and Music Literature Selection" (2000), Cooksey identified five stages of change. In Stage I (midvoice I) the young man loses notes in his upper range. In Stage II (midvoice II) the young man notices a general narrowing of the entire range. At Stage III (midvoice IIA) the young man is able to sing more notes in his lower range. When the young man reaches Stage IV (new voice), a young baritone voice emerges. The unchanged, soprano qualities are completely gone, but the adult sound is not yet present. The last stage, Stage V (emerging adult voice), is when the young man may begin to be labeled a baritone or tenor, and the voice is more resonant and agile. Cooksey (1977–1978) noted that young men move through each stage at different rates and linger at different stages for varying amounts of time. Eventually, the voice settles, often during the early years of high school. Range and tessitura change with each stage as well. Therefore, if middle school music teachers are committed to singing with young men in their general music classes, they must not only be sensitive to the social and emotional trauma the voice change causes their male students but also accommodate the changing physiology by selecting repertoire that is appropriately voiced. Middle school music teachers should hear the boys in their classes sing individually and often to competently monitor progress as the young men pass from one stage to the next.

Girls' Changing Voices

The change in the female voice does not seem so dramatic because it changes in quality and strength of tone rather than range. Casarow (n.d.) identified several characteristics of the female changing voice:

- The speaking voice lowers three to four half steps.
- The larynx grows about three to four millimeters in length.
- There is increased breathiness, huskiness, and hoarseness.
- There is insecurity of pitch.
- Like the males, the voice may "crack."
- Like the males, there may be noticeable register "breaks."
- There is a decreased and inconsistent pitch range capability.

Gackle (1994) identified four stages of voice change in females, similar to Cooksey's (1977–1978) stages for males: Stage I—prepubertal (unchanged, ages eight to ten); Stage IIA—premenarchal (ages eleven to twelve); Stage IIB—postmenarchal (ages thirteen to fourteen); and Stage III—emerging adult female (age fifteen and beyond). Table 3.1 compares the changes between male and female adolescent voices. The chart clearly shows that both boys and girls move through stages of vocal change during adolescence and that this change affects their ability to sing in tune, sing with a uniform vocal quality, and feel comfortable and secure when participating with the other students.

USE ONLY THE HIGHEST QUALITY MUSIC

Choose music carefully and present only music of the highest quality to your singers. The basal music series are good resources for literature. Defining high quality is a personal issue. It is informed by teacher preferences and biases, context, and culture and is often generational. Music considered radical in one generation is considered standard fare by the next. Teachers influenced by Kodály's teaching typically have programs

Table 3.1.   Comparison of Male and Female Adolescent Voice Change

Stages of Voice Changes in Males (Cooksey, 2000)		Stages of Voice Changes in Females (Gackle, 1994)	
Maturational Stage	Voice Classification	Maturational Stage	Voice Classification
	Unchanged (premutational)	I	Prepuberty (unchanged)
I	Midvoice I (initial period of voice change)	IIA	Pubescence/Premenarche (beginning of mutation)
II	Midvoice II (high mutation period)		
III	Midvoice IIA (climax of mutation and key transitional period)	IIB	Puberty/Postmenarche (peak of mutation)
IV	New Voice (stabilizing period)		
V	Emerging Adult Voice (postmutational development and reexpansion period)	III	Young Adult Female/Postmenarche (timbre begins to approximate that of the adult female)

rich in folk music. Teachers trained in contemporary musical styles have different ideas. Discuss with the students what they consider to be quality music. They make very sophisticated decisions when choosing what to download onto their playlists.

In middle school, in addition to range, the text is a very important consideration. Students are more likely to sing when the text is appealing. A class blog on Edmodo (which will be described later in this chapter) provides a venue for such ongoing discussions. Students feel comfortable sharing their thoughts and exchanging ideas on blogs. When students can contribute and know that their contributions are valued and considered by the teacher, it will be easier to engage them in classroom singing activities.

Part Singing

If students are singing in parts, choose music where the voices are labeled part I, II, and III rather than soprano or alto. This allows teachers to easily mix the sexes when assigning voice parts. In addition, the young men will feel comfortable singing treble until they can move to a lower part. Do not force boys into the tenor range before they are ready just to stroke their emerging male egos. Do not be afraid to move the young men from one part to another as their voices change. A boy's range in January or May might be different than it was in September. Singers can also move among parts from song to song, or even within a song. I sometimes map out an individualized part for each young man in the midst of the change using a highlighter. That is, for each song, there will be a roadmap. The singer might sing part I for several measures and then move to another part if part I becomes too high. Similarly, a singer might start in part III or part IV and move up for several measures when the range becomes too low. This practice works for boys or girls and makes each student feel special, valued, and cared about. It also ensures that students are singing in healthy ways. Figure 3.1[1] shows the ranges of the male changing voice.

TREAT STUDENTS AS ARTISTS, AND THEY WILL RESPOND AS ARTISTS

When singing with students in general music classes, treat the students as artists, and they will respond as artists. For example, use standard musical vocabulary when speaking about the music. Select the term *messa di voce* instead of "hairpin" and call a fermata sign a *fermata* and not a "bird's eye." Use *alla breve* instead of "cut time" and *anacrusis* for the common term "pick-up."

Incorporate Critical, Musical Thinking

Ask students in general music classes to be critical listeners of their own singing and of the singing in the class. Ask follow-up questions when the

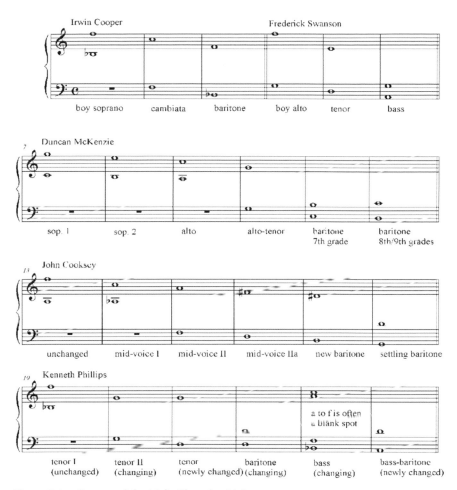

Figure 3.1. Ranges of the Male Changing Voice

response is, "The dynamics were good." Suggest to students, "Can you be more specific?" "Can you use a more precise word?" "Can you tell me where?" "Can you make a suggestion that might make the dynamic contrasts more obvious?" Ask students to share with their neighbor two suggestions they might have to remedy sloppy attention to dynamics. Ask students if they believe that what they just sang was a *musical* performance. If not, ask them what might make it more musical. Use informal cooperative learning where students work in pairs to find solutions together. In language arts, this strategy is called "Think-Pair-Share."[2] Ask them, "What will you do differently when we sing this again?" Students behave the way they are expected to behave. Set and maintain high standards and insist that every engagement students have singing in your class be a musical one. Don't add musicality later. Build it in initially.

DESIGN SINGING EXPERIENCES TO
APPEAL TO MIDDLE SCHOOL STUDENTS

It will take careful planning and time to build a singing culture in your class-room. What works in one school with one group of students may not be effective in another. Use singing experiences that will appeal to your students.

Connect Singing to Something Else

Many of my colleagues find that their students will sing in general music class when singing is connected to something else. For example, in Rio de Janeiro, Lucas Ciavatta has his middle school students sing Bach chorales in four parts using solfège on numbers when they are stepping to the beat. They do native Brazilian drumming, also while stepping, and often sing songs with the rhythms they are playing. His process, called *O Passo*, connects the body, including singing and stepping to the beat, with written and oral notation and drumming (Abrahams, 2010). In the United Kingdom, Lucy Green (2008) places students into cooperative learning groups, which she calls *friendship groups*, and instructs them to re-create the arrangements of popular music from listening to recordings, without formal intervention from their teacher. Her research shows that this is often the way popular musicians learn. We know that the Beatles began copying arrangements from recordings of their contemporaries in the early years as they were honing their own style. Green's research demonstrates that students in general music classes enjoy this activity. Once completed, students will freely sing their arrangements for the teacher and their classmates. Because this is an activity within the confines of the classroom and nothing is recorded or archived, posted on the Internet, or presented publicly, it falls under the fair use provisions of U.S. copyright law.

In personal correspondence and my own observations in their classrooms, several of my colleagues have shared their successes with me. Grant Mech, a middle school music teacher in Robbinsville, New Jersey, has a project with seventh-grade students where they rewrite the lyrics to a Gilbert and Sullivan patter song. "The students never seem to have any inhibitions in singing this 'old' music," he explains, "once they have had a hand in reworking it." In eighth grade, his general music students often imitate or mock opera singers in a lesson where they select operatic music to create a commercial. Mech feels that this is a good ice-breaker and facilitates singing in later activities. He notes that boys are often the ones to be goofy and poke fun, but are willing to vocalize without much fear of reprisal once class is finished. Like Ciavatta, whose students sing along while drumming, Mech finds that students will sing along as they play hand-chimes. In this instance, the singing helps them navigate where they are in the music.

Maureen Fernandez at Community Middle School in Plainsboro, New Jersey, connects singing to pieces the students play on Orff instruments. "They pick a melody, sing it through on note names, add another layer for a different part, and then try to sing the two parts against each other." She adds, "When they are composing they will at some point sing their composition with me on a neutral syllable. I often sing to them as they listen for musical elements, and invariably they sing back. When analyzing a score, they track a melody that I sing on a neutral syllable and then sing with me after we have noted measures, time [signatures, and other elements in the score]."

Fernandez's colleague Jodi Johnson at Grover Middle School, in the West Windsor -Plainsboro school district in central New Jersey, includes a unit on vocal anatomy and production in her seventh-grade general music classes. She finds that "[t]alking about what's going on from a physical standpoint, complete with viewing a recording of a laryngoscope, keeps it all about them! [It also] takes the focus off of singing in front of their peers (as a group, of course, but still scary to some!)."

Connect Technology and Singing

Music teachers with access to computers in their classrooms can use Auto-Tune to entice students into singing. With the appropriate hardware and software, one can synthesize the most modest of voices and make it sound like a singer. Middle school students are especially excited to hear their voices transformed by the software. There are many videos on YouTube to describe and demonstrate the process. An original accompaniment composed by the students on GarageBand turns the shyest singer into a rock star. For the more adventurous, several video games that engage players in singing would be worth investigating. *Rock Band* incorporates singing, drums, and two guitars and features songs that are the cornerstones of rock'n'roll. *Karaoke Revolution* comes in a *Glee* edition. *Disney Sing It* also teaches harmony. *Def Jam Rapstar* caters to hip hop and offers multiple options for the player/singer/student to manipulate the content. There are other games dedicated to specific artists such as Green Day, Michael Jackson, and the Beatles, as well as many more options you can explore on the Internet.

ADDRESS VARIOUS LEARNING STYLES

Use singing strategies that work with various learning styles. Recognize that with middle school students there are diverse learning needs and that their musical aptitudes vary. Accommodate those needs by differentiating instruction. Whenever possible, include imagery. Add kinesthetic activities where you can. Having students sing using hand signs is one easy option. As explained earlier, include cooperative learning strategies. For example, ask students to find a partner. Have one partner sing while the other listens for something specific. It may be intonation, phrasing, diction, or the like. Afterward, have the listener tell the singer what was good, what was not, and what he or she might do to remedy the situation. Repeat the activity with the partners switching roles. This informal cooperative learning can provide support for students who are having a difficult time or who are uncomfortable singing in class. In addition, this type of activity empowers musicianship and encourages critical listening and problem solving. Build independent musicianship in each student. Engage them in musical thinking and authentic musical behaviors. And again, always use music vocabulary.

TEACH FOR UNDERSTANDING

In their book *Understanding by Design*, Wiggins and McTighe (2005) discussed six facets of understanding: explain, interpret, apply, have perspective, empathize, and self-knowledge. These facets can guide teachers toward ways to deepen and enrich student learning. Find techniques to involve students in conversations both in class and online to ensure understanding. Help singers transfer what they learn in one context to a new and different context instead of just learning through imitation. This promotes long-lasting learning and facilitates the ability of singers to connect the content of the general music class to the context of their reality.

Encourage dialogue between students and their teachers to uncover problems and solve them together, changing how both students and teachers perceive the world. Engage in experiences that are transformational. Teachers who embrace this ideology believe that the results of teaching and learning should add value to the lives of those who participate by changing the perceptions that learners have as they interact in and with the world. Engaging students in reflective thinking is one way to foster such a transformation.

Problem Solve to Learn

Remember that all learning is problem solving. Take an experience singing in general music class out of the realm of low-level thinking (rote experiences) into higher levels (analysis, synthesis, and evaluation). Set up a website using one of the social networks available on the Internet. D. Cressman (personal communication) at William Penn Middle School in Fairless Hills, Pennsylvania, uses Edmodo, where students can blog thoughts and feelings, discussion groups may be created, and MP3 files of the parts of a song may be posted for downloading. Other music that the director feels students should hear can be posted there as well. Parents can also enter the site and see what is happening. Short video or audio clips of rehearsals can be included, and students can be asked to reflect and comment on what they see and hear. Does everyone look engaged? Is the music in tune? Such reflective thinking will pay dividends later.

USE BOTH FORMATIVE AND SUMMATIVE ASSESSMENTS

While assessment in and of itself is not a strategy to engage students in singing, many students are motivated when they know that teachers will assess their performance. Plan assessments that will not only provide information for you to know when a concept has been mastered but also help you document students' understanding of themselves.

Wiggins and McTighe (2005) recommended setting a goal and then designing a plan to meet it. They suggest that summative assessments (those items that can be measured at the end of a particular marking period, cycle of classes, or unit) be articulated up front and be considered when designing and planning the lesson sequence and selecting the most appropriate strategies to fulfill them. They also suggested integrating formative assessments, evaluations that are ongoing. Good music teachers do this instinctively: in every class they listen, analyze, and remediate. In addition, the Achievement Standards described in the National Standards for singing in grades 5–8 can also be used as guidance for assessment (Consortium of National Arts Education Associations, 1994, p. 42). They may be found at www.nafme.org/resources/view/the-school-music-program-a-new-vision. Teachers can easily construct a rubric to assess these skills on a formal or informal basis.

Student self-reflection is very effective for assessment. One way to promote self-reflection is to use a rubric. Table 3.2 shows a sample rubric for student self-assessment. Students check the appropriate box and then add a comment in the box if they wish.

USE IDEAS FROM THE MUSIC
STUDENTS HEAR OUTSIDE CLASS

Remember that students engage with music outside of school in significant ways. According to Parker-Pope (2008), adolescents listen to an average of 2.5 hours of music each day. A significant amount of that listening is vocal music. Thus, middle school students already have an image of what they

Table 3.2.   Student Self-Assessment

Benchmark	Yes	Sometimes	No
In class, I use good breath support and strive to produce good tone quality.			
My diction is precise. I pay attention to beginning and ending sounds in words.			
I sing with expression.			
I am comfortable singing alone.			
I contribute positively and with enthusiasm when singing in a group.			
I can carry my own part when the class sings in 2- or 3-part harmony.			
I enjoy singing music from diverse cultures.			
I enjoy singing music in foreign languages.			

think singing should be. In class, use that as a jumping-off point or bridge to the kinds of healthy singing you expect from your students.

Students search for and download music from the Internet and listen to music on MP3 players, much of it unfamiliar to their music teachers. Students sort music into playlists by genre or artist, making relatively sophisticated decisions about what they hear and how it is categorized. They compose using GarageBand. All of this is informal and often unconnected to school music.

Designing a lesson or group of lessons using *mashup* songs is one strategy to incorporate the music students know outside of school and engage them in singing during general music classes. In recording, a mashup is a song that blends or combines the recordings of two different songs by overlaying the vocal track of one onto the instrumental track of another. Entering "mashup song" in a search engine on the Internet yields numerous hits. One list of songs may be found at http://en.wikipedia.org/wiki/List. In addition, several Internet clips explain and demonstrate the process. Most likely, middle school students are very familiar with mashup songs, as they are used frequently on the popular TV series *Glee*.

TEACHING IS NOT TELLING

Remember that teaching is not telling. Teaching is motivating, informing, coaching, and evaluating. It is a dialogue between teachers and student-singers. Students do not come to middle school general music as "empty slates." Most likely, they have been singing in music classes since kindergarten. In addition, they have rich, varied, and extensive musical lives outside school. The challenge is to make those musical lives the bridge to in-school music learning. Use what they bring to take them from *is* to *ought*.

CONCLUSION

Chris Macedo's supervisor gave her much to think about. Since Lowell Mason introduced music as a formal subject in schools in 1837, singing has been at the core of the curriculum. It is the first of the nine content areas that frame the National Standards for Music Education.

Although singing is considered a feminine activity, middle school music teachers successfully get their students to sing in general music classes when the singing is connected to another activity. Adding a kinesthetic response such as *O Passo* or writing parodies of patter songs, or singing accompanied by Orff instruments, or creating GarageBand accompaniments are effective strategies. Integrating technology through Auto-Tune or video games is another option. Applying a self-assessment in the form of a reflective rubric fosters critical thinking and problem solving. In sum, *singing alone and with others* fosters collaboration, communication, and creativity. All are twenty-first-century skills that prepare students for success in the future.

I teach my college music education students that the purpose of music education in any school setting is to empower musicianship and in the process change the students and teacher in ways that enrich their lives. I believe that experiences in music education inside school should make lives better in some way. This happens when learning is meaningful to students and connects to their world, their lives, and their inner selves.

REFERENCES

Abrahams, F. (2010). O Passo (the step): A critical pedagogy for music education from Brazil. In A. C. Clements (Ed.), *Alternative approaches in music education: Case studies from the field* (pp. 177–88). Lanham, MD: MENC/Rowman & Littlefield Education.

Billmeyer, R. (2003). *Strategies to engage the mind of the learner: Building strategic learners*. Omaha, NE: Dayspring.

Casarow, P. (n.d.). *Changing voices*. Retrieved from www.faccs.org/assets/PDF.../ CasarrowP-Changing-Voices.pdf

Consortium of National Arts Education Associations. (1994). *National standards for arts education: What every young American should know and be able to do in the arts.* Reston, VA: MENC.

Cooksey, J. M. (1977–1978). The development of an eclectic theory for the training and cultivation of the junior high school male changing voice (four-part article). *Choral Journal, 18* (October 1977), 5–14; (November 1977), 5–17; (December 1977), 5–15; (January 1978), 5–17.

Cooksey, J. M. (2000). Male adolescent transforming voices: Voice classification, voice skill development, and music literature selection. In L. Thurman & G. Welch (Eds.), *Body mind and voice: Foundations of voice education, book five: A brief menu of practical voice education methods* (2nd ed.). Collegeville, MN: Voicecare Network.

Freer, P. K. (2009). *Getting started with middle-level choir* (2nd ed.). Lanham, MD: MENC/Rowman & Littlefield Education.

Gackle, L. (1994). Changing voice. In J. Hinckley (Ed.), *Music at the middle level: Building strong programs* (pp. 53–59). Reston, VA: MENC.

Green, L. (1997). *Music, gender, education*. London: Routledge.

Green, L. (2008). *Music, informal learning and the school: A new classroom pedagogy*. Burlington, VT: Ashgate.

Hanley, B. (1998). Gender in secondary music education in British Columbia. *British Journal of Music Education, 15*(1), 51–69.

Parker-Pope, T. (2008, February 5). Under the influence of . . . music? *New York Times.* Retrieved from http://well.blogs.nytimes.com/2008/02/05/under-the-influence-ofmusic

Svengalis, J. N. (1978). Music attitude and the preadolescent male. Doctoral dissertation: University of Iowa.

Wiggins, G., & McTighe, J. (2005). *Understanding by design* (2nd ed.). Alexandria, VA: Association of Supervision and Curriculum Development.

ADDITIONAL RESOURCES

Abrahams, F., & Head, P. D. (2005). *Case studies in music education* (2nd ed.). Chicago, IL: GIA.

Adcock, E. (1986). Junior high singing . . . Wow! . . . Yuk! *North Carolina Music Educator, 36*(2), 40–41.

Adcock, E. (1987). The changing voice: The middle/junior high challenge. *Choral Journal, 28*(3), 9–11.

Adler, A. (1999). A survey of teacher practices in working with male singers before and during the voice change. *Canadian Journal of Research in Music Education, 40*(4), 29–33.

Barham, T. J., & Nelson, D. L. (1991). *The boy's changing voice: New solutions for today's choral teacher.* Miami, FL: CPP/Belwin.

Barresi, A. L. (1986). *Barresi on the adolescent voice* [videotape]. Madison, WI: University of Wisconsin–Madison Department of Extension Arts.

Barresi, A. L. (2000). The successful middle school choral teacher. *Music Educators Journal, 86*(4), 23–28.

Barresi, A. L., & Bless, D. (1984). The relation of selected variables to the perception of tessitura pitches in the adolescent changing voice. In M. Runfola (Ed.), *Proceedings. Research symposium on the male adolescent voice* (pp. 97–110). Buffalo: State University of New York Press.

Brodnitz, F. S. (1983). On change of the voice. *The NATS Bulletin, 40*(2), 24–26.

Collins, D. (1987). The changing voice: A future challenge. *Choral Journal, 28*(3), 13–17.

Collins, D. L. (1981). *The cambiata concept.* Conway, AR: Cambiata Press.

Cooksey, J. M. (1977–1978). The development of a continuing, eclectic theory for the training and cultivation of the junior high school male changing voice. Part I: Existing theories; Part II: Scientific and empirical findings; Part III: Developing an integrated approach to the care and training of the junior high school male changing voice; Part IV: Selecting music for the junior high school male changing voice. *Choral Journal, 18*(2, 3, 4, 5), 5–13, 5–16, 5–15, 5–18.

Cooksey, J. M. (1984). The male adolescent changing voice: Some new perspectives. In M. Runfola (Ed.), *Proceedings: Research symposium on the male adolescent voice* (pp. 4–59). Buffalo: State University of New York Press.

Cooksey, J. M., & Welch, G. F. (1998). Adolescence, singing development and national curricula design. *British Journal of Music Education, 15*(1), 99–119.

Demorest, S. M. (Ed.). (2000). Music and middle school chorus [Special Focus]. *Music Educators Journal, 86*(4).

Ekstrom, R. C. (1959). Comparison of the male voice before, during, and after muta- tion. *Dissertation Abstracts International*, 20–09A, 3569.

Emge, S. W. (1996). The adolescent male: Vocal registers as affecting vocal range, register competence and comfort in singing (boys). *Dissertation Abstracts Interna- tional, 57*(05), 1987A.

Fowells, R. M. (1983). The changing voice: A vocal chameleon. *Choral Journal, 24*(1), 11–15, 17.

Freer, P. K. (2005). *Success for adolescent singers* [DVD]. Available from www .choralexcellence.com/

Freire, P. (1970). *Pedagogy of the oppressed.* New York, NY: Continuum Press.

Friar, K. K. (1999). Changing voices, changing times. *Music Educators Journal, 86*(3), 26–29.

Friesen, J. H. (1972). Vocal mutation in the adolescent male: Its chronology and a comparison with fluctuations in musical interest. *Dissertation Abstracts Interna- tional* (UMI No. 73-7891).

Gackle, L. (1987). The effect of selected vocal techniques for breath management, resonation, and vowel unification on tone production in the junior high school female voice. *Dissertation Abstracts International*, 48-04A, 862.

Gackle, L. (1991). The adolescent female voice: Characteristics of change and stages of development. *Choral Journal, 31*(8), 17–25.

Gates, J. T. (1989). A historical comparison of public singing by American men and women. *Journal of Research in Music Education, 37*(1), 32–47.

Groom, M. A. (1979). A descriptive analysis of development in adolescent male voices during the summer time period. *Dissertation Abstracts International*, 40- 09A, 4945.

Gustafson, J. M. (1956). A study relating to the boy's changing voice: Its incidence, train- ing, and function in choral music. *Dissertation Abstracts International*, 16-09A, 1696.

Harris, L. D. (1993). An investigation of selected vocal characteristics in young male singers at various stages of maturation. *Journal of Research in Singing and Applied Vocal Pedagogy, 17*(1), 17–30.

Harrison, L. N. (1978). It's more than just a changing voice. *Choral Journal, 19*(1), 14–18.

Harrison, S. D. (2004). Engaging boys: Overcoming stereotypes—Another look at the missing males in vocal programs. *Choral Journal, 45*(2), 24–29.

Killian, J. N. (1997). Perceptions of the voice-change process: Male adult versus adolescent musicians and non-musicians. *Journal of Research in Music Education, 45*(4), 521–35.

Koza, J. E. (1993). The "missing males" and other gender issues in music education: Evidence from the *Music Supervisors Journal*, 1914–1924. *Journal of Research in Music Education, 42*, 212–32.

May, W. V., & Williams, B. B. (1989). The girl's changing voice. *Update: Applica- tions of Research in Music Education, 8*(1), 20–23.

McKenzie, D. (1956). *Training the boy's changing voice.* New Brunswick, NJ: Rut- gers University Press.

Nycz, T. J. (2008). A description of a gender separate middle school choral program (master's thesis, Bowling Green State University). Retrieved from http://drc.ohiolink.edu/handle/2374.OX/104779

Phillips, K. (1998). *Teaching kids to sing.* New York, NY: G. Schirmer.

Phillips, K. H. (1995). The changing voice: An albatross? *Choral Journal, 35*(10), 25–27.

Rutkowski, J. (1981). The junior high school male changing voice: Testing and grouping voices for successful singing. *Choral Journal, 22*(4), 11–15.

NOTES

1. Figure 3.1 shows how various experts identify the vocal ranges of middle school boys. Information comes from the following sources:

- Cooksey, J. (1999). *Working with adolescent voices.* St. Louis, MO: Concordia Publishing.
- Cooper, I., & Kuersteiner, K. O. (1965). *Teaching junior high school music.* Boston, MA: Allyn and Bacon.
- McKenzie, D. (1956). *Training the boy's changing voice.* New Brunswick, NJ: Rutgers University Press.
- Phillips, K. H. (1996). *Teaching kids to sing.* Belmont, CA: Wadsworth Group/Thomson Learning.
- Swanson, F. (1961). The proper care and feeding of changing voices. *Music Educators Journal, 48*(2), 63–66.

2. Information about "Think-Pair-Share" and other appropriate strategies may be found in Billmeyer (2003).

Chapter Four

Middle School Keyboard Ensemble Class

Kenneth R. Trapp

Early in my career, I found myself teaching keyboard in middle school general music classes consisting of a diverse population of about thirty students per class. As is typical in a middle school, the difference with regard to physical and emotional development was significant; some students were very outgoing while others were painfully shy.

What I found most challenging was the fact that these students came to me with such divergent musical experiences and levels of musical development. Some students had taken piano lessons for years and others had never played a keyboard. Some could read from piano books and play with two hands, while others could only play a simple melody by ear. I remember asking myself, "Why can't I get just one class where all of the students are at the same level so I can teach them all the same thing, at the same time?" What I discovered after working with many ensemble classes over the years is that there will never be a class where all of the students are at exactly the same level in regard to any skill, including music. I then began to ask myself a different set of questions. I wondered how I could unify instruction for such a group of diverse students, and how I might develop the music skills of all students while keeping instruction relevant to their musical needs.

RETHINKING TRADITIONAL INSTRUCTION

When I was a young boy, I would listen to my older brother practice his piano lessons. I was fascinated with how he played and I became very focused on the musical selections he was learning. When he finished practicing, I would go to the piano and try to play the songs that I heard him working on. I was amazed to discover that I could learn to play these songs on my own by using a method of trial and error. I learned several songs in this manner, and they sounded pretty good. Upon hearing me play, my parents decided it was time for me to have piano lessons.

When I began piano lessons, I was surprised to find out that I was not asked to play songs by ear, but to read them exclusively from a piano book. I was unfamiliar with most of the music that was presented to me in the books and I found it difficult to make sense out of the activities. Frustrated, I struggled to get my left hand to move with my right as I tried to play the correct combination of white and black keys while attempting to make the rhythm match the notes on the page. The results were not exactly musical. I now realize that I was frustrated because I did not have enough prior knowledge with the material I was being asked to read. The notation did not have meaning for me—I needed to have more musical experiences to draw upon in order to bring meaning *to* the notation.

Essential Music Skills

While piano and keyboard books are great for presenting students with literature to play, they may not engage students in the development of essential music skills. When thinking of developing music skills, four music vocabularies should be considered: listening, performing, reading, and writing. Most piano methods focus exclusively on reading without addressing the other vocabularies, which are critical for students to become comprehensive musicians. These vocabularies are best learned from a person who knows how to model them in a way that helps students to organize music aurally, without a dependence on notation. Instruction should be driven, not from a book, but by a teacher who investigates the achievement level and music potential of individual students and of the class as a whole. Generally, students in the middle school general music class are there by default; that is to say, they do not play a band instrument nor do they want to sing in choir. This is a group of students that warrants a music teacher who is willing to explore the most effective ways to meet their musical needs.

The Power of Modeling

The teacher must be a model for all music learning at the initial stages of instruction. This means that the teacher must be willing to sing, move rhythmically, improvise, arrange, read, and notate music for students. The teacher must model any music behavior that students will be asked to demonstrate. Activities that focus on making music should become the first priority, with intellectual discussions *about* music coming later when that information best describes the musical experiences students have had.

AURAL SKILL DEVELOPMENT

Aural skill development is what enables students to express themselves musically on an instrument and, most importantly, away from an instrument. Students should be given opportunities to internalize music before they play an instrument. As a result, a student who is thinking musically, or audiating, will be able to transpose songs, predict and play harmony, accompany others in an ensemble, improvise, and play with good rhythmic feel. Additionally, reading skills are strengthened when students understand the music they hear. When students are not limited to reading activities, but are taught how to audiate and feel music, they will develop into comprehensive music readers.

The middle school general music keyboard class is an ideal setting to embrace the development of aural skills, as the teacher can address the individual differences of all of the students at the same time. This task is harder to achieve if the instruction is presented exclusively from a book.

Tonal Skills

It is important for the teacher to help students organize the sounds that they hear when listening to music by presenting songs with similar tonal and rhythmic characteristics. For instance, students should have experiences singing many songs in major and minor tonalities. The first songs chosen should have the harmonic functions of tonic and dominant; later, songs with the subdominant function may be added. These songs should be in duple and triple meters and clearly define macrobeats, microbeats, and divisions of the microbeat.

Singing and movement activities should become a part of the class on a daily basis. A routine of singing melodies and root melodies should be established for no more than five minutes at the beginning of each class period. The teacher will sing a song for the class and have the class echo the melody. When it is apparent that the class can sing the melody in tune and with a good rhythmic feel, the teacher will sing the root melody of the song as an accompaniment. For songs in major tonality, the root melody will be *do* for the tonic function and *sol* for the dominant function. This two-part activity may require repetition or need to be taught over several class periods because it is more difficult to sing the melody accurately while the root melody is being sung than it is to sing the melody alone. When students are first developing aural skills, they will have a tendency to "split second" sing (imitate) the melody with the teacher. However, to develop singing independence, the teacher will start the activity and then drop out to allow the students to sing alone.

In addition to singing songs and root melodies, students should be encouraged to audiate the resting tone as it relates to those songs. Give students many opportunities to sing the resting tone in an informal manner as well as a more direct, formal approach. For instance, sing the last phrase of the song "Yankee Doodle" and highlight the last note. Later, sing the same phrase and pause before the last note, and have the class sing it on their own. The class will hear how the song sounds incomplete without a resolution to the resting tone. This is an important skill that will help students begin to learn songs by ear.

When students learn to sing root melodies to songs, they not only learn to harmonize the songs they are taught by rote, they also learn to predict the harmony for new songs that are not taught by rote. For instance, students who are taught to sing, by ear, many melodies and root melodies (such as those shown in figure 4.1) will be able to hear a melody such as this and predict the root melody (in figure 4.2).

In addition to root melody instruction, the teacher should teach students to sing tonal patterns that define tonic and dominant harmonic functions in major and minor tonalities. The teacher establishes the tonality and key center by playing a tonic, dominant, tonic cadence on a keyboard and then

Mexican Hat Dance

Aunt Rhody

Figure 4.1.   Listening and Singing

Camptown Races Melody

Camptown Races"Root Melody

Figure 4.2.   Hearing and Predicting

sings tonic and dominant patterns, one pattern at a time. After each pattern, the class echoes the teacher. These patterns should first be learned without notation, so that students are focused on listening to the teacher and then repeating the pattern. Also, patterns should first be introduced on a neutral syllable until they become familiar to the students and they can sing them in tune. Later, the patterns should be presented and echoed using tonal syllables. I have had success using a moveable *do* system that incorporates a *la*-based minor. Learning to audiate tonal patterns will assist students in making musical connections when playing songs, creating harmony, improvising, reading, or writing.

The patterns notated here are in the keys of F major and D minor. Singing activities are not restricted to those keys and should be transposed to different keys to accommodate the students' vocal ranges. This is especially true when dealing with middle school students whose voices are changing. Establish major tonality in the key of F major and sing the corresponding tonal patterns. On another day, establish minor tonality in the key of D and sing those corresponding tonal patterns (see figure 4.3).

From Rote to Inference Learning

A specific lesson that I teach middle school students focuses on demonstrating how rote learning can lead to inference learning. In this lesson, I play the accompaniment to the song "Silent Night" on the baritone ukulele and ask the class to audiate the melody to the song as I play. At the end of the accompaniment performance, I ask the class to sing the resting tone. After the class sings the resting tone, I ask them what the dominant root would sound like. I then ask them to sing the other bass note (subdominant). Next I have the class audiate the melody to "Silent Night" while I strum the har-

Establishing F major

Singing F major Patterns

Establishing D minor

Singing D minor Patterns

Figure 4.3.   Singing Tonal Patterns

mony. As they do this I ask them to sing the root melody. I only play simple chord voicings at this time so the class has to infer what the resting tone and the bass notes will sound like. The students are typically accurate when singing the root melody as an accompaniment, though I sometimes help them by walking the bass line from the tonic up to the subdominant note on their first attempt. I do not sing the subdominant note for them; I only lead them to the note and they infer what the root melody for the subdominant chord will sound like.

The reason the class is able to demonstrate such a depth of understanding is that they have had repeated experiences echoing the teacher singing songs with similar harmonic content. These experiences allow them to predict and then ultimately decide what harmony is appropriate for songs in major or minor tonality. This skill is not effectively learned through a lecture approach or by studying theory from a textbook; it is best learned through the aural experiences that the teacher models.

Rhythmic Skills

In addition to tonal skills, students should develop rhythmic skills. Rhythm instruction should always include movement. The teacher should demonstrate how music moves in duple meter with a feeling of two microbeats for every macrobeat, and how music moves in triple meter with a feeling of three microbeats for every macrobeat. An effective way to help students achieve a rhythmic feel is to show them how to move their heels down on the macrobeat, as they pat their thighs on the microbeat. Students should be encouraged to move to different meters and to chant rhythm patterns by echoing the teacher's performance. The teacher should establish the feeling of duple meter through movement and then chant patterns in duple meter that consist of macrobeats and microbeats, lasting for the duration of four macrobeats per pattern. The class, following the teacher's model, should move to the feeling of duple meter and echo the teacher's pattern.

On another day, the teacher will move in triple meter and perform triple meter patterns for the class to echo. It is a good idea to alternate duple patterns one day and triple patterns on another day. When students hear, move, and chant patterns in triple meter, it helps them to solidify their understanding of duple meter. At first, they subconsciously compare the different rhythmic feelings and then, later, consciously compare the meters and notice what is different about them (see figure 4.4).

CONNECTING TO STUDENTS

Developing music skills by singing and moving may be a challenge in the middle school due to the social and emotional makeup of the adolescent. Additionally, students may or may not have had positive singing and moving experiences in their elementary general music classes. If the class is reluctant to sing, the teacher could model this concept on a keyboard and then be willing to sing examples as students just listen. I have found that going back and forth from playing a keyboard to singing helps students feel more comfortable with singing activities. I always try to create an environment where students feel safe and are not embarrassed in any way. Later, students will join in the singing activities because this routine has been established and will begin to make musical sense.

Repertoire

The teacher can demonstrate how a simple tonic and dominant root melody can be coordinated with both hands to accompany many songs in many

Duple Meter

Figure 4.4.   Chanting Rhythm Patterns

styles. When the teacher is modeling how melodies and bass melodies work together, pop songs that students are currently listening to should be included. Many reluctant students will develop interest if the teacher demonstrates how simple bass lines are a part of popular songs that they are familiar with.

Using songs in a wide range of styles is a powerful way to connect to students. Included in the range of songs should be simple folk songs that consist of fundamental harmonic and rhythmic functions. These songs are wonderful teaching tools because they are familiar to the middle school students from their elementary school experiences and they include simple harmonic functions such as tonic, dominant, and subdominant. They will generally move in duple or triple meter and contain rhythm patterns that are easy to comprehend. I have found that middle school students will be more accepting of folk songs if the class is also learning songs of varying styles that they enjoy. Maintaining a balance with song material is important as folk songs provide a pedagogical foundation and pop songs are very engaging. As students begin to develop aural skill, they will make connections between many styles of music as each style is being presented in the same manner. The presentation of many musical styles will serve as a medium for music learning. The content of a musical style becomes married to the development of musical skills.

Some students may not be comfortable singing, especially at the middle school level. Even so, the teacher should be willing to model music behaviors and address this issue by continuing to enthusiastically sing melodies and root melodies. The reluctant singers may be expected only to play simple melodic patterns or solos of songs they already know. It is reasonable to anticipate that the entire class will be learning music skills with varying degrees of success.

BEGINNING KEYBOARD INSTRUCTION

Once the routine of developing aural skills through singing has been established, students will develop a deeper understanding of music that they play. Keyboard instruction could begin with the students turning the volume down on the keyboard, or using headsets, and singing a familiar tonic pattern as they imitate the teacher's demonstration of correct hand position and fingering of this pattern. This way, students are making a connection between what they audiate and what they are going to play. It is a good idea to have students use their thumbs and their index and middle fingers for most of what they play initially. Once the students are using their hands correctly, the class can turn up the volume and play the patterns aloud. Several more familiar patterns can be taught this way with students using headsets to practice what they have just learned. A keyboard graphic could also be projected to enable the entire class to see the keyboard demonstrations at the same time.

Melodic Patterns

In addition to learning tonal and rhythm patterns, students should learn to play melodic patterns. Melodic pattern instruction begins when the teacher plays four macrobeat patterns using only two notes. These notes should be related to a familiar tonality and a familiar meter. The students listen to the teacher's pattern and then they try to play what they hear. The teacher plays several variations of those two notes, and the students continue to decide if what they are playing sounds the same as or different from the teacher's performance. I make a point of expressing my assessment in the terms of

same or *different*. I do not tell a student that his answer was *wrong*; I say that
it sounded different from what I played. This gives the student permission
to make mistakes and to keep trying again and again. When students play
something that is *different*, this shows that they are learning. Learning occurs
when a student plays something different from what he wants to hear and he
tries variations until he plays what he wants to hear.

The difficulty level of the patterns can be adjusted within one five-minute
melodic pattern session to challenge the more advanced students and to keep
the beginning students engaged. Melodic patterns should be expanded to become song melodies. For instance, students can start playing melodic patterns
on C-*do* and *ti* for several minutes. Then the teacher can instruct the class
that two more notes are being added: *la* and *sol*, which will sound below *do*.
The melodic patterns will now begin to sound like the melody to the familiar
song "God Bless America." Next, add *re* and *mi*, and the first phrase can be
completed. If some students are not having success, the teacher should play a
simpler melodic pattern. If students are progressing more quickly, the teacher
can demonstrate the more difficult patterns to complete the song.

When students are having success playing melodic patterns and songs in
one key, transpose them to another key. Doing this will strengthen student
understanding of harmonic function because the melodies that they are
comprehending can be found in different keys. When aural skills are driving
keyboard performance, it is easy for students to transpose melodies and learn
songs in many keys.

After the class has played melodic patterns as a group, they should be given
time to practice on their own using headphones. This gives the teacher an opportunity to circulate around the room and monitor each student's progress.
I encourage students to take chances and make many attempts at playing a
melody until they hear the melody that they want to hear. I find that it is effective to make the entire class aware of examples of good individual solo
work that I have observed. I might say, "Hey, everybody listen to what Mary
did. She played part of 'God Bless America' but got stuck at the end of the
first phrase. I heard her play this [teacher plays the wrong ending] and then
she tried this [teacher plays another version that sounds closer] and then she
played this [teacher demonstrates the correct version]. Who can tell me what
is so important about what Mary did?" The class will answer that she kept
trying different variations until she found the one that was correct.

Technical Concerns

Technical concerns should be addressed as the need arises. I do not spend
excessive time teaching students technical drills at the expense of making

music. For instance, I will allow a student to play a new song in its entirety as I observe his questionable fingering, then demonstrate better fingering choices when he is finished.

Generally, students who play melodies using their thumb, index finger, and middle finger can be successful playing most folk songs. I encourage students to curve their fingers and to keep them above the keyboard, not letting them curl under. I will model any technical element that needs to be learned by letting students see how my hand looks as I play musical passages.

Differentiating Instruction

Each year I am amazed at how quickly students learn to play songs on the keyboard. I continually encourage them to learn more songs as we build on each success. However, some students may feel overwhelmed and have difficulty making corrections to the songs they are trying to play. If students do not experience success, they could become frustrated, causing them to stop taking the chances they need to take in order to learn. If I sense this is happening, I will find ways to keep these students engaged and will give them the answers they need to start making music. For instance, I might have the students look at my hand and watch how I play a melody. Some music educators may think that this type of instruction is not good pedagogy because the students are imitating by rote. While students are learning by rote, they are also learning significant music behaviors, such as using good hand positions with comfortable fingering on the keyboard. They are also learning to play in a musical tempo and to phrase in a way that the teacher demonstrates. Most importantly, the students are not shutting down or having a negative experience. When students engage in this activity, they begin to relax as they watch how I play melodies. Eventually, I will play a phrase that is so long that they can't possibly remember what it "looked" like. As these students begin to play, they inevitably forget what they "saw" and they start playing the melody by ear. Of course, this is the goal all along: to have students experience playing melodies by ear.

Another technique to engage tentative students is to ask them to play five versions of the melody that are "wrong." This gets students' attention! I tell them that I want them to start the melody on the correct note, which I show them, but then play five versions that sound "wrong" or different from the melody they are trying to learn. This technique can be very liberating to the student because it's easy to play something that is incorrect. What I find is that after the second or third try, the student starts to play the melody correctly. Many times students go from being frustrated to being amazed that they can learn melodies by ear.

Sometimes a student will be working diligently on a song but have difficulty fitting a particular passage into the flow of the entire song, such as the fast-moving phrase of "Frère Jacques." Have the student isolate that passage and focus on how it should be played. Then the teacher will play the song as the student listens and waits to play the newly learned passage at the correct time. This way, the student is hearing the entire form of the song and entering at the appropriate time and with a good rhythmic feel. This can be fun, as it allows the student to be successful with a difficult passage while also learning to play with a sense of ensemble.

When students are not successful, the teacher needs to ask, "How can I move the level of instruction backward to meet this struggling student?" Conversely, if a student is not engaged because the lessons are too easy, the teacher should ask, "How do I move this student forward?" There are two outcomes from not differentiating instruction: some students will become frustrated and some students will become bored. Neither of these is a favorable state of mind and often leads to discipline problems, especially at the middle school level. Through aural skill activities the teacher is able to constantly monitor and differentiate instruction to keep all students engaged.

Solo Sharing Sessions

A solo sharing session is when students play something on their own for the class. I like to have sharing sessions as soon as possible during the year. The first day of class is not too early to ask students to show what they can play. This gives students a chance to demonstrate their ability level to the teacher in an informal manner. This is good information for a teacher to have, as it will guide future instruction. Sometimes students' performances are very musical and others are not so musical, but all of the performances are accepted.

As the year progresses many students share songs that they have learned in class while others play songs that are more advanced. This can be fun because I learn many songs from these sessions, as do the students. During these sessions, the teacher models an attitude that respects many different styles of music and different levels of achievement, and students learn that it is safe to play in front of others and safe to learn. Solo sharing sessions motivate students. Students who anticipate playing a solo will prepare for it rigorously. Also, students hear excellent music performances from their peers, which present positive models for future learning.

Accompanying Solos

Solo sessions also give the teacher an opportunity to demonstrate how to create harmonic and rhythmic ensembles. This can be done very informally.

While the class is focused on the student playing the solo, the teacher creates a simple but musical accompaniment. The teacher might sing the root melody, play the root melody, play the root melody and a simple harmony part with the right hand, or play an underlying drum beat.

When the teacher sings or plays an accompaniment with a student who is playing a solo, the teacher validates the student's work. The teacher shows that the student's performance is worthy of being expanded into an ensemble piece. While doing this, the teacher is also modeling to the rest of the class how an ensemble works.

Creating ensembles can be a challenge for the teacher and is a lesson in simplicity. For instance, some students might play classical pieces that they have learned in a piano lesson. The trick for the teacher is to play a simple accompaniment that includes only the root melody for the harmonic progression of the piece. Some students might play a pop tune that they listen to outside of school. Once again, the teacher should try to find the most basic accompaniment to the song using just chord roots. This activity allows instruction to account for the individual differences of the students while reinforcing aural skills. Later, students can be asked to join the teacher in creating simple accompaniments to solos. Witnessing the teacher's informal ensemble performances is beneficial to the class because they serve as a model for the development of student ensembles.

Hesitant Soloists

There may be some students who do not volunteer to play a solo because they may not have the ability to play a song that is as difficult as they hear other students play, or they might be shy. This is acceptable and easy to deal with. The teacher could make a point of assigning the entire class to play a song that is easy enough for the non-soloing student to play. Then, after the group has had time to work on this easier assignment, the teacher can ask for volunteers to play a solo. Many times the non-soloing student will volunteer or, if not, the teacher might ask this student to play a solo. It may take some time before a student is willing to "solo" for the class, even under these conditions. The teacher could instruct the class to work independently with headphones. While the class is focused on their individual work, the teacher could move to the non-soloing student and ask him to play a solo at a volume that is loud enough for the teacher to hear but not necessarily the entire class.

Creating Ensembles

Students should have success playing as an ensemble because of their past experiences singing melodies and root melodies to familiar songs. They have also witnessed multiple demonstrations of ensemble performances by the teacher during the solo sessions. The teacher can begin ensemble instruction by singing a familiar song like "Skip to My Lou." The class is shown how to find the tonic and dominant roots on the keyboard. The accompaniment will start on *do* and the class will try to anticipate when the accompaniment will move to *sol*. The teacher plays the root melody and the class echoes by ear without looking at the teacher. When the root melody is learned, the class can be split with some students playing the melody and others playing the root melody. Songs in minor tonality like "Joshua Fit the Battle of Jericho" and "Snake Dance" should also be learned in this manner. Later, songs with subdominant functions should be learned. I always like to introduce the subdominant function with songs such as "Camptown Races" and "O Susanna." These songs work well because they have an A section and a B section. The A section is harmonized with tonic and dominant, and the B section makes an obvious move to the subdominant chord. This is helpful when students are first learning to harmonize a subdominant function.

Students should be made aware of the difference between playing solo and playing in an ensemble. When practicing alone, they should try many different options until they can play a melody correctly. When students make a mistake as they are playing in an ensemble, they should keep the song in their audiation and think forward as they join the group again. When students learn to practice using these two models, they learn to play melodies independently and they also learn how to get back on track when something goes wrong in an ensemble performance. They learn to become sensitive to what they are playing in relation to the ensemble as a whole.

PLAYING WITH TWO HANDS

One of the unique characteristics of playing a keyboard instrument is that it is possible to play two parts simultaneously. Playing with two hands is very satisfying when successfully achieved but can be overwhelming when first attempted. Piano books generally provide a notated accompaniment part for the left hand that students are expected to play from the initial stages of instruction. These accompaniments are sometimes difficult to coordinate, and many times the rhythmic feel of the piece suffers as the student tries to read the left- and right-hand parts simultaneously.

Harmonizing through Singing

Students need to have alternate experiences playing with two hands before they attempt to read the accompaniments in piano books. Their first experiences playing with two hands should be an extension of their ability to sing and play simple harmony parts in an ensemble. Accompaniments can be expanded when the class sings the root melody to a familiar song as the teacher sings a different harmony part, based on the particular chord function, using good voice leading. The teacher has the class audiate the melody of the song "Mary Had a Little Lamb" while singing the root melody on *do* and *sol*. The teacher listens to check that the class is singing the root melody accurately and then adds another voice by singing the chord tones of *do* moving to *ti* (see figure 4.5).

Make a loop out of this activity and repeat it several times so that students hear the two parts working together. Then, the roles are switched and the teacher sings the roots while the class sings the harmony part.

Next, a different harmony can be learned when the class sings the root melody as before, but this time the teacher sings *mi* moving to *fa*. Once again the roles are reversed and the teacher sings the roots as the class sings the new harmony part (see figure 4.5). This is a good way to give students multiple experiences with harmonic accompaniment.

Playing Roots and Chord Tones Hands-Together

Students should learn to play these parts on the keyboard as an accompaniment while the teacher sings or plays the melody. Instruction should be

Figure 4.5. "Mary Had a Little Lamb" Root Melodies

expanded to include several songs with the same harmonic functions as "Mary Had a Little Lamb," such as "Hot Cross Buns," "Skip to My Lou," and "Mexican Hat Dance." The root melody will be played in the left hand at the same time as the single voice harmony part is played in the right hand. The process is repeated with the roots in the left hand and a different single voice harmony part in the right hand. It is important that students continue to anticipate when the harmony is about to change and coordinate both hands to accurately move to the next harmonic function.

When students can hear the harmonic progression and successfully coordinate the two parts, they can next play the two harmony parts together in the right hand while playing the root melody in the left hand. It is a good idea to also learn to play the inversion of the right-hand part. This activity should also be learned in other keys to help solidify the concept of harmonic keyboard accompaniment (see figure 4.6).

Playing Melody and Roots, Hands-Together

When teaching students to play the melody of a song while playing the root melody in the left hand, keep in mind that it will be more difficult to play the melody with the roots because the right hand will not always move exactly with the left hand similar to the previous exercises.

Figure 4.6. Chords, Inversions, and Root Melody for "Hot Cross Buns"

Movement for Coordinating Hands-Together

Movement activities help students coordinate their hands to play melody and roots simultaneously. I ask students to move their feet to the biggest beat possible that will fit with the song rhythmically. This is different than tapping quarter notes; we are trying to find a comfortable beat to move to as we feel the music. Many times the big beat that we find would be notated in cut time, as we would end up moving to the half note instead of the quarter note.

While the students are moving, I demonstrate how the right hand and the left hand meet on the big beats. Next, I point out how the left hand stays on the key while the right hand continues. I will make a loop out of both of these feelings, the hands meeting on the beat and then the left hand sitting on the key while the right hand moves on. After each performance, I take a slight pause to let the feeling of both hands interacting with each other register with the students. Next, I ask students to imitate what I have just demonstrated. Students can quickly learn to coordinate their hands in this manner as they draw upon their previous experiences with creating harmonic accompaniments.

Many classical pieces sound good when accompanied by the root melody. Beginning students can play a classical melody in the right hand and the root melody in the left hand after a month or two of instruction. When the student learns the traditional left-hand part, it will make more sense because the student comprehends the harmonic structure of the composer's arrangement while gaining experience coordinating the two hands.

Playing Drum Beats for Coordination

Another way to help students develop coordination with both hands is to teach them to play drum beats. Some students may experience their first success playing on the drum machine. This success is transferable to the keyboard. Most drum machines and keyboard drum patches are set up so that the bass drum can be played with the left hand and the snare drum can be played with the right. When students play bass and chord tones as an accompaniment on the piano, they will use the same configuration—bass notes in the left hand on the first beat and the chord tones in the right hand on the off beats.

Students can be taught drum beats (see figure 4.7) that are appropriate to use as accompaniments by ear, without notation.

Rock

Swing

Waltz

March

Hip Hop

Figure 4.7. Drum Beats

IMPROVISATION

Improvisation is an important skill that all musicians and music students should learn. Improvisation is to music as conversation is to language. An entire chapter could be written about this subject as more and more teachers are realizing the power of this wonderful, sometimes mysterious form of musical expression. There are many approaches to teaching improvisation from playing pentatonic scales to modal practice. In this section, I will describe some activities that have proven to be successful in my classes. The best way to learn to improvise proficiently is to repeatedly model improvisation for your students in an honest, authentic way.

Tonal Improvisation

Improvisation activities are initiated when students give novel responses within a given parameter. For instance, the teacher can establish major tonality and sing a tonic pattern, and ask the students to sing a *different* tonic pattern than the one they just heard. On a different day, the teacher could establish minor tonality and sing a tonic pattern followed by a dominant pattern, and ask the students to sing a *different* tonic pattern followed by a dominant pattern. Once the parameters are set, students demonstrate their understanding of the music content by their responses to those parameters. You cannot fake improvisation when singing responses in this way.

Rhythmic Improvisation

Rhythmic improvisation can begin much in the same way: the teacher establishes the feeling of duple by moving to macrobeats and microbeats, then chants a pattern and asks the students to chant a *different* pattern in duple meter. Rhythmic improvisation should not be limited to duple meter, so on another day the teacher will establish triple meter by moving, chanting a pattern, and asking the class to chant a *different* pattern in triple meter.

Teaching Improvisation

The teacher should model different examples of improvisation as students listen without responding. Later, students could be asked to listen to the teacher's example and then improvise an answer as a group. Students generally will feel more comfortable improvising as a group because there is safety in numbers, but the teacher should be sure to ask for solo improvisations. The best way to determine if students understand a given musical content is by assessing the quality of their solo improvisations.

Many times I will initiate improvisation in a playful way. I might sing the beginning of a song in a gregarious voice but not sing the last phrase. Many times my relaxed singing style will get students' attention and they will answer by either singing the last phrase of the song or by making up a melody of their own. Other times I will sing part of an improvisation to a song and once again leave off an ending and wait to hear what students do next. The results are usually fun and musical.

Often, students are not aware that they are improvising. For instance, a student might try to play a song by ear but have difficulty playing it accurately. They may make a "mistake" that sounds like a perfectly good melody. I have students remember these melodies and we treat them as song variations.

READING NOTATION

Reading activities should give students opportunities to make connections from the sounds that they have organized by ear to the notation on the page. In order for reading to be meaningful, students must draw upon their prior music experiences. To accomplish this goal, students should first be asked to read music that is familiar to them before they are asked to read music that is unfamiliar.

Reading Tonally

When starting tonal reading instruction, I present a series of familiar tonal patterns in major tonality (see figure 4.8). Students are only asked to look at each pattern as the teacher reads all of them to the class, much in the same way that a parent would read a book to a child before the child is asked to read on his own. Next, I point out that there is one flat in the key signature, which indicates that the F will sound like *do*.

Solfège syllables are always sung and never spoken. The power of using solfège syllables is that they are sounds; they are not words describing sounds, but the sounds themselves. Solfège provides a way to organize and express musical sounds that are heard.

I read each pattern again individually and the class echoes. I then point out that a tonic pattern in F major falls in the spaces and the dominant pattern seems to be mostly on the lines. Students are then asked which patterns are the tonic patterns in the series. When a student gives an answer, I sing the pattern they have chosen.

I and V in F major

I and V in D minor

Figure 4.8.   Reading in F Major and D Minor Tonalities

Students can be further engaged by playing simple games with the notation. For instance, I may sing a pattern and ask the class what pattern they think they hear by holding up their finger for the harmonic function of the pattern. Many students will give correct answers because they are familiar with how tonic and dominant patterns sound from their aural skill development. However, if one or two students give an incorrect answer, the entire class can be engaged by asking them to look at the incorrect pattern and listen to hear if it matches what is being sung. More likely than not, the class will hear that the pattern being sung does not look like the pattern that was chosen in notation. Then, I sing the correct answer. By engaging the class in this manner, the students are constantly audiating as they are reading rather than just identifying the notes on the staff. The goal is for the notation to "sing" to students and lift off the page as a musical thought, much in the same way that words and phrases speak to us as we read a book.

Students should also learn that, in the bass clef, the F is on the space below the staff. I demonstrate that when the F sounds like *do*, the C sounds like *sol*, yet I do not read all of the bass note patterns to the students. Students next look at the bass clef notation and sing the chord roots for each pattern on their own. They read successfully due to their prior experiences with singing melody and harmony. Reading lessons are made more challenging when, eventually, students can look at any of the patterns in the series, audiate them, and sing them. Note that patterns should be transposed to different keys so that students gain facility with transposition.

When students are guided by their aural skills to interpret notation, they will quickly learn to read in minor tonality as well as major tonality. I begin the lesson by showing students that there is one flat in the key signature,

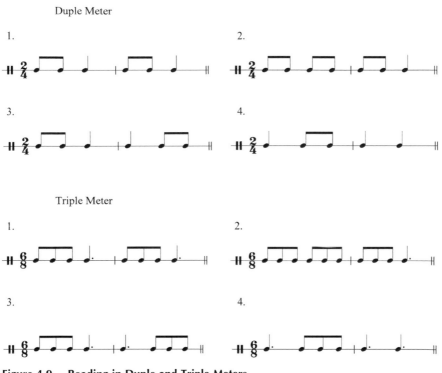

Figure 4.9. Reading in Duple and Triple Meters

which tells us that F sounds like *do*. I remind students where F is on the staff and then establish the tonality of D minor. I sing through the series of patterns for the class, and students notice that we are in minor tonality. I show them that the music rests on D-*la*, which indicates that the tonality is D minor (see figure 4.8).

All of the previous reading activities will apply to this activity in D minor. Students are encouraged to match the sounds that they hear with the notation that they see by singing solfège. Patterns should also be presented in different keys such as A minor and E minor to develop transposition skills.

Reading Rhythmically

When beginning rhythm reading instruction, I present a series of familiar rhythm patterns in duple meter (see figure 4.9). These patterns have an element of familiarity for the students because they remind them of rhythms learned in folk songs. For instance, the first two patterns are the same as the folk songs "Hot Cross Buns" and "Twinkle, Twinkle Little Star," respectively.

Figure 4.10. Melodic Reading Exercises

My experience is that once I read one or two patterns to the class, they are able to read many patterns of a similar content level on their own. Each pattern represents a rhythm and a feeling that students have had experience with. If students are not successful, I will model one or two more examples and then present them with more patterns to read on their own. After reading in duple meter, students will learn patterns in triple meter (see figure 4.9).

Figure 4.11. Reading Familiar Songs

Combining Tonality and Rhythm

Students next learn to combine tonality and rhythm in the same reading activity. The patterns notated here are very similar to the melodic patterns that students played by ear during their initial keyboard lessons. Notice that the patterns begin with simple two-note variations (see figure 4.10). Melodic reading exercises can become more complex and eventually lead to reading songs.

Reading Familiar Songs

The reader may notice that there are no song titles associated with the notation. These songs are presented this way intentionally. The goal is for the notation to "sing" to the student, so that the student is able to look at the notation and audiate the song. If a student is having trouble doing so, solfège is used as an aid. For instance, I will ask students to look at one of the songs and lead them through a process of inquiry to read the song (see figure 4.11). I ask them whether a song begins on *do, mi, sol,* or *la* (singing the solfège) and then ask where the melody moves to after the starting note.

Reading as a Developmental Skill

Reading music is not a matter of students either having the ability to read or not; it is a developmental skill, similar to language literacy. One can read English, yet there is a level of difficulty to reading based on our prior knowledge and interest in the subject matter that we read. Reading fluency is less dependent on knowing the letters on the page than it is on having an understanding of the content matter that we are reading. The music reading activities presented here have been sequenced to help students make connections from what they have already experienced musically. Because the materials are presented sequentially, the teacher is able to adjust instruction to help students if they are not succeeding at a particular level. For instance, if students are not able to read songs accurately, they can go back and read melodic patterns to become more aware of the similarities between the melodic patterns and the songs they are reading. If students are unsuccessful with reading melodic patterns, they can be asked to read rhythm patterns and notice the similarities of the rhythms in the melodic patterns. Further, students could be asked to read tonal patterns and then find those patterns in songs that they are reading.

Repertoire for Skill Development

The reader may be thinking that middle school students will not be interested or motivated to sing and play simple songs like "Hot Cross Buns" or "Mary Had a Little Lamb." However, when students learn how to correctly harmonize or play a song using two hands in good rhythm, they become very excited and want to share their performance. In addition, simple folk songs are not the only song material that students are learning in class; they are also engaged in a wide variety of other styles. When a variety of styles are treated respectfully and used as a springboard to develop music skills, students focus on the process of learning and less on what others might consider to be an acceptable music style. Students enjoy developing the ability to hear a melody and play it on their own, without any assistance. They also become excited to hear how a melody they are playing fits harmonically and rhythmically with another student's melody. Making music becomes the driving force behind class activities. The students will accept the music selected for these activities because they realize that it is the vehicle for their skill development.

Classical Literature

Most piano books present arrangements for the left hand that create harmony for the melody. While these left-hand parts work well as accompaniments, they do not teach students the process of creating harmony, as they are difficult to sing. An effective way to learn how to harmonize piano music is to sing the root melody, which clearly defines the harmonic progression of a piece. The root melody is easier to coordinate when the student first attempts to play a piece with two hands. I have created the following arrangements of classical themes as a way to enable students to audiate the harmonic progression of the piece as well as coordinate the left and right hands for performance (see figure 4.12).

Sonatina, Op. 36, No. 1

Muzio Clementi

Invention No. 4 in D minor

J.S. Bach

Figure 4.12.   Classical Music Arrangements

When students read this arrangement of Clementi's Sonatina in C Major, op. 36, no. 1, they notice the use of a C major tonic pattern in the first phrase. They also can hear how the piece modulates to the dominant key, G major, and the use of tonic and dominant patterns in the new key. In the original score of this piece, tonic and dominant patterns are used as an accompaniment in the left hand. Students will be much more successful playing the original version after they have sung and played the version presented here. This is also true of Bach's Two-Part Invention no. 4 in D Minor.

ACCOMMODATING DIFFERENT SKILL LEVELS

An effective way to accommodate students of differing levels of achievement is to begin at the skill level they are at and challenge them to develop their skills. This means that within one class, some students will learn to play simple folk songs by ear while other students will work on more difficult music. The student with less skill may work at learning difficult songs with the assistance of the teacher while at the same time play easier songs and melodic patterns by ear without the teacher's help. In the same class, high achieving students may be challenged to transpose classical pieces or to listen to difficult melodies and play those by ear.

Building an Ensemble

As the learning activities proceed, novice students can play simple accompaniments or learn short portions of the melodies that more advanced students are working on. For instance, the A section to the song "Winter Wonderland" is a simple melody to learn; however, the bridge is more difficult. When a class is learning that song, the more advanced students can play the entire song, including the bridge, while students who are not as advanced might only play the A section. When beginning students are working on a simple song like "London Bridge," more advanced students could play an improvisation to the harmonic structure or create an expanded accompaniment in a different style —such as an Alberti bass or broken chord accompaniment—while the novice students play only the melody.

Some students who have had extensive piano lessons may be reluctant to play by ear. They may get a feeling of satisfaction from reading piano music and not feel a need to play songs that are not in their piano books. However, these students benefit greatly from aural skill and ensemble activities. Many times students who take piano lessons do not play naturally with a consistent rhythmic feel and the tempo may change during their performances. Sometimes piano students playing from written music are not focused on balance between the melody and accompaniment, or expressive phrasing. The nature of formal piano lessons is that the performances are primarily solo, with no accompaniment or ensemble to respond to.

One way to create an ensemble with students who have had piano lessons is to sing the root melody to a classical piece that the piano student may be playing. For instance, the piano student might play Beethoven's Sonatina in G as written while the teacher sings the root melody. After modeling this several times, the teacher has the entire class, including the piano student, sing the root melody. Next, the class can play an accompaniment to the sonatina using the root melody and some very fundamental harmonic lines. The class can begin to accompany in a way that an orchestra functions in a piano concerto and the piano student is encouraged to hear how the piano part fits with the accompaniment.

CONNECTING TO POPULAR MUSIC

Students often enjoy playing music that they listen to outside class. To facilitate this, ask them to bring examples of recorded music to class. The teacher can listen to the songs and then demonstrate to the class how to learn a song by ear. The teacher accomplishes this by modeling the process of learning the music, while thinking the steps out loud for the benefit of the class to hear. For instance, the teacher will play a student's recording and say, "Let me listen for a little bit and then I will pause the music." The teacher then listens and pauses the recording and says, "The resting tone sounds like . . ." and sings the resting tone. Finding the resting tone will determine the key and the tonality of the song. Next, the teacher says, "I think this song is in minor because the resting tone sounds like *la* and a tonic pattern sounds like *la–do–mi*." The teacher then sings and plays the bass line to the song. (Many times the bass line to the song begins and ends with the resting tone.) After that, some melodic patterns from the song could be learned. The teacher continues to think out loud for the class and says, "I will pause this part of the song and try to play the melody. I think I'm playing the first part of the phrase correctly but the ending sounds different. Let me try again. It still sounds different to me. Let me give it another try. Oh, wait, that's it! Now my melody sounds the same as the recording. Now, let me try to fit the bass part with the melody that I just learned."

This process of learning by ear is very entertaining for the class to witness as the teacher is modeling important steps needed to play music without any outside assistance. This is a powerful lesson that motivates students and enlightens them to the reality that all music is connected and is more accessible than they might have previously believed.

CONCLUSION

The ideas presented in this chapter are a departure from the approach taken by traditional piano method books. However, a traditional approach may not address the variety of needs students have in a middle school general music classroom. A teaching style that welcomes diversity is likely to be more successful. Undoubtedly, reading is an essential skill and should be taught to all students; however, aural skill development acts as a prenotational literacy skill. Reading comprehension is dependent on what students have experienced *before* they read notation.

The teacher plays a critical role in the success of his students. This new role can be exciting for a teacher who is willing to learn new teaching strategies and take some chances. How exhilarating it is for a teacher to witness students, with no prior keyboard experience, successfully playing classical music and functioning musically in an ensemble, or to see a student who has had traditional piano lessons begin to play by ear, improvise, and create accompaniments for fellow classmates! There are no limits to the learning outcomes for students and teachers alike as they work together to create an environment that fosters lifelong music making.

RESOURCES

Azzara, C. D., & Grunow, R. F. (2006). *Developing musicianship through improvisation*. Chicago, IL: GIA.

Bastien, J. (1978). *Easy piano classics*. San Diego, CA: Kjos West.

Grunow, R. F., Gordon, E. E., & Azzara, C. D. (1989). *Jump right in: The instrumental series*. Chicago, IL: GIA.

Runfola, M., & Taggart, C. C. (Eds.). (2005). *The development and practical application of music learning theory*. Chicago, IL: GIA.

Chapter Five

Teaching the Guitar as a Tool for Creative Expression

Clint Randles

Is there a middle school general music student who would not like to play guitar? An instrument that naturally engages students because of the music that has glamorized it over the years, the guitar is a natural choice for inclusion in a general music class. The instrument can be found in classical, popular, folk, sacred, blues, and jazz music. Video games feature the simulation of being a great guitarist, yet students spend hours mastering a game when they could be engaged in actually learning the instrument! The guitar has been the iconic symbol of rock'n'roll music for the better part of five decades and can be seen on all of the music video channels. Moreover, video clips on how to play nearly every riff from the great guitar solos of the last forty years can be located on the Internet. In my experience, students will exhaust innumerable hours picking up guitar riffs to songs simply for the fun of being able to play them. The guitar is an instrument that sells itself. I find this analogy useful, seeing that often at the secondary level students can choose whether they take music classes.

For these reasons, guitar instruction is a logical and necessary addition to the general music curriculum for the middle school student. In this chapter, I will draw upon numerous resources from music educators, music education researchers, and my own personal experience as a general music teacher, band director, and private lesson guitar instructor. I seek to give you, the practicing or future teacher, a number of resources that will help you to set up a class for guitar instruction in your middle school general music program.

ADOLESCENTS AND MUSIC

Music is often embraced as an identity badge in the lives of middle schoolers. Their music—as represented by playlists on their MP3 players and posters in their lockers—is a powerful signifier of who they are as individuals. Each adolescent student would not only like to fit in to a larger cultural group, but would also like to be different than everyone else in some way. Adolescent students also deal with anxiety and self-esteem issues in their daily lives. The guitar, as the primary instrument in popular music and culture, can help facilitate adolescents' need to be similar yet different from their peer groups, while providing a musical outlet for self-expression.

GUITAR ANATOMY

A few basic aspects of guitar anatomy must first be understood in order for the following sections to be helpful. The acoustic guitar is essentially made up of the body, the neck containing the fret board, and the headstock where the tuners can be found. Other important components include the strings, the sound hole, the bridge, and the nut. Components unique to the electric guitar include pick-ups and electronics (volume and tone). (See figure 5.1.) The frets are numbered, starting with "1" just after the nut, and continue until the end of the fret board.

Guitar Selection

When choosing guitars to purchase for classroom use, one must think not only of quality sound but also of a number of other factors including durability and versatility. These points are important to consider, as the instruments will likely be handled by a number of students over an extended period of time, providing quality sound for multiple applications over years of use. There is not a definite recipe for making quality choices in this regard, other than making sure that the guitars are made by a reputable company such as Fender, Martin, Gibson/Epiphone, or Yamaha. A good place to consult for quality, sale-priced instruments is Musician's Friend (www.musiciansfriend.com).

Another important consideration when selecting guitars for classroom use is the action, or the proximity of the strings to the fret board. The strings must be close enough to the neck to allow ease of playing, but far enough away so that the strings do not rattle against the frets. Having to overwork to press down the strings can lead to poor practice habits and discouragement on the part of students. Rattling strings can also be a practice inhibitor as poor sound quality can lead to discouragement. Sometimes quality strings can help compensate for poor action.

String Selection

String selection should be considered when setting up a class guitar environment. Generally speaking, medium gauge strings work best for rhythm guitar work—such as when a guitar is used for accompanying voice. Medium gauge strings can also work for solo guitar playing. Beginners will benefit from the use of nylon over metal strings, and students may find unwanted rigidity in medium gauge strings and desire a lighter gauge string for solo playing. Students who desire to play heavy metal and punk may wish to use heavy gauge strings. A number of companies manufacture very light to very heavy gauged strings for both acoustic and electric guitars. Some of these companies include D'Addario, Dean Markley, Elixir, Ernie Ball, GHS, Fender, and Gibson.

Once the instruments and accessories have been purchased, it is time to take a serious look at curriculum. The next sections provide a focus for building a meaningful middle school general music curriculum with the guitar in mind. These ideas can be adjusted to fit your particular setting and teaching situation.

DIGITAL SOUND DESIGN

Important to my conception of a vibrant middle school general music program, with a focus on class guitar, is the centrality of digital sound design. In order for the focus of a general music class to be on using the guitar to create songs, the teacher must develop a strong understanding of how sound can be recorded, artistically manipulated and refined, produced, and distributed. What I mean specifically is the inclusion of music production workstations in the classroom. A workstation of this kind would include a computer, recording software, a recording microphone, and an audio interface (see figure 5.1). These components in a student workstation allow teachers and students to create and perform music that could in turn be burned to a CD or transferred to a digital sound player. Using technology in this way allows teachers and students to capture, analyze, and share their music within the class community in a way that is forward thinking and refreshing. This type of sound manipulation and sharing fits nicely with the emerging musical identity demonstrated by adolescents around the world.

Developing a musical community—based on the collection and manipulation of personally produced works—will make the daily structure of class

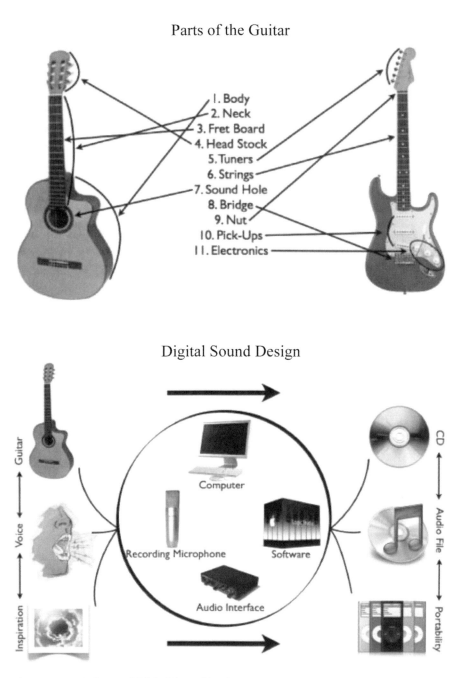

Figure 5.1. Guitar and Digital Sound Design

guitar come to life for students. With these skills at hand, the music teacher can present music as a process—which is in and of itself personally rewarding—as well as a product, reflecting the current focus of students with regard to music as a product most often consumed as MP3 tracks played on an iPod. The world of musical products can be closely aligned with class guitar instruction, thus enhancing the experience of students taking the class.

DAILY CLASS STRUCTURE

Just as in all areas of classroom music instruction, class guitar will need to be planned out in a way that maximizes time for multiple aspects of music making. Certainly, the National Standards for Music Education (National Association for Music Education, n.d.) should serve as a guideline for planning which aspects of musicianship merit inclusion in instruction, specifically, playing an instrument (Standard 2), improvising (Standard 3), composing (Standard 4), and reading and notating music (Standard 5) Because the guitar is an instrument that students seem to naturally want to play, the principles and processes of music can be taught in a way that minimizes classroom management issues related to students not being interested in the subject matter. While no single class plan will work for every student population, there is one particular model that might work well for a teacher who desires to begin a general music class with guitar instruction as a primary component in the middle school setting.

Here is an example of how a daily, fifty-minute class guitar session might be laid out:

1. Playing pop songs (ten minutes)
2. Skills—strength, stretch, strumming, picking, slurs (five minutes)
3. Scales, harmonic progression, and theory—all tonal materials including triads (five minutes)
4. Improvisation and Songwriting—class and individual (sixteen minutes)
5. Guided or open student practice time and private lessons (fourteen minutes)
6. Grand finale—playing a piece students have been working on during class (optional)

This class layout is based on the work of Eckels (2006), but is modified to address the centrality of musical creativity in the general music classroom. The practicing teacher should adjust the times to meet the specific demands of the particular school context.

Recognizing the source of students' motivation is important to how the class period is structured. Desirable skills must be taught in a way that relates to what students want to accomplish with the guitar. I suggest structuring the class in relationship to the end goal of having students write songs that foster their ability to accompany themselves on the guitar. The desire to write more meaningful, sometimes more complex songs will motivate students to seek out the skills needed to bring musical ideas to fruition, setting the stage for the music teacher to present and teach guitar skills. In this model, both the student's musical needs and teacher's pedagogical desires are satisfied.

Playing Pop Songs

Songs that are engaging should be chosen by both students and teacher, and introduced in the beginning regimen of class. Carefully chosen songs can draw students into what you want them to learn. Students will be all the more invested in learning if they are allowed to be a part of the song selection process. As far as criteria for judging good songs, I recommend that the music teacher keep an open mind. If the song choice excites students about practicing and learning guitar skills, then the song is a good one for that purpose. Skills such as strumming and technique can be taught while in the comfort of a catchy popular song. Numerous online guitar chord databases exist as resources to efficiently locate basic chord progressions for songs. Important, though, is the value of picking out the chords of familiar and unfamiliar songs by ear. This type of activity can be a satisfying exercise that will help students develop aural skills in relationship to their technical and deductive abilities on the guitar. The following section provides one such way of setting up such an activity.

Lesson Idea 1: Determining a Chord Progression by Ear

First, choose a song to use as a basis for this lesson. Generally, most pop songs are some derivative of tonic (I), dominant (V), and subdominant (IV). Next, as a class, establish the key that the song is in. Then, the teacher (or a student) can project or write on the board all of the possible chords that the song could contain. Sketching these chords for the students and then playing them as a class can help prepare students for what they will hear in the song. Provide a lead sheet with the lyrics, with blank spaces for students to write in the appropriate chords. Then, by listening to the song and experimenting on the guitar, help students discover the harmonic progression and overall structure of the piece. Then, have students fill in the chords on the lead sheet. This activity can take place as a whole class, or within smaller groups of students.

Again, choosing the right songs for these types of exercises is critical to grabbing students' attention, which can be difficult to do! Choosing music that intrinsically motivates students will address the need to maintain their attention with nonmusical persuasion.

SKILLS

Guitar skills that students need in order to play the songs they are working on should be built into the regular routine of class. When implemented this way, the skills students learn carry more personal meaning and value. Further, students will be more motivated to learn additional skills if they have a use for them. Among these skills are stretches, strength exercises, strumming styles, finger-picking (arpeggios), fast hand drills, and finger efficiency training.

Stretches and Strength Exercises

Stretches and strength exercises are necessary for the developing guitarist because of the physical exertion that is needed to finger and position the hands for playing. A number of resources exist that address teaching students to stretch before playing the guitar. Some of these resources can be found in table 5.1. This part of the performing process is often overlooked, making playing for long periods of time more difficult. The simplest, and perhaps most important, stretch is extending the fingers of each hand out in front of the body and using the opposite hand to stretch the hand and fingers down gently for a count of eight and then up for a count of eight. Switch hands and do the same two exercises with the other hand. This exercise can be performed every twenty minutes of class to help lessen students' finger fatigue.

Strumming Styles

Strumming styles should be based on the songs that the class and individuals are learning at the time. Learning strumming styles is important for students when generating ideas for performance and song creation. Certain strumming styles lend themselves better to particular styles and genres. A variety of different styles should be taught as a foundation for guitar playing. Some examples of strumming patterns in duple and triple meters are found in table 5.2. Students should be expected to listen to music and develop strumming patterns that fit with the musical material they are hearing. They should also be expected to create their own strumming patterns to share with the class. Oftentimes, the patterns that they create are more meaningful to the group than those that the teacher supplies for them. An example of how to teach a strumming pattern can be found in the following section (see table 5.2).

Table 5.1.   Guitar Class Resources

Class Guitar

Title	Author	Publisher
The Complete Beginning Guitarists	Aaron Stang and Bill Purse	Alfred Publishing
The Total Rock Guitarist	Tobias Hurwitz	Alfred Publishing
The New Complete Guitarist	Richard Chapman and Les Paul	DK Publishing
Chords and Scales for Guitarists	David Mead	Sanctuary Publishing Limited
1st Steps for a Beginning Guitarist Volume One: Chords and Chord Progressions for the Guitar	Bruce Arnold	Muse Eek Publishing
The Pro-Guitarists Handbook	Paul Lidel	Alfred Publishing
Guitar Expressions Student Edition	Alfred Publishing	Alfred Publishing

Classical Guitar

Title	Author	Publisher
Solo Guitar Playing 1	Frederick M. Noad	Hal Leonard Publishing
Pumping Nylon	Scott Tennant	Alfred Publishing
Christopher Parkening Guitar Method Volume 1: Guitar Technique	Christopher Parkening	Hal Leonard Publishing
Sight Reading for the Classical Guitar	Robert Benedict	Alfred Publishing
Arpeggi Per La Mano Destra	Miguel Abloniz	Berben Publishing
Diatonic Major and Minor Scales	Andres Segovia	Columbia Music
Slur Excercises and Chromatic Octaves	Andres Segovia	Columbia Music
Esercizi Essenziali Per La Mano Sinistra	Miguel Abloniz	Berben Publishing
Metodo Per Chitarra Op. 1	Mauro Giuliani	Ricordi Publishing
Foundation Studies in Classical Guitar Technique	John W. Duarte	Backbeat Books

Lesson Idea 2: Teaching Strumming Patterns

First, sing the strumming pattern to the class while pantomiming the strumming motion. Then, have the class sing the pattern back to you, while demonstrating the strumming motion in unison. You may wish to have individual students volunteer to sing the pattern back to the class. Then, demonstrate the pattern, strumming the strings of the guitar with your right hand, while your left hand mutes the strings. (To mute the strings, simply rest your left hand on the strings without pressing them down to the point that they vibrate and consequently ring.) Muting the strings isolates the playing task to the pure execution of rhythms, so that the students do not have to worry about making the correct strings ring properly.

Fast Hand and Finger Efficiency Training

Fast hand drills and finger efficiency training should be inserted into the skills portion of the class routine in order to ensure that chords can be played without pause in transition. An example of a fast hand drill that I have done with my students can be found in figure 5.2.

Lesson Idea 3: Fast Hand and Fingers

In figure 5.2, the dark circles represent the fingers that are a part of the exercise—the second and third finger in the left hand. Have someone call out the name of the chord, while students only move the dark-circled fingers to the chord. While performing this activity, students begin to see how the chords are connected. Seeing and feeling the connections between chords, specifically with regard to the fingers in the left hand, helps bridge the neurological gap between playing isolated chords and playing progressions of chords.

Scales, Harmonic Progression, and Theory

This portion of the daily class schedule should be devoted to teaching the scales and harmonic content needed to (a) learn the songs and (b) improvise on the songs that students are creating and working on. As with all of the class segments, learning scales and theory should come into play when learning this material is personally meaningful to the students—namely, when they are creating songs or trying to pick out the harmonic or melodic structure of songs they wish to perform.

Scales ranging from major and minor, to pentatonic and blues should be taught in order to facilitate improvised solos within created songs. Sometimes playing around with scale patterns will prompt the development of riffs and melodic ideas. Some scales lend themselves better to inclusion within created songs in the popular music genre. Certainly the blues scale is valuable for students to learn because it is incorporated within numerous popular music

Table 5.2. Strumming Patterns

Duple Meter

Sixteenth Note Sub-Division

Possible Strumming Patterns	**1**	e	&	a	**2**	e	&	a	**3**	e	&	a	**4**	e	&	a
1	D				D				D				D			
2	D		D		D		D		D		D		D		D	
3	D		U		D		U		D		U		D		U	
4	D	U	D	U	D	U	D	U	D	U	D	U	D	U	D	U
5	D				D		U		D				D		U	
6	D				D		U		D				D			
7	D				D				D		U		D		U	
8	D				D		U				U		D		U	
9	D				D		U		D		U		D		U	
10	D				D	U		U	D				D	U	D	U

Triple Meter

Sixteenth Note Sub-Division

Possible Strumming Patterns	**1**	e	&	a	**2**	e	&	a	**3**	e	&	a
1	D				D				D			
2	D		D		D		D		D		D	
3	D		U		D		U		D		U	
4	D	U	D	U	D	U	D	U	D	U	D	U
5	D				D		U		D		U	
6	D				D		U		D			
7	D				D				D		U	
8	D		U		D				D		U	
9	D				D		U		D		U	
10	D				D	U		U	D	U	D	U

styles. Figure 5.2 shows the moveable pattern for fingering the notes of a blues scale; the example is in the key of F. In addition, the same scale is provided in the keys of G and B-flat. Similar scale patterns can be found in the materials listed in table 5.1, or located on numerous websites that detail scale patterns such as the resource All-Guitar-Chords.com, which can be found at www.all-guitar-chords.com/guitar_scales.php.

I recommend that in the context of the scales, harmonic progression, and theory portion of class that the teacher introduce classical guitar—both performance literature and theory—to the general music class. Some techniques will not be as readily applicable in this setting, such as hand position and foot placement (as with the classical guitar foot rest), as students will likely have a variety of different guitars, both acoustic and electric, nylon and steel stringed. Yet the wealth of historically sound pedagogical and performance resources—more than any other instrument besides the piano—should be used. In table 5.1, you will find a number of resources for group and individual classical guitar instruction.

Harmonic progressions common to popular music should be inserted into the daily regimen of guitar instruction, along with those found in the classical guitar repertoire. Sometimes chord progressions from the classical realm provide inspiration for new music; indeed, students recognize some progressions as music that they have heard before on the radio. These kinds of connections are exciting for both students and teachers. Much of the knowledge and experience from this portion of the class will carry into the next segment of class: improvisation and songwriting.

Improvisation

When improvising, students should be encouraged to "mess" around with the tonal and harmonic material from the pop songs that they are learning, as they build their own songs. Care should be taken in this daily portion of the class time to allow students to produce and refine musical ideas in real time. When students know the scale that was used to generate a melody of a song, they have the material at hand to improvise within the harmonic structure of the piece.

In order to facilitate the improvisation segment of the class period, the harmonic progression that is being used to improvise over should be recorded on a music-sequencing program so that the progression can be played back and looped for student performance. This looped progression can be performed and recorded on acoustic or MIDI instruments. Of course, the harmonic progression can also be performed acoustically, but recording it via a music sequencer will allow you to post the progression on a class website, e-mail the progression, or burn it to a CD for students to access at home or wherever

Fast Hand Drills

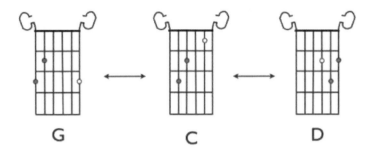

F Blues Scale

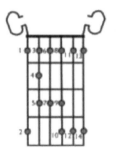

G Blues and Bb Blues Scales

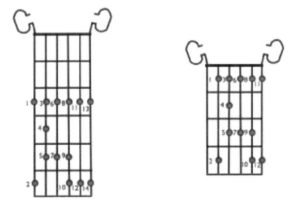

Figure 5.2.   Drills and Scales

they wish to use it. Lesson Idea 4 provides an idea on how you might teach improvisation over a recorded loop.

Lesson Idea 4: Improvising over a Prerecorded Harmonic Progression

Once a harmonic progression is recorded with the music-sequencing program, you are ready to use it to provide a harmonic accompaniment for student performance. Depending upon your specific setting, you will need to provide students with strumming patterns or riffs as material to improvise with. In order for the students to have a creative role model for the lesson, you will need to be the lead improviser at first. For example, if students are learning the F Blues scale, you might play scale segments for the class to echo back; doing this will allow the students to hear a model and to pick out riffs by sight. Try to encourage students to rely on their own ears to make musical judgments when they are comfortable doing so. Once the routine has been established, incorporate the students into the class-leading portion of this exercise. When sufficient riffs have been taught and performed by the class, it is time to play the recorded loop and have student volunteers improvise over the prerecorded harmonic progression. This exercise can be an exciting aspect of the class time, especially when you have presented a good model of what the improvisation could sound like. This portion of class time will likely be some students' favorite part of the day!

Songwriting

Songwriting could very well be the central act of the student in a middle school general music class that has a strong class guitar component. The act of creating something that is unique and original is something that will stay with a student for a lifetime. Because songs contain words, students can create songs that are personally meaningful to them, about subjects that resonate with them, using musical styles and genres that they enjoy. Songwriting puts students in the driver's seat of their own musical development. The desire to create original songs can motivate students to push themselves to acquire new skills and knowledge. In the next section I provide a lesson that will help you to begin songwriting with your class, in the context of a class guitar setting.

Lesson Idea 5: Songwriting with the Guitar

One way of teaching songwriting is to study a popular song that the students enjoy listening to. Examine how the songwriter created the song and the form that was used—for example, verse, chorus, and bridge. Identify why the song is interesting to listen to. Then, begin to brainstorm about topics that interest them. Your students will likely come up with interesting ideas—sometimes inappropriate—that can be redirected into suitable topics. Generating new ideas will come more easily for some students than others. With the students, choose one of their generated topics to base their song upon, then use the form of the chosen class song as a way of structuring the student song project. This way, students have a framework to work within. Create the song together, as a class, using your students' ideas for the key, meter, and the overall feel of the song. Students can contribute ideas for strumming patterns, riffs for motivic material, and the melody line for the different parts of the song. In order to preserve students' progress at the end of each songwriting segment, record the song or have students notate the music with traditional or graphic notation. Because the song is a work in progress, keep in mind that structure is key to all music-learning situations that focus on student creativity.

Student Practice and Private Lessons

A good chunk of the class time should be allotted to students practicing the guitar—individually, in groups, or in a private lesson setting. This is the second largest section of class time, allowing the teacher flexibility in setting up the class for maximum student learning. Differentiated instruction is at the heart of this part of the class period and should be a mix of teacher-guided and student-driven instruction. If some students are ready to work in groups to create their music or perform covers of other artists, they can spend this time doing that. If there are students struggling with learning basic chords, these students can receive extra help from the teacher, either individually or within a small group. Advanced students can receive instruction that will take them to the next level. With careful planning around the skill levels of your students, you will create conditions that allow for the maximum growth of learning guitar for all of the students in your class.

Grand Finale

This portion of class should be similar to the opening of the class: something that is fun, that showcases the skills students have learned in class. The activity might take the form of performing a well-known song or a song that a student has created, or may be an activity similar to a jam session that features some students playing twelve-string guitar, some playing bass, some playing rhythm guitar, and some playing lead guitar. Improvised solos would be great to hear at this point! The grand finale is the final experience students have before leaving class and is the experience they will likely think about when recalling the events of the day with regard to music class. The teacher should wisely plan this portion of class time so that it has the potential to be something special and memorable.

CONCLUSION

Incorporating the guitar as a tool for musical expression should be considered in light of the other areas described in this book. The daily class structure that I have described should be adjusted to fit each unique setting and student population. The guitar can be a motivating and engaging entry point for teachers who value giving students opportunities for original music creation. The guitar is an instrument that sells itself and can be used to accompany students' original songs. If the focus of instruction is on providing students with the skills that they need to play the guitar for personal satisfaction, student interest and motivation will drive the curriculum forward. The teacher's role, then, is to guide the unfolding and unveiling of student interest.

REFERENCES

Eckels, S. (2006). Getting started with class guitar. *Teaching Music*, April, 26–32.

MENC: The National Association for Music Education. (1994). *The school music program: A new vision*. Retrieved from www.nafme.org/resources/view/the-school-music-program-a-new-vision

ADDITIONAL RESOURCES

Kratus, J. (2007). Music education at the tipping point. *Music Educators Journal, 94*(2), 42–48.

Kratus, J. (2008, April). *Teaching songwriting at the secondary level*. Paper presented at the MENC National Biennial Conference, Milwaukee, WI.

Moore, P. (2011). Guitar class makes a Georgia school's music program the "envy" of the district. *Teaching Music*, February. Retrieved from www.nafme.org/documents/journals/tm/feb_2011_tm_guitar_class.pdf

Purse, W. E., Jordan, J. L., & Marsters, N. (1998). *Strategies for teaching middle-level and high school guitar*. Reston, VA: MENC. Retrieved from www.nafme.org/lessons

Chapter Six

Drumming and Percussion

Gareth Dylan Smith and Brian D. Bersh

The rhythmic aspects of music are intuitively accessible for all people to understand and engage with. It is rhythm that people dance to; it is rhythm that pumps out of car stereos and to which people tap their feet; it is rhythm that keeps people motivated as they run and work out in the gym; and it is rhythm to which rappers articulate their thoughts and feelings. As one of the oldest forms of instrumental music, playing percussion instruments connects us with an ancient and vital pastime—an art and a craft that transcends cultural boundaries, and engages musicians of all ages in diverse musical settings; one that is associated with dancing, rituals, battles, celebrations, and the richness of human culture. These significant and authentic musical experiences serve as a vehicle to engender genuine interest within the general music classroom. To that end, the intent of this chapter is to provide practical methods of introducing percussion instruments using group-based and teacher-centered approaches. The wonder and allure of percussion is just waiting to be released, nurtured, and tamed in your classroom . . .

When you strike a drum, it produces an instantaneous response. This immediate success in producing a sound on an instrument is an exhilarating and captivating experience for students. Yet each drum, percussion instrument, or drum set contains an infinite number of subtle sounds and nuances that can be teased, coaxed, and battered to emerge from within. Entrancing and captivating when played quietly, and exhilarating when played loudly, a world of rhythmic sound is contained within drums.

DRUM SET AND PERCUSSION ENSEMBLE

Perhaps the most engaging percussion instrument in today's society is the drum set. It is also the instrument that students hear most often in the context of their daily lives, such as through the radio, at concerts, or on television. Whether your students listen to rock, country, reggaeton, or hip hop, a person playing the drum set (or drum kit) is likely to be *laying down the groove*. As educators, it is important to find out what students are listening to and incorporate student interests into the music curriculum, using creative ways that meet state and national standards. However, with 30 students in your classroom, you may be wondering how to incorporate a single drum set into your curriculum without causing conflict among your students. The following lesson offers one approach to introducing the drum set in an inclusive way.

In order to play the drum set (see figure 6.1), an individual must develop a certain level of interdependence and coordination with his or her body. Operating three to four limbs at a time can be challenging, and many students will not be ready to sit down at the kit and provide a *pocket groove* (maintaining

Figure 6.1. Drum Set

solid time with good feeling). Therefore, playing the drum set must first be approached aurally. If students cannot audiate (or hear) what they are going to play before they play it, the resulting experience is bound to be frustrating. Fortunately, rote teaching of those rhythmic aspects included in drum set grooves provides an opportunity to incorporate other percussion instruments, reinforce ensemble and listening skills, and broaden students' rhythmic vocabulary. Breaking apart the intricacies of a drum set groove also presents a sequential teaching process. Here is one example for teaching standard drum set rhythms.

Step 1: Rote-Based Instruction

The collection of rhythms, consisting of the hi-hat, bass drum, and snare drum, will be referred to as a *drum set rhythm*. A notation key is provided in figure 6.2.

Drum Set Rhythm 1, found in figure 6.3, will be familiar to students, as it is the fundamental rhythm played on the drum set or programmed into a sequencer in numerous styles of popular music including funk, soul, hip hop, R & B, country, and rock. Other method books and students might refer to the drum set rhythm as a *rock beat* or *rock groove*, but it is important to realize the all-encompassing utility of this single drum set rhythm. It is easy to play and to master, and students can use this rhythm as a base from which to improvise and create variations.

Note that no single standard for notation has been established for drum set rhythms; thus, we have chosen to write them with the hi hat and snare drum beamed together and the bass drum beamed separately so that the reader can easily discern how the bass drum is changing each time. For this section of

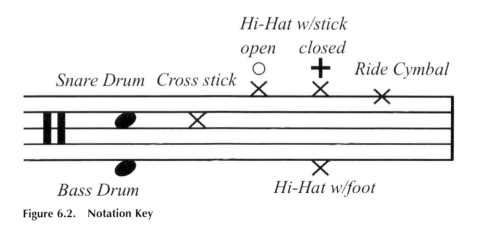

Figure 6.2. Notation Key

Figure 6.3.   Drum Set Rhythms

the chapter, only the bass drum rhythm will change. However, it has been the authors' experience that students will be able to read the patterns with greater ease when the snare drum and bass drum are beamed together. This style of writing promotes the continuity of the line, with (in most circumstances) no rests that often confuse young students.

First, play Drum Set Rhythm 1 on the drum set, providing a model of what your students will be able to achieve through their participation in the lesson. Playing something as simple as this rhythm will provide a foundation from which to continue new ideas. Remember, at this point students have not seen the notation for this rhythm, so make sure your playing is consistent.

Next, create a percussion ensemble with your class to provide a context for your students to successfully master the components of Drum Set Rhythm 1. To teach this groove, separate it into its three parts, teaching each part by rote through call-and-response (for now students will imitate your call—more on improvisation later!). Teach students the hi-hat part. As the smallest subdivision of the beat in the drum set rhythm, internalizing this hi-hat part will provide students with a metrical foundation to contextualize the rest of the rhythms in the groove. Kinesthetic learning is a great supplement to an aural approach to rhythmic understanding. Therefore, whatever rhythm counting system you use, it is important that students first vocalize and feel what they are going to play. To prepare students to play shaker instruments on this part, have them air-play and vocalize the hi-hat part in time. Then give one-third of your students a shaker instrument and have them practice their part with the instrument.

After your students have mastered the hi-hat part, you will lay down the *backbeat*. As the first group of students is keeping time with the shakers, have the rest of the class vocalize and air-play the snare drum hits on beats two and four. Once the class is able to perform these two parts together, give another group of students an instrument to play representing the snare drum. One option is to use a tambourine. Now the snare drum and hi-hat are accounted for, and the bass drum part (represented by hand drums) may be taught. The same steps can be taken to teach this final part of the groove. As two-thirds of the class sustain the rhythmic ostinato of the hi-hat and snare drum using shakers and tambourines, teach the bass drum part by rote to the last group of students. At this point, the percussion section is complete, and the class can play the drum set rhythm together as an ensemble. Listening carefully to each other in order to maintain time and stay together, have the groups switch parts so that every student has a chance to become familiar with each component of the drum set rhythm. Next, place this groove within musical contexts that students relate to, such as real-world recordings, to further engage students.

Technology: A Music Teacher's Best Friend

Incorporating technology into the classroom is a fun and useful way of musically engaging students, providing a musical context while you teach. Furthermore, effective use of technology can serve as a second teacher, an aid for helping students throughout the lesson. This added context increases the significance of what you are playing. Within the current lesson, playing shakers in a percussion ensemble becomes a more meaningful experience when it can be done *with* music, whether it is provided by the teacher using a chordal instrument or through the use of a recording.

There are many other opportunities for technology to be used to assist your instruction throughout this lesson. For example, playing a recording of the drum set groove while teaching the class the rhythmic components of Drum Set Rhythm 1 will allow you to spend less time with the hi-hat/shaker group while teaching the bass drum section. While it is important that students do not allow an external timekeeper to become a crutch for keeping good time, such devices can enhance student performance and become a source of motivation. Other possibilities for incorporating technology into the classroom could include playing a drum loop of Drum Set Rhythm 1. Loops can be found on the Internet at sites such as free-loops.com, within computer programs such as GarageBand or AcidPro, and from recordings. You could also insert the groove into notational software such as Sibelius or Finale, or play a track from an album that students would be familiar with. A groove such as Drum Set Rhythm 1 is found in a plethora of music heard on the radio, such as "Sweet Home Alabama" (Lynyrd Skynyrd), "Respect" (Aretha Franklin), "California Love" (Tupac), or "Proud Mary" (Creedence Clearwater Revival). Even simplified versions of Drum Set Rhythm 1 (consisting of just a quarter note in the bass drum on beats one and three) are used in hits such as "Island in the Sun" (Weezer) and "September" (Earth, Wind and Fire). Get your students involved to help you find more examples!

Another idea is to use a program such as Band in a Box, which allows you to pick a style of music, adjust the tempo, and insert chord changes. The program then generates accompaniments that can be looped. If there is a song that you are currently teaching to the class, students could sing the song as they provide the underlying rhythm with the preprogrammed harmonic changes or accompaniment.

Step 2: Improvisation

The call-and-response, aurally based rote method of instruction that has been used up to this point requires no prior theoretical knowledge from the student. After you have cycled the instruments through the class once, so that each group has played each part of the drum set rhythm, provide your students with further challenges. While you have introduced them to a foundational groove on the drum set, many variations are possible. In most cases, the backbeat will remain on beats two and four, but the bass drum will offer a platform for improvisation. The following is an example of one way to engage students in improvisation.

Bring the hi-hat and snare drum to the front of the classroom. While playing the hi-hat and snare drum parts together, engage your students with different bass drum rhythms using a call-and-response approach (see figure 6.3). Chant four-beat rhythm patterns for the class to imitate, changing it up so as to provide variety within the context of the rhythm being played on the hi-hat and snare drum. To simplify this exercise, you might play these rhythm patterns on the bass drum and have the students echo the bass drum part.

After students are comfortable with their newly acquired bass drum vocabulary, ask them to respond vocally to your four-beat rhythm patterns with their own different patterns. They are now improvising the bass drum part of the drum set rhythm. If you wish to be more mobile during your teaching, you could once again use technology to create a loop or play a recording of yourself playing the hi-hat and snare drum with no bass drum part. Taking this approach allows for each of your students to practice improvising in the safety of numbers: the entire class can improvise at the same time. For more practice, students could improvise with a partner. As an extension, teach students to play any of the drum set rhythms presented thus far with the instruments used in step 1. Have those students playing the bass drum part improvise on hand drums while the hi-hat and snare drum parts remain constant. Change instrument groups so that all students have an opportunity to improvise the bass drum part. All of these skills developed so far are preparing the student for the big prize coming up—playing the drum set!

Step 3: Using Notation

Up to this point your students have engaged in rhythmic imitation and dialogue. They have improvised and arranged bass drum beats using a familiar set of rhythm vocabulary without having seen any notation. If students are audiating, performing, and improvising using these rhythms, they have developed the readiness to read notation. Transcribing familiar information that students are comfortable manipulating will be less intimidating and more meaningful musically than having students decode unfamiliar and foreign notation. From this perspective, teaching students to read rhythmic notation also gives them a valuable tool to write down their own compositions. Use the rock patterns that students have successfully performed in order to work through the process of reading and writing rhythmic notation. Drum Set Rhythm 1 may be used as an introduction for demonstrating how the hi-hat, snare drum, and bass drum look on the staff. Another benefit of using drum grooves to teach rhythmic notation is that notes are naturally aligned vertically so that the relationships between note values become even more apparent to students. We suggest that you do not introduce rhythmic concepts visually through notation that students have not already been exposed to aurally through performance. With that being said, use the bass drum patterns from drum set rhythms 2, 3, and 4 to continue to model reading and writing rhythm notation for students. Next, have students share their bass drum improvisations, and show them how to notate them on the board. Ask students to attempt writing their own improvisations down on manuscript paper and share them with a partner as you survey the class and provide necessary scaffolding. Now students are gaining an understanding of writing and reading rhythm notation in the context of drum set rhythms.

Step 4: Composition

At this point all students have played each part of the drum set rhythms using an auxiliary percussion instrument, and have improvised new bass drum parts to change the feel of the groove. They have also been introduced to reading and writing rhythmic notation. To begin composition activities, have students split into smaller groups with one to two students on each part, hi-hat, snare drum, and bass drum. You have created multiple ensembles within the classroom, each using shakers, tambourines, and hand drums. Using their experience of improvising new bass drum parts, instruct students to compose their own drum set rhythm as a group. Initially, have students concentrate on composing one new part—the bass drum. The hi-hat and snare drum parts from drum set rhythms 1–4 serve as the structure to support the newly composed bass drum part. Then have each group share their compositions with the class through a short performance.

Have students preserve their compositions by writing down their drum set rhythms on manuscript paper. As a cooperative learning exercise, have students notate their group's newly composed drum set rhythm. This allows students to help each other rather than having one student who understands music notation keep the record. If you are not ready to introduce students to standard notation, brainstorm other ways for students to "record" their compositions. You may find that if students do not have the proper readiness for standard notation, too much attention toward writing their composition down could stifle creativity within the group.

Step 5: Developing ~~Independence~~ Interdependence

Your students are now comfortable with how different drum set rhythms function, and have fully experienced each of its components; it is time to further their rhythmic interdependence. There is a myth that implies that drummers need to control each of their limbs independently of one another. *Independence* is the term traditionally used by percussionists when referring to one's ability to play different rhythmic patterns at the same time using multiple limbs. We would prefer to re-label this term as *interdependence* because the myth of the independent-limbed drummer is simply not true! For the vast majority of drumming situations, independence would be a disaster, and would run counter to the whole point of playing the drum set—namely, that the different rhythms all fit together seamlessly. What drummers require instead is *inter*dependence of their limbs. This is far more easily achieved, and is also a much less daunting task to place in front of a novice drummer. Taking this approach with our students will help to get all three drum set rhythms working in tandem. Bass drum, snare drum, and hi-hat parts all fit together around one another; this is the secret to playing drum set rhythms well.

Air drumming or body drumming are great ways to begin this process. The easiest step to begin with is having students play the hi-hat and snare drum parts together. With students sitting in chairs, have them pat their thighs. The right hand plays the hi-hat, and the left hand plays the snare drum (all directions are being given as if the student is right-handed, and can be reversed if the student is left-handed). Engage students in rhythmic conversation (call-and-response) as they keep time on their right and left thighs, although, when actually playing the hi-hat and snare drum, your right stick will be crossed over your left (see figure 6.4). You may want to keep your right hand (hi-hat rhythm) on your right thigh, and left hand (snare drum rhythm) on your left thigh as it may be physically awkward to cross your hands when playing on your thighs. Students will make the proper connections when actually sitting at the drum set. Additionally, although your sticks are crossed when playing hi-hat and snare drum, drumsticks are long enough that your hands will not actually cross over one another.

This call-and-response step is very similar to when you were engaging your students in improvisation. The only difference is that while you were the one keeping time on the hi-hat and snare drum, the students are now fulfilling that role. Once students are comfortable vocalizing rhythm patterns while patting the hi-hat and snare drum parts, ask them to double their vocalizations with their right foot. Students are now playing all three parts of the drum set rhythm, with their voice doubling the bass drum part. Through a call-and-response approach, students will be imitating your patterns and varying the feel of the rock pattern while maintaining the ostinato of the hi-hat and snare drum in their hands. Adjust the difficulty of the bass drum pattern to reflect your students' current skill level. In some cases, it may be necessary to simplify the bass drum pattern to only quarter notes (see figure 6.5). Next, engage students in rhythmic conversation with Bass Drum Pattern A and other variations.

Next Steps

At this point a majority of your students will have developed the coordination necessary to play the drum set, and will be looking for opportunities to use

Figure 6.4.   Playing the Hi-Hat and Snare Drum

Bass Drum Quarter Notes

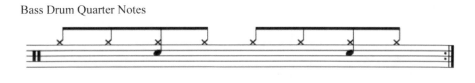

Bass Drum Pattern A

Figure 6.5.   Bass Drum Patterns

their skills. There are a number of ways in which full class instruction can continue even though only one student at a time will be playing the drum set.

Small group work can once again be useful in promoting the development of new skills. Invariably, certain students will be more able to play the drum set than others, and placing students in heterogeneous groups will allow you to differentiate your instruction, benefiting everyone. Depending on what resources you have in your classroom, the drum set could be one of the many segments you teach while introducing students to the instruments of the modern rock or pop band. If this is the case, then students could take turns rotating among the instruments, playing guitar, drum set, keyboard, and bass.

You could also identify those students who are ready to be challenged, and have them play along with other classroom activities. Imagine a standard American folk tune (such as "Go Tell Aunt Rhody"), most likely in major tonality and duple meter. This song develops an entirely new feel and will be more interesting for your students when a drum set rhythm is played underneath it. The basic drum set rhythm, first presented, can be extended as your students progress with their ability to play the three parts together. Eventually, you will be able to modify underlying percussion grooves to incorporate a variety of rhythmic styles such as those found in Latin and Afro-Cuban music.

Lesson Extensions

With the presence of MP3 players, CD players, and the Internet, many recordings can be easily accessed at minimal cost. After you have introduced students to these basic drum set rhythms, give them the challenge of finding new variations. They could bring in music that they listen to at home, and you can direct them to free resources on the web. There are many high quality videos on YouTube and an abundance of resources on websites such as vicfirth .com and drummerworld.com. These sites provide educational materials for students, as well as biographical information on performers, videos of performances, and other features that are sure to capture students' attention. Provide an initial listening list or scavenger hunt of songs, musicians, and bands for your students to research on the Internet, and expand your students' musical experiences with a variety of musical performers and styles.

Some famous drummers who are well known for their sense of groove and musical good taste are Carter Beauford, John Bonham, Jon Christensen, Vinnie Colaiuta, Steve Gadd, Omar Hakim, Steve Jordan, Harvey Mason, Joseph "Zigaboo" Modeliste, Neil Peart, Bernard Purdie, Questlove, Phil Rudd, Chad Smith, and Tony Williams. All of these artists may be viewed on YouTube. Homework for novice, aspiring drummers could consist of no more than a fifteen-minute daily dose of watching and listening to eminent drummers and practicing along on a rubber practice pad.

For those students who continue to excel and are looking for more challenges on the drum set, a resource list of materials that go much more in depth into drum set playing for percussionists is provided at the end of this chapter.

LATIN RHYTHMS IN THE CLASSROOM

As people of numerous cultures with various musical traditions have migrated to and settled in the United States, musical styles have merged in different ways, providing constantly evolving types of music. For percussionists, this is a dream come true! Music outside of the boundaries of the Western classical tradition, such as the music of Latin America, South America, and Africa, tends to consist of complex and intricate rhythms that are exciting to listen to and challenging to perform. As with the introduction of any new style of music, immersing your students in listening to examples of the following styles will enhance their understanding and help to familiarize them to new stylistic subtleties.

Bossa Nova

The following lesson will present the rhythms of the *bossa nova* and *samba*, two popular styles of music from Brazil (see figure 6.6). The folkloric traditions of these styles open many opportunities for creativity and ensemble performance, but in order to create a situation that is most likely to result in success for your students, we suggest that you once again break the grooves into three parts. The bossa nova was developed from the samba and has a slower tempo and less rhythmic complexity than the samba, so it is a good place to begin learning about Brazilian music.

Even though the bossa nova is exemplified in its traditional form by nylon-stringed classical guitar and vocals, it is rare that you would hear bossa nova music today without its distinct percussive element. This rhythm uses some of the same material that your students are already familiar with from the previous drum set lessons. Notice that in Bossa Nova Pattern 1 the hi-hat pattern is the same as the initial Drum Set Rhythm 1, and includes the bass drum pattern from Drum Set Rhythm 2. All that has changed is the snare drum pattern, which is played using a cross-stick technique (see figure 6.7).

To achieve the cross-stick sound, place the tip-end of a drum stick in the center of the drum head, and, keeping the tip in contact with the head, strike the rim of the drum. It is worth experimenting with striking the rim at different points along the shaft for the stick to achieve the ideal sound, something like a wood block or claves. This rhythm can be taught and learned using the teaching procedure presented above in step 1. Whereas, with drum set rhythms 1–4, the bass drum part was more likely to vary as the hi-hat and snare drum provided an ostinato, the snare drum part is likely to play an improvisatory role in the music of Latin and South America. As seen in figure 6.6, Bossa Nova Pattern 2 presents a different snare pattern.

1.

2.

3.

Figure 6.6.   Bossa Nova Patterns

Figure 6.7.   Cross-Stick Technique

Take this opportunity to share with the class some popular bossa nova tunes. Antonio Carlos Jobim, Vinicius de Moraes, and João Gilberto are Brazilian musicians who were instrumental in developing this style of music. Songs such as "Chega de Saudade" (No More Blues) and "The Girl from Ipanema" are popular tunes and may be recognized by your students. Try to play along with the recording as a class or in small ensemble groups. Identify one part of the groove and learn it using the method from step 1. Occasionally, you may find that the groove will clash with the music. In these instances, change the groove to better complement the phrasing of the melody. Playing this style of music with your students can allow for creative and authentic uses of auxiliary percussion instruments. Bossa Nova Pattern 3 (see figure 6.6) uses a new hi-hat rhythm, and can be imitated by a number of instruments. A pattern such as this one can easily transfer to classroom ensemble performance. Try having students imitate the hi-hat pattern with the guiro, triangle, or cabasa.

Latin Percussion Instruments

Guiros come in all shapes and sizes (see figure 6.8). If you have a traditional guiro, made of wood or hollowed gourd, use a rattan shaft to strike the instru-

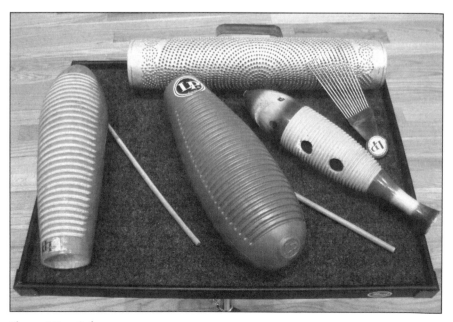

Figure 6.8.   Guiros

ment. If you have a metal gourd, a metal hair pick should be used. Playing the guiro is a combination of scraping and tapping. Scrape the pick or shaft along the ridges of the instrument in a motion that is away from the body for beat one, and tap the instrument for the following two eighth notes. If there are two holes in the bottom of the guiro, you can insert your fingers to hold the instrument.

Figure 6.9 demonstrates how to hold and play several Latin percussion instruments. The triangle can be used to mimic the hi-hat rhythm. Triangles should always be struck with a metal beater, not pencils or drumsticks! See the diagrams of Triangle 1 and 2 for an easy and effective method of holding and playing the triangle. The clip being used can be purchased at any hardware store at minimal cost, and fishing line is used here to hold the instrument. Two loops are tied in the event one should break. When striking the triangle, the beater should hit at a forty-five-degree angle. You will find that if you strike it parallel or perpendicular to the ground, you will get a distinct pitch, yet the sound you are looking for is a blend of the instrument's overtones. When playing the pattern found in Bossa Nova Pattern 3, let the triangle ring free on beat one, and gently muffle it with your fingers for the eighth notes on beat two.

The cabasa is another popular instrument found in Latin American music that can impact the groove of any piece. A combination of scraping and tapping is used to play this instrument. To get the scrape sound on the first quarter note of this pattern, play the cabasa by turning the handle with one hand while the other remains stationary holding the beads. Tap the beads with the hand that was stationary to sound the eighth notes on beat two.

To play the cross-stick rhythm of the snare drum, try using rhythm sticks or claves. In order to get the best sound out of the claves, create a sound chamber with one hand. The clave in this hand will remain stationary, balancing on your palm and fingertips as it is struck from above by the other clave.

Finally, we suggest using some sort of drum for the bass drum pattern, such as hand drums, world drums (tubano, djembe, etc.), or some type of variation.

Samba

The bossa nova provides a foundation for learning the rhythms for the more up-tempo samba. The bossa nova originally evolved from the style of samba. Perhaps the most popular samba tune is "Aquarela do Brasil," by Ary Barroso. This song continues to be used in television and movies; it was used for the trailer of the Disney-Pixar film *WALL-E*.

There are different patterns for the snare drum that are appropriate for the samba, but the pattern from Bossa Nova Pattern 2 can work in both styles. With the substitution of the hi-hat pattern from Bossa Nova Pattern 3, the

Guiro

Triangle 1

Triangle 2

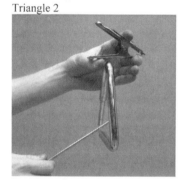

Cabasa

Claves

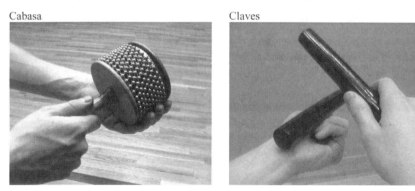

Figure 6.9.   Holding and Playing Latin Percussion

resulting groove becomes the first samba pattern (see figure 6.10). The samba style opens the door for more challenging rhythmic improvisation. Engage your students with the additional rhythmic patterns from figure 6.10. Then, play prerecorded samba music and have your students play along with the recording. (Tip: Use looping software to keep the music going while you

Samba Pattern

Additional Samba Patterns

Figure 6.10.   Samba Patterns

change the sections of students so that they may play the different grooves.) The highly syncopated and dance-like rhythms of this style of music are exciting to participate in.

There are certainly inherent differences in the music of Latin and South America in comparison to American popular music. As long as your method of instruction accounts for the similarities and differences in these new styles of music, the teaching techniques presented in step 1 of this chapter should still be effective.

RESOURCES FOR PERFORMANCE, COMPOSITION, AND IMPROVISATION

We have included two pieces of music that are extremely versatile with many applications in the general music class. Gareth Dylan Smith's composition "3 & 6" (see appendix A) is designed for use with classes with a wide range of skill levels. The piece is presented in such a way as to encourage creativity among students, and can be rehearsed for performance. "Percs of the Job" (see appendix B) also by Smith is loosely based on West African traditions of playing rhythms with six eighth notes per measure. To the ears of a musician socialized in North America, it is likely to sound as though there are simultaneously measures of 3/4 and 6/8 being played. However, as the separate rhythmic components lock in together, a unified groove is created.

Teaching "3 & 6"

New instruments used in this composition are the congas, bongos, and maracas. The pictures in figure 6.11 offer a basic representation of how to play these instruments. Detailed information regarding techniques specific to playing congas and bongos is out of the scope of this chapter but can be found in the methods books listed in the resources section. In the pictures, notice how the bongos are positioned (player is right-handed) and how the maraca is held.

The following are some suggestions on how to teach the class "3 & 6":

1. Have the whole class vocalize and air-play the first shaker (maracas) rhythm until it is rhythmically solid.
2. Have the whole class vocalize and air-play the second shaker rhythm (tambourine) until it is rhythmically solid.
3. Split the class in two and have one half of the class vocalize and air-play the maraca rhythm while the other half vocalizes and air-plays the tambourine rhythm.
4. Give one half of the class maracas and the other half tambourines. Combine these two parts vocalizing and playing instruments.
5. Have students mark time or move in rhythm around the classroom, with their feet stomping out the pulse; the pulse to mark is on the downbeat of every measure, giving the impression of triple meter. Do not be intimidated by the kind of tempo implied by this—these rhythms are probably easier to pick up when not performed too slowly, thereby feeling un-groovy.

You can choose any two rhythms to try this exercise with, and most any combination of percussion instruments as well. Note that the bongo rhythms work most effectively with bongos due to the two pitches required to articulate each rhythm correctly; however, they may be played either as hand claps or as rhythms between one leg and another, or with a hand slapping each thigh. It is possible to repeat the above exercise with any combination of three, four, or more rhythms. If students are in rhythm-groups of three or four to a part, you may be surprised at how quickly they can play what sounds like a highly complex piece of music. You may wish to input the rhythms into a notation software program and play combinations of the rhythms for your students so that they can hear how rhythmically complex this composition can become. This technique also allows students to follow other classmates' parts and is a great exercise for developing ensemble listening skills.

Congas

Bongos

Maraca

Figure 6.11. Instrumentation for "3 & 6"

Once the class successfully performs a few rhythms (two or three is plenty), brainstorm ways for the groups to make the performance their own. One idea is to see how quietly a group can play without losing the groove. Also, students often find it almost impossible to decrescendo without slowing down the tempo, and equally difficult to crescendo without speeding up! Ask groups to monitor this themselves while they play and suggest ways in which they might monitor issues arising in performance and rehearsal. For instance, can they hear one another, or are some musicians too quiet or too loud? Can they think of ways to structure their performance with different players dropping in and out? How might it work if the dynamics are raised and lowered in different places? How does the music sound if they play/strike the instruments in different places? By asking students to think of ways in which the sound and structure might be altered, you will involve them in thinking musically and creating performances that are uniquely theirs.

Once you have any number of rhythms working together, a fantastic way to engage students further is to allow them to improvise. A good way to approach this is to play an agreed-upon rhythm (or rhythms) from "3 & 6" for a number of measures, and then improvise the same number of measures before returning to the original rhythm (see figure 6.12). Improvising in the context of "3 & 6" can be organized as a call-and-response exercise, with one group playing the set rhythm and others responding with improvisations. Modeling improvisation is helpful to students who may be wondering what to play. The key is to let students be creative, and to let them discover what works.

Another, perhaps less chaotic, way to have students improvise is to have each student or small group of students improvise in turn while the others in the class maintain their rhythms from "3 & 6" and the steady pulse. Students can be very creative in this way by playing quieter or louder than one another. To make this a more creative endeavor, consider incorporating rests, eighth notes, or a quiet section, or even playing the instrument in a way that the student has not yet tried (for instance, the side of a drum, the underneath of a cymbal, shakers played side-to-side instead of back-and-forth) in the planning stages of the performance.

"Percs of the Job"

This piece of music is a great resource that can be used in several ways to make music in your classroom. As with "3 & 6," you may choose the instru-

Figure 6.12.   "3 & 6" Improvisation Exercise

ments and the parts to be played (or omitted). Like "3 & 6," "Percs of the Job" is ideal as a platform for call-and-response, improvisation, performance, and assessment/evaluation activities. With an overall feel of duple meter in 4/4, it provides an alternative to "3 & 6" with its common time signature framework (see appendix B).

A New Piece of Music

Teachers and students are encouraged to remember and to take note of new rhythms or ideas that occur by accident during improvisation. What begins as "3 & 6" or "Percs of the Job" could end up as a completely different piece of composed or composed-and-improvised music. There is a joy in creating and re-shaping, just as there is in honing a performance that follows a set of strict rules. "3 & 6" or "Percs of the Job" can be used in any way that feels comfortable to teachers. However, some of the best results are likely to be achieved through embracing elements of creativity on the part of students.

JUNK: ALTERNATIVE RESOURCES FOR PERCUSSION INSTRUMENTS

"3 & 6" and "Percs of the Job" are compositions that, in addition to many other applications, could be used for a junk percussion project. Substitute an upside-down trash can for the bass drum, an empty milk jug filled with pennies for the cymbal(s), and a frying pan struck with drumsticks for the hi-hat. Recycling bins can be effectively converted into tom toms. Small shakers can easily be fashioned from cans of all sorts. Tubes used to hold potato chips or nuts are especially good as shakers when partly filled with rice or lentils. The soles of old shoes or pieces of plywood can be struck at various angles with drumsticks; lightweight drumsticks can be cheaply replaced with the thin wooden supports used for planting shrubs, or sticks used to stir paint. For further creative ideas, see the section "Inventing Notation for Found Sounds" in chapter 11 of this book, which deals with the use of found sounds for compositions.

ASSESSMENT AND REFLECTION

As a cumulative activity, student ensembles could perform their completed compositions for one another. A performance for family and friends in an informal environment will give your students a sense of accomplishment and support for their musical achievements. Such a performance will also highlight your music program.

A performance also provides time for you to evaluate your students' work and for your students to assess each other's compositions and performances. In this regard, students should clearly understand the standards by which their work will be judged. Begin with a class discussion of what should be assessed and how. By collectively deciding on the assessment criteria for the compositions and/or performances, students will feel a valuable sense of ownership and authority regarding the music they have created and will perform for their peers. Next, create the actual assessments to be used. Bringing students into this process facilitates reflective learning as they consider their work, that of their peers, and what they have learned.

Keep the Groove Going!

To help students think deeply about music and reflect upon what they are learning, have them document their music experiences. There are numerous ways in which students could record their experiences, thoughts, and opinions of their in-class participation. Provided here are a few suggestions:

1. Have students write an essay at the end of a project.
2. Have students keep a weekly journal throughout the compositional process.
3. Create a weekly blog for your students to maintain, either in groups or individually; if in groups, a different member could be assigned each week to write the blog.
4. Create a wiki page as a class, in small groups, or as individuals. Setting up groups on social networking sites such as Ning.com or Facebook and inviting peers to join is an easy way to set up an online forum.
5. Create a scrapbook of your students' work using photos, drawings, and text.
6. Create a wall display for the classroom or another part of the school.
7. Share videos of your students' performances on protected sites such as www.schooltube.com.

TIPS FOR MAKING MUSIC WITH PERCUSSION

Keeping *It* Together

The vision of teaching drum set and percussion ensemble lessons to a room full of middle school students may invoke feelings of trepidation, apprehension, and perhaps a touch of consternation. However, these lessons need not appear unwieldy. Here are some ideas to bear in mind that can keep your students' musicking from descending into mayhem:

1. *Signals:* There should be a simple set of clear and agreed-upon signals for instruction such as *start, stop, repeat, improvise,* and *back to the beginning.* Have students participate in the decision-making regarding the signals to use for different instructions. Everyone should agree to follow the teacher when the chosen gestures are made.

2. *The Pulse:* This is the most important element in any piece of music involving percussionists. For percussion-based compositions, it is essential that each performer feel the pulse. This is not to say that the tempo cannot change. With beginning students, try to maintain steady beat at one tempo, but if you feel the pulse change, keep in mind that you can spoil the musical moment if you stop the music just to adhere to a strict tempo.

3. *The Groove:* Groove comes through (a) practicing, (b) listening to your fellow musicians while you're playing with them, and (c) being relaxed and comfortable with your playing. Through the lessons in this chapter, students will develop a desire to practice because they are enjoying what they are learning. Students will have to work with each other and listen to the ensemble in order to improvise and play their compositions, and they will develop a skill set that will allow them to comfortably and confidently engage rhythmically with music.

4. *Listening:* Listening is the conscious and subconscious immersion in a given sound-culture that helps us to know what is and is not music, and what music we do or do not like. Students listen to music all the time. Therefore, it may be crucial to the success of school music that teachers do at least as much listening as their students do—to a wide range of music that their students enjoy, and to which teachers judge it educative to introduce their students. Also, getting students to listen to *their* music in a detailed way that offers new perspectives can be interesting and musically satisfying for them. Ask students to remember rhythms that they may wish to have the class reproduce with percussion instruments, body percussion, beat-box, or the drum set. Students' rhythms can be used as component parts of collaborative class compositions, or as springboards for improvisations by other members of the class. Additionally, students could be encouraged to teach rhythms to their peers—either in small groups or as a whole class.

5. *Perseverance:* It may take some time in music class to establish an atmosphere of mutual encouragement and respect, where students feel able to contribute creatively. Some students will find certain activities easier than others, and ability level will vary from student to student—that is why

differentiating your instruction and having parts of varying degrees of difficulty within each activity is so important. By planning for parts that require varying skill levels and that have equal importance to the overall groove, each student can be empowered and adequately challenged, resulting in a feeling of enjoyment from being in music class. Once the hard work has paid off and a safe environment for creativity has been established, students will feel free to express themselves and support their peers.

THE DRUM SET

This section is provided to give advice for the purchase, maintenance, and assembly of a drum set. The first step is to become familiar with the names of the numerous components that make up a drum set. Figure 6.1 at the beginning of the chapter serves this purpose.

Setting Up the Drum Set

There is a fairly standard set-up for the basic five-piece kit (see figure 6.1). Five-piece kits are the most common, but you are also likely to come across four-piece kits, which would still be appropriate for a classroom setting, and may be cheaper to purchase. In the instance of a four-piece kit, the middle-sized tom is left out. When sitting at the drum set (the stool is called a drum throne), adjust the throne so that when your feet are on the pedals of the bass drum and hi-hat, your thighs stay parallel to the ground, with a slight downward angle. The snare drum will be between your legs, raised to just below your waist (see figure 6.13).

The bottom cymbal (which is the heavier one) of the hi-hat should be placed about six to eight inches above the head of the snare drum. The small tom should be placed above the snare drum with a slight downward tilt. The floor tom, which is set up on the right-hand side, should provide enough space for your right leg to be untouched. If you have a third tom, it can be placed at a similar height and angle to the small tom. This middle tom will be above the floor tom and to the right of the small tom.

There are three types of cymbal stands for the drum set: the hi-hat stand, straight cymbal stand, and the boom stand. Boom stands are useful in placing cymbals where drums or other hardware might be in the way of a straight cymbal stand. Cymbals should also be set in a downward angle. The ride cymbal (above the floor tom) will usually have a greater angle, because the majority of the time the bead of the stick will be used to strike the topside of the cymbal. (The shoulder of the stick may be used on the bell.) The crash cymbals are set at a forty-five-degree angle; the shoulder of the stick should be used to strike them. Make sure that none of the drums are touching each other, and that none of the cymbals will hit any of the drums upon being crashed.

Playing the Drum Set

When holding drumsticks, the fulcrum of your grip lies between the pad of your thumb and the first knuckle of your forefinger (see figure 6.14). The rest of your fingers should form a natural and relaxed curve around the stick. (These fingers help to control the stick from flying out of your hands.) Your grip should lie about one-third of the way up from the shoulder of the stick. When you play the snare drum, your palms will face the head of the drum. When playing the ride cymbal, it may be more comfortable for your thumb to point upward, as if you were giving a handshake. Yet, when playing on the bell, it may be comfortable again to have your palm face the surface of the cymbal.

The three most common ways to play the hi-hat cymbal are as follows: (a) bead of the stick to be used to strike the top cymbal while your foot is depressed on the pedal (closed hi-hat), (b) shoulder of stick to be used to strike

Figure 6.13. Position of the Snare Drum

Figure 6.14.   Drum Stick Grip

the edge of the cymbal (closed hi-hat), or (c) shoulder of stick on open hi-hat. As shown in the drum notation key (figure 6.2), an open hi-hat is designated when a circle is above the notation, and closed is designated by a plus sign. When there is no marking, it means the hi-hat is closed.

Purchasing a Drum Set

A drum set can be purchased for a manageable price. One place to look for a drum set is your local music store, where you can often find good prices on used instruments. Websites that we have found to be useful are listed in the resources section. Quality equipment can be found on websites such as eBay and Craigslist; however, whenever making an online purchase, seek the advice or opinion of a percussionist or teacher whom you trust.

Drum Set Maintenance

The most common problem, when caring for the drum set, is the maintenance of the cymbal stands. You must make sure that the cymbal stands have felts and sleeves. If a cymbal is left touching the metal of the stand, it can weaken the cymbal, eventually leading to a crack when it is struck with a stick. It will also be necessary to change the drumheads every so often. When heads begin to lose their resonance, or are dented from improper playing, it may be time to change them. As long as you make sure that the heads of the drums are not overly tight, and that the drums are played correctly, drumheads should last the course of a year.

CONCLUSION

This chapter is by no means the be-all and end-all of percussion instruction. Results will vary according to the interests of students and the music background of the teacher. The models we have presented are those that reflective practitioners will be able to adapt to their unique classroom situations. These examples and lesson ideas will guide you to create your own curriculum that will reflect the needs of your circumstances, and successfully engage your students in meaningful music making!

ADDITIONAL RESOURCES

Included below is a short list of some of the drum set and percussion education resources that we use in our practice.

Internet Resources

www.mikedolbear.com (This site provides news about drumming events, interviews with drummers, and journalistic pieces covering a wide array of drum-set-related subjects.)

www.musicradar.com (This is the online home of *Rhythm* magazine; the website provides reviews of drums, cymbals, drum kits, album releases, and gigs. Each month there are interviews with various professional drummers.)

www.drummerworld.com (As the name implies, this is a website for all things drums! One of the best features of this site is its encyclopedic pages of information about hundreds of the world's best drummers.)

www.moderndrummer.com (This site provides information regarding professional drummers, contests, clinics, and events. It also archives videos and music that are referenced in the pages of the *Modern Drummer* magazine.)

www.youtube.com (YouTube offers a platform for viewing musical performances and tutorial videos for drumming and percussion.)

www.vicfirth.com (This site has an education resource center with videos and play-along tracks, information on artists, and clinic schedules.)

Software Programs

Sibelius: music notation software

Finale: music notation software

Noteflight: online music notation software

Audacity: free recording software

GarageBand: www.apple.com/ilife/garageband

ACIDPro: www.sonycreativesoftware.com/acidpro

Instructional/Method Books

Drum Set

Erskine, P. (2004). *The Erskine method for drumset.* Van Nuys, CA: Alfred Publishing.
Hassell, D. (1989). *Graded course for drum kit book 1.* Woodford Green: International Music.
Hassell, D. (1989). *Graded course for drum kit book 2.* Woodford Green: International Music.

Latin/Afro-Cuban Percussion

Mauleon, R. (1993). *Salsa guidebook for piano and ensemble.* Petaluma, CA: Sher Music.
Sulsbruck, B. (1982). *Latin-American percussion: Rhythms and rhythm instruments from Cuba and Brazil.* Copenhagen: Den Rytmiske Aftenskoles Forlag.
Uribe, E. (1996). *Afro-Cuban percussion and drum set.* Van Nuys, CA: Alfred Publishing.
Uribe, E. (1994). *Brazilian percussion and drum set.* Van Nuys, CA: Alfred Publishing.

General Percussion

Bruford, B. (1988). *When in doubt, roll!* Cedar Grove, NJ: Modern Drummer.
Casella, J., & Ancona, J. (2003). *Up front.* Portland, OR: Tap Space.
Hart, M., & Stevens, J. (1990). *Drumming at the edge of magic: A journey into the spirit of percussion.* New York, NY: Harper.
Persip, C. (1987). *How not to play drums: Not for drummers only.* Milwaukee, WI: Hal Leonard.

Rothman, J. (1983). *Basic drumming*. Voorhees, NJ: Charles Dumont & Son.

Starr, E. (2003). *The everything drums book*. Avon, UK: F & W.

Pedagogy

D'Amore, A. (2009). *Musical futures: An approach to teaching and learning resource pack* (2nd ed.). London: Paul Hamlyn Foundation.

Green, L. (2008). *Music, informal learning and the school: A new classroom pedagogy*. Aldershot, UK: Ashgate.

Online Stores for Purchasing Equipment

www.steveweissmusic.com

www.musiciansfriend.com

www.westmusic.com

Gareth Dylan Smith and Brian D. Bersh

APPENDIX A: "3 & 6"

Gareth Dylan Smith

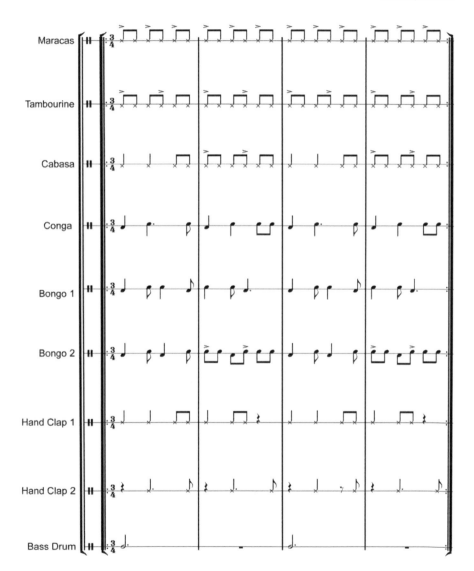

APPENDIX B: "PERCS OF THE JOB"

Gareth Dylan Smith

Chapter Seven

Steel Band in the Middle School General Music Classroom

Harvey Price

Whether it is the captivating sound of the instrument, its technical ease, or the ability to facilitate playing in all twelve keys, teaching musical concepts and skills with the steel drum is easy and inspirational for student and teacher alike! Invented in Trinidad about sixty years ago, the steel drum, or *pan*, developed out of the desire of an underserved population to make music. The use of the pan grew into both a musical statement and a political and socioeconomic movement. Over the past fifteen years of teaching pan at all levels of education and with typical and special needs school students, I have found that this instrument is an excellent means to educate all students musically. In this chapter, I will take you through the process of acquiring your first instruments to learning how to play and giving your first performance, to maintaining your band.

LEARNING TO PLAY

Getting Started

Learning to play pan is an easy and organic process. As a teacher, you can teach yourself how to play pan over the course of a few weeks, since very little time is needed to learn how to get a good sound out of the instrument.[1] To teach yourself, I suggest starting with either a *lead* or *tenor pan* (two names for the same instrument), or a set of *double seconds*. Begin your instruction with scales on the lead pan (see figure 7.1). Notice that the intervallic pattern of the drum is in fourths and fifths. This instrument is referred to as a *fourths and fifths* lead. You will see that the *naturals* are on the right side of the drum whereas the *sharps* and *flats* are on the left side of the drum. Regardless of the initial scale degree to be played, the pattern will always be the same as in this C major scale example: The first three notes will be counterclockwise, C, D, E; the next note across the drum, F; then the next three notes will be counterclockwise, G, A, B; and the last note, C, across the drum.

If you start learning how to play on a set of double seconds (see figure 7.1), you will notice that in front of you are two whole tone scales on each drum. To play a C major scale, your left hand will play C, D, E on the left drum. Your right hand will then play F, G, A, B on the right-hand drum; your left hand will finish with the C on the left-hand drum. An F major scale would work the same way; however, you will start on the right-hand drum. Chromatic scales operate by alternating both hands and drums, with C on the left side, C-sharp on the right, D on the left, and so forth.

Another positive aspect of using this instrument to teach music is that your students can start to play melodies immediately due to the *built-in* sound of the drum. Mastery of scales is not necessary to begin playing melodies and there are no tone production obstacles to overcome. Both conjunct (stepwise) and disjunct (intervallic) melodies are simple to teach and attain since the layout of the drums is readily visible, without physical barriers. You and your students will find that playing pan is easy and comfortable.

Chords are also easy to learn on these instruments. On the lead pan, the root and the third (in a major triad) are four notes apart moving counterclockwise, with the fifth being right next to the root. For a minor triad, the root and the third are three notes apart moving clockwise, with the fifth next to the root. When playing on the double second pans, the root and third in a major triad are next to one another with the fifth being on the opposite pan. In a minor triad, the root is by itself with the minor third and the fifth next to one another. As you can see, the patterns of the notes on these two instruments are very logical. Just as with melodic playing, don't be afraid to start right away with playing scales, melodies, and chordal harmonies. You can apply everything you already know about music to the steel drums.

Other Voices of the Steel Band

While the lead pan and double seconds are generally the best pans for beginners, there are other voices used in the steel band. Presented here are the double guitars (figure 7.1), triple guitars—or cellos (figure 7.2)—and the six bass (figure 7.2).

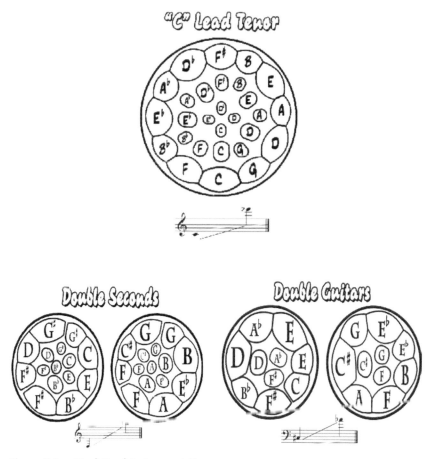

Figure 7.1.   Steel Band Instrumentation

SETTING UP THE STEEL BAND

Once you have learned the basics of playing the steel drum, the moment comes when you ask yourself or your school administrator the question, "Where can I get these instruments?" This section will provide detailed information on the selection and purchase of steel drums.

Pan Manufacturers and Cost

There are two types of steel drums sold in the United States: those manufactured within the United States, and those manufactured abroad. Of these types,

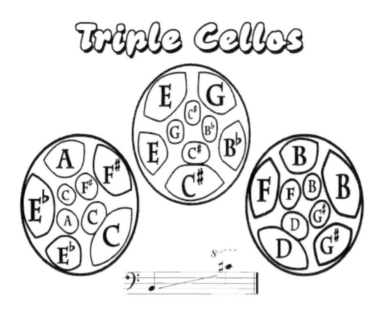

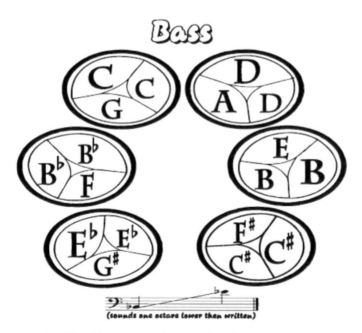

Figure 7.2. Steel Band Instrumentation (continued)

there are several U.S. manufacturers and an even smaller number of companies that import drums from Trinidad. The imported drums are made by Trinidadian pan makers and are shipped to the United States. Well-manufactured foreign instruments generally sell for less money than those manufactured in the United States. Pans imported directly from Trinidad sell for lower prices than those that are sold by U.S. importers. The problem with importing pans is that there is no guarantee that the drums will arrive properly tuned or undamaged. Returning an out-of-tune or damaged drum back to a Trinidad manufacturer is costly and time consuming. Fortunately, the few companies that sell imported drums in the United States often will guarantee their products.

Because these instruments are handmade, the layout of the steel pan voices varies from builder to builder. A set of double seconds from one builder will look different than a set of double seconds from a different builder. If you order a set of pans and have to switch builders or suppliers, it is advisable to ask the new builder to stay with the pattern that your band is used to.

Table 7.1 presents a number of websites that sell either imported or U.S.-manufactured drums. This is a partial list, searching steel drum websites, chat rooms, and message boards will most likely reveal more suppliers.

The pricing of steel drums varies greatly. Table 7.1 also shows an approximate cost for each voice.

Accessories

The accessories required for each pan are stands, sticks, and cases. There will be additional delivery or shipping fees that vary depending on where you live and the geographical area of your supplier. A quick perusal of the above prices will help you to calculate the cost of a five-piece beginning steel band consisting of two leads, a double second, a triple guitar, and a set of basses. Equipping each with stands, sticks, and cases, with the addition of delivery fees could cost between $12,000 and $30,000. Don't be put off by the price, however. This will be one of the best investments in music education that you will ever make!

Funding Your Steel Band

You may wonder how you will pay for all of this equipment. Purchasing these instruments is very different from purchasing traditional band instruments. The cost of a pan set and the necessary accessories may exceed most schools' music budgets. Since the investment is quite large, school districts as well as local granting organizations may be asked to help defray all or portions of the cost. Funding entities are often more eager to give money for capital in-

Table 7.1. Steel Drum Resources

Websites for Steel Drum Suppliers

1.	http://www.steelpans.com/
2.	http://www.panyard.com/
3.	http://www.mannettesteeldrums.com/
4.	http://www.kdsteeldrums.com/home.html
5.	http://www.coyledrums.com/

Imported and Domestic Costs for Steel Drums

Type	Cost
Imported Leads	$900 - $1500 depending on the drum finishes (chrome-plated or painted)
U.S. Manufactured leads	$2200 - $5000 depending upon the manufacturer
Imported Seconds	$1200 - $2200 depending on the drum finishes (chrome-plated or painted)
U. S. Manufactured Seconds	$2800 - $7000 depending on the drum finishes (chrome-plated or painted)
Imported Guitars	$1900 - $2500 depending on the drum finishes (chrome-plated or painted)
U. S. Manufactured Guitars	$2500 - $4000 depending on the drum finishes (chrome-plated or painted)
Imported Cellos	$2200 - $3500
U. S. Manufactured Cellos	$2500 - $8500 depending on the drum finishes (chrome -plated or painted)
Imported Basses	$1900 - $2500
U. S. Manufactured Basses	$3000 - $10,000 depending on the drum finishes (chrome-plated or painted)

vestments that will involve a wide population of students rather than to those that are more narrowly based. With that in mind, consider maximizing the use of the instruments by forming a faculty/PTA or community steel band in addition to your student bands. These instruments can be taught to the entire student population of your school; extending instruction to the adult staff members of your school and also to your community will ensure that you will have support from school administrators, parents, and the community at large. With such a large base of support and popularity, requesting and receiving funding will be a much easier task!

DIAGRAM OF THE CLASSROOM

A typical instrumentation for a steel band consists of two leads, a double second, a triple cello, bass, and drum set. You will want to set up your classroom so that you can teach from in front of the ensemble. If you think of the steel band as an SATB chorus, the leads are the sopranos, seconds are altos, cellos are tenors, and basses are the basses. Place the two leads and the seconds in front. The cellos and the bass can be together behind the leads, and for rehearsal purposes, the drum set, if you (the teacher) are playing it, can be in front. If you are not teaching from the drum set, that player will be in the back of the ensemble. See figure 7.3 for an initial classroom layout. As your band gets larger, add an additional lead (see figure 7.3). Then, add a double second, followed by a double guitar pan (figure 7.4). Increase your ensemble to include a cello pan, further extending the band by adding a bass (figure 7.5). Additional leads and double seconds may then be incorporated to your instrumentation.

FIRST LESSONS

At the first lesson, allow the students to explore the pans to hear the beautiful sound that they produce. Have the students hold the sticks lightly between the thumb and forefinger with the rest of the fingers curled loosely around the stick. The students then should strike lightly on the various notes of the drum that they are playing. It will take no time for them to realize that the larger notes (the lower notes) take much less effort to produce a sound than the smaller, higher notes. Each player will have to learn where the sound threshold is for the entire range of the drum. If they strike the lower notes with the same intensity as the higher ones, they will produce a harsh, *barking* sound. Encourage your students not to let the notes bark! Determining which student plays on what drum is entirely up to you. You can let each student try the different drums to decide which one he or she prefers, or you can assign each student a drum to play.

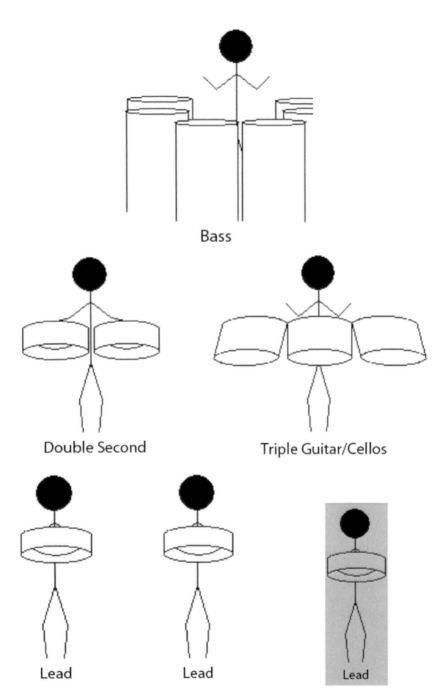

Figure 7.3. Class Layout I

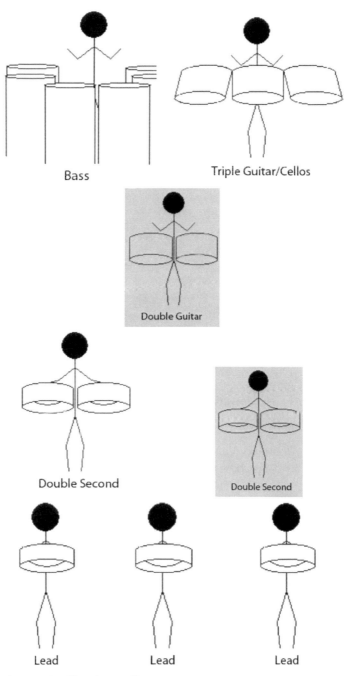

Figure 7.4.   Class Layout II

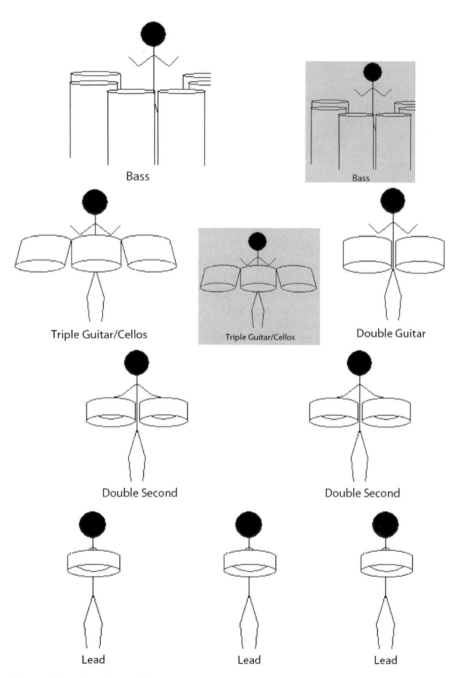

Bass

Bass

Triple Guitar/Cellos

Triple Guitar/Cellos

Double Guitar

Double Second

Double Second

Lead

Lead

Lead

Figure 7.5.   Class Layout III

Scales

Once the students are standing at their instruments, you can start teaching scales. It really does not matter which scale you start with, since the patterns are all the same, depending on where you start. For example, here is a process for teaching a D major scale: Have everyone find D. Then have them play it in whole notes, half notes, quarter notes, and eighth notes. Create different rhythms to play on the note D. Next, move to E, then F-sharp, and eventually each scale degree on up to D. Then explore the D scale using a variety of rhythm patterns.

When the students are comfortable moving up and down on the D scale, start to work with smaller-scale combinations. While having students trill on each note, use *toggling*, or moving back and forth between two notes in various rhythms. For instance, toggle D, E, D, E repetitiously in eighth notes. Then move to E, F-sharp, E, F-sharp, in the same rhythm. Next, play F-sharp, G, F-sharp, G and up to C-sharp, and D. Explain the difference between half steps and whole steps this way and the configuration that comprises the major scale.

You can add other notes and create three- and four-note toggled rhythms. It is important at this point to make sure that the students have a way of identifying the scale degrees that they are playing. Whether you use a solfège-based system (*do–re–mi–fa*) or a numbers-based system (1–2–3–4) does not matter; use the system through which your students will learn the best. All of these techniques engage students in exploring their pans, helping them feel comfortable with the notes in each scale, while allowing them to see how melodies are created. Moreover, these techniques provide an opportunity for them to play together as a hand, a concept that is probably the most beneficial element that steel band performance has to offer: students love being part of a group and experiencing a sense of camaraderie.

First Tunes/Teaching Chord Progressions

Once your students are familiar with the D major scale and the many ways they can move around within it, it is time to introduce chords. Because you have emphasized that scales move in a *step-wise* fashion, introducing chords as *moving by skips* helps to solidify the difference between the two.

Teaching chords and their relationship to melody is a good first step in introducing your students to functional harmony. Begin with the D major triad in root position. From there you can move to the IV chord in root position and then to the V chord. By adding a dotted quarter, dotted quarter, quarter note rhythm to each of those chords you have created the chorus to the Calypso classic, "Matilda." Not only have the students just learned their first song but they have also been introduced to the world of music theory. (To listen to a recording of "Matilda," go to www.akh.se/harbel/lyrics/matilda.htm.)

Having already introduced your students to the concept of scale degrees, you can now start to string together common chord progressions such as ii–V–I, or vi–ii–V–I. Explore uncommon progressions for fun. You will find that with steel drums students will be thinking harmonically sooner than on any other instrument that they encounter.

Getting back to the example of "Matilda," after learning the three chords there is a scale pattern that travels in descending order: *do–la–sol–sol–fa–mi–mi–mi–re–do* (or, if you prefer, 1–6–5–5–4–3–3–3–2–1). Moving this song around in multiple keys emphasizes the impact that I–IV–V–I has on our Western music. Transposition becomes easy because the pattern layout of the steel drums makes the playing of a tune like "Matilda" in multiple keys attainable within the first couple of weeks that your band is together.

It is a good idea to have the entire ensemble learn to play the melody on any tune that you teach to your steel band. Try using songs that every student knows, such as "Mary Had a Little Lamb," "Twinkle, Twinkle, Little Star," "Are You Sleeping?," or "Happy Birthday." Once your students have learned the tunes, you can arrange the songs in any manner you want. For example, have the cellos and the leads play the melody in octaves; add the double seconds using a *strumming* pattern on the harmonic progression (see figure 7.6), and have the bass play a combination of the melody and the root and the fifth of each chord in the song. There are multiple ways to arrange for steel drums. Treating traditional songs as Reggaes or Calypsos adds different colors and dimensions to familiar songs. Be sure to play songs in as many keys as possible, or modulate within a song. All of these techniques make the musical experience more interesting!

Another way to teach songs is by letting the students experience the chord progression of the song first. Using the song "Jamaica Farewell," have students on the bass and cello pans play the root and fifth of the chord with those on the leads playing the third and fifth. The double seconds play the root and the third. (To hear "Jamaica Farewell," go to www.akh.se/harbel/lyrics/jamaica_farewell.htm.)

Have your students switch the voicing, allowing them to hear how different the same progression sounds in alternate voices. With only two sticks to play three notes of a chord, decisions will have to be made; let the students decide which two of the three notes of the chord they want to play. The results will be that your students will be arranging on the spot! After the chords to "Jamaica Farewell" are learned, teach them the melody. You can do this either by writing out the notation or by teaching it by rote.

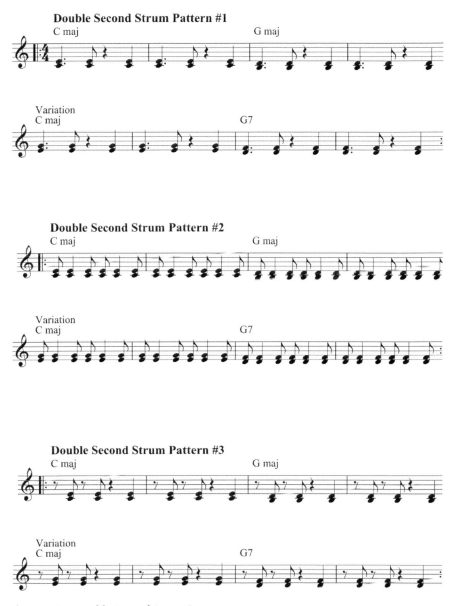

Figure 7.6.   Double Second Strum Patterns

There are many musical elements and musicianship skills that you will teach through the use of simple songs. Form, harmony, rhythm, voicing, ensemble playing, listening, and decision-making are but a few, and all have great merit; each will have an impact on each student's musicianship. While decision-making is not typically considered to be a musical element, it is an excellent concept for a middle school student to grasp. Insightful questions such as "If I play the third and fifth as opposed to the root, will I like the sound of the chord better?" or the consideration of "My fellow pan player is playing the root and fifth so I'll choose the third and fifth" are advanced musical decisions. You will find that playing in a steel band facilitates these types of musical thought processes.

LEARNING BY ROTE

The traditional way of learning steel pan in Trinidad is by rote. A leader stands in front of one or more players and teaches them by either playing or singing the notes of a particular passage. Our Western sensibilities often deride this type of learning, yet the pan players in Trinidad may very well have the best *ears* in the world. They can learn incredibly complex music just by listening. Naturally, having musicians who can both hear and read music is an ideal situation. Trying to attain this ideal may be frustrating, especially at the beginning stages of instruction. Yet don't be afraid to teach your first steel drum lessons through rote learning. You will be amazed how quickly your students develop listening skills, how readily they accept and learn new material, and how easily a transition to reading music is accomplished.

With rote learning, start with the simple scale concept. Try singing and playing two- to four-note scale patterns using the toggling method described earlier. Then use rote learning to explore the concept of step-wise movement for scales and skipping movement for chords, remembering to work in multiple keys. Finally, teach the songs mentioned above. You can sing using solfège or with numbers.

TEACHING READING

If the students in your steel band are already reading music, it is relatively easy to learn how to read on pan. If your students are new to reading, however, it will not take long to get them to grasp this concept on steel drum. The key to reading on pan begins with knowing the instrument's layout well enough so that your students do not have to look down at the instrument, taking their eyes away from the page or whiteboard. Encourage your students to keep their eyes on the page, even if they strike the wrong notes. Eventually they will feel comfortable not looking down into their drum when they go to strike a note. Remember that to become proficient readers, students need regular opportunities to read music. As with any novice music reader, keep the range of the music small—confining it to a fifth or an octave. Music in beginning oboe books work really well for the range of leads and double seconds. Then, there is always a question whether to use treble clef or bass clef with guitars and cellos; the preference is yours.

STYLISTIC ACCOMPANIMENTS: CALYPSO, SOCA, BOSSA NOVA, AND REGGAE

Developing rhythmic accuracy and time is one of the biggest benefits to playing in a steel band. Because the music that you will perform with your band is dance based, it is important that students understand the feel of macro and micro beats (the overall pulse and its subdivision). Accompaniment patterns to the melodies that you have taught by rote or through reading are naturally broken up so that some players play on downbeats while others play on upbeats, such as the typical double second "strum" patterns in figure 7.6. Notice the interplay between the voices. Each voice has to work with the other and change chords together in order for the performance of the song to be successful. The rhythmic benefits as well as the overall cooperative nature of playing in a rhythm section cannot be overstressed.

Calypso

There are four basic patterns that come out of the drum set/percussion section of a steel band, which is called the *engine room*. The most traditional steel band groove is the Calypso (see figure 7.7). When playing Calypso, the drum set player can play a pattern as simple or as complicated as the Calypso pattern. Other members of the engine room (iron, conga, and cowbell) play rhythms that sound like those in figure 7.7.

Soca

The Soca pattern is a close relative of the Calypso so the engine room parts are similar.

The drum set player could play something as simple or complex as the Soca patterns shown in figure 7.7. Other members of the engine room would play the same iron, conga, and cowbell rhythms illustrated.

Calypso

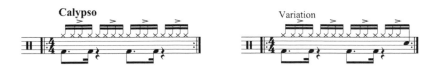

Variation

Soca
open H.H optional

Variation #1

Variation #2

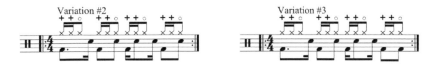

Variation #3

Reggae 1-drop

ENGINE ROOM INSTRUMENTATION

Iron

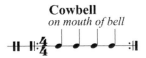

Conga
with steel drum cello mallets

Cowbell
on mouth of bell

Figure 7.7. Calypso, Soca, Reggae One Drop, and Engine Room Instrumentation

Reggae

The Reggae pattern hails from Jamaica and comes in several different forms. The *one drop* drum set pattern is found in figure 7.7. It shares the conga and cowbell rhythms with the Calypso and Soca patterns.

Bossa Nova

The Bossa Nova is a dance pattern from Brazil but is commonly used in the steel band. The drum set player could play the pattern demonstrated in figure 7.8. The engine room instruments are a bit different in the Bossa Nova. Rhythms to be played on the clave, guiro, and bongos (see figure 7.8) add an interesting timbre to the conga pattern found in figure 7.7.

By teaching these stylistic accompaniments, your students will have learned numerous ways to enliven the most rudimentary of songs while developing a feel for a variety of Latin dance rhythms.

YOUR FIRST PERFORMANCE

Getting the band ready for its first performance is always an exciting venture. The audiences for steel band are some of the most enthusiastic that you and your students will encounter. Your first performances can consist of two or twenty tunes; no matter the number of tunes, you can be sure that you will receive excited applause and leave the audience begging for more.

When you feel ready, take the band on the road. A performance at another school, school music festivals, or your state MEA conference will generate interest for your program. Keep in mind that you will need to rent a truck to get the instruments to the concert site as well as secure a van or bus to transport your students.

Moving the instruments is another aspect of steel band that helps students feel like they are part of something special. Teach them how to carefully place these valuable instruments in cases and, just as carefully, break down the stands to be loaded into the vehicles that are transporting the equipment. This group effort develops important team building skills within the ensemble.

MAINTAINING THE BAND

Like an acoustic piano, steel drums need to be tuned on a regular basis. Your students will play better on instruments that are in tune, and your au-

Bossa Nova
snare drum played cross stick

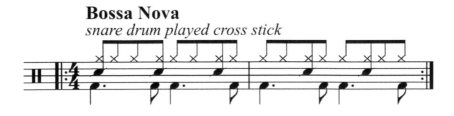

Engine Room

Clave
3-2

Guiro

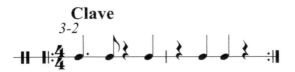

Bongos
Martillo

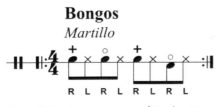

R L R L R L R L

Figure 7.8. Bossa Nova and Engine Room

dience will appreciate the sound. Rehearsing the band on a daily basis and moving the pans several times a year for performances can wreak havoc with the drums' intonation. Therefore, it is a good idea to have the drums tuned twice a year.

Typically, a good tuner will charge between $100 and $150 per drum for tuning. The same price applies for a lead and for a set of basses. (Note that a tuner tunes the number of notes on a drum or set of drums, not the number of drums in a set.) The tuner will or should spend about twenty minutes to an hour *blending* or putting each drum or set of drums in tune. A tuner may charge more if a drum has accidently been dropped, as more work is required to fix a damaged drum.

It is important that the drums are well maintained, as they are more fragile than they appear. Tuning and maintenance is a necessary expense that needs to be budgeted within your program. If you have a ten-piece band that needs to be maintained and tuned twice a year, you will need to budget around $2000 annually for these expenses.

You can raise money specifically for tuning and maintenance by dedicating certain amounts of your band's activities and performances to that end. If you decide to make and sell a CD of your band, make sure you obtain a mechanical license and pay the royalty for each song on the CD. The Harry Fox Agency has a mechanical licensing tool called Songfile to make licensing easier. Activities such as bake sales and car washes can bring in funds. Be creative with funding ideas—after all, your band is worth it!

NOTE

1. Several workshops offered at the University of Delaware, the University of West Virginia, or Villanova University provide support during the summer months if you are not feeling intrepid enough to try learning pan on your own.

Chapter Eight

Informal, Intuitive, Interdisciplinary, and Interactive: Middle School General Music with a Twist

Gena R. Greher

Learning in school need not, and should not, be different from children's natural forms of learning about the world. We need only broaden and deepen their scope by opening up parts of the world that children may not, on their own, have thought of thinking.

Duckworth, 1996, p. 49

To listen intelligently, you must clearly understand not only your own role but also that of composer and interpreter and what each one contributes to the sum total of a musical experience.

Copland, 1988, p. 265

SETTING THE STAGE

The room darkens and the screen fades in from black. We are in the middle of a vast ocean at what appears to be dusk. On the screen is a lone woman who seems to be floating peacefully; we think this is so because the background music is calm and serene, and gives the impression of drifting. After a brief discussion with your students regarding the mood of this film excerpt and what might be taking place, you play the same footage again. But wait . . . something strange seems to be happening. There is tension and a sense that something frightening is about to occur. Nothing in the film excerpt is visually different. What changed?

Congratulations! You have now reeled your students in to your lesson. They are experiencing the power of music firsthand. And you accomplished this by entering their world through the realm of film and music. You have activated the teenage brain, and you have done this by defying their expectations.

The above scenario has taken place in many classrooms with many skeptical teenagers throughout the country. The footage in question is a short scene from the beginning of the movie *Jaws*, where we, the audience, encounter the shark for the first time. What makes this short excerpt so engaging is that, for all the talk of danger and sharks, in this particular scene there is no shark—at least not in a physical sense. For in this scene the air of danger is completely intuited and virtual. In reality, it is the shark as musical motif (Greher, 2002). The twist in this presentation is that, during the first playing, the sound has been turned off and an excerpt from Debussy's *La Mer* has been substituted. The second viewing uses the original music, demonstrating the role that a well-crafted soundtrack can play in the making of a film.

Now that you have your students' attention, there are a variety of ways to pique your students' interests, while finding the right musical balance for meeting the standards within a student-relevant context. The purpose of this chapter is to suggest a framework for developing strategies and techniques for music learning that builds on what the students know and understand intuitively; a framework fashioned closer to what is considered *informal* learning. As evidenced by the research of Allsup (2003), Bamberger (2003), Folkestad (2006), Green (2006), and Resnick (1987), middle school students come into the classroom with a great deal of musical understanding through the kind of learning and acquisition of knowledge that takes place outside of the formal structure of school. For this chapter, the objective is to draw upon students' media-centric "cultural capital" as a starting point for musical listening, composing, and performing, in a manner supporting Folkestad's (2006) description that "the intention of the activity is not to learn about music, but to play music, listen to music, dance to music, or be together with music" (p. 136).

No doubt, these activities will take place in a school setting that is not exactly informal, but the goal is to create situations where the context for learning mirrors the types of learning situations likely to be encountered informally outside the classroom. In this case, the context for the activities being presented is steeped in the artifacts of popular culture. Pogonowski (2002) stated, "Contexts are designed to engage students in music making that describes real-life situations as closely as possible. . . . As seen though the eyes of children, music can make sense in school only if it has validity in the here and now" (p. 28). While a great deal of the literature on informal learning centers on using popular music in the classroom and adapting the techniques of learning popular music to classroom situations, one needn't have to choose between the popular music our students are listening to and everything else. We can and should incorporate a diversity of musical genres into the mix. Nor should we assume that our students choose their music as a monolithic group. Because teenagers define themselves by the music they listen to, they often take a fairly narrow view of music when it is not of their choosing (North & Hargreaves, 1999).

Film music's origins are rooted in the traditions of classical music, but like all musical styles through the ages, it has evolved and mutated into new styles that are reflective of the changing times. Working within the realm of film music can be an entry point for students into learning important musical concepts such as thematic development, form, harmonic language, rhythm, meter, tempo, instrumentation, and orchestration. The variety of musical genres that are used in contemporary films can help to defuse the tension teachers often feel when they include popular forms of music, which have not traditionally been valued in schools, in the curriculum.

To promote active listening, the idea is to devise listening prompts in such a way that students get involved through purposeful listening and decision-making. The students can enter the discussion through their own language, observations, and individual points of reference. As the listening exercises, activities, and discussions evolve, musical terminology can then be added to define their observations. In these types of activities, students will:

1. think like a composer, through listening, creating, and performing
2. collaborate with their peers
3. analyze and reflect upon their musical decisions as well as the musical decisions of others
4. research and communicate their findings and ideas to others

In the process, you, as the teacher, will be able to take your students on quite a musical journey with opportunities to integrate music history, film music history, music literature, musical terminology, and literacy development into your curriculum.

In the following sections, we will expand on these ideas with several listening and creating activities and see what happens when a director uses music that goes against the expected: Suppose a director uses music that works with the timing of the action, but the genre of music does not fit our expectations? How might your students react? This will be followed by an activity where you will have the students experiment with putting music and sound effects against a film and, if resources permit, create their own short videos. In so doing, they will experience firsthand how different moods, rhythms, and melodies affect the pacing and feel of a film or story, eventually learning to think more deeply about the role of music in film and not take it for granted. In this context the student is placed in the position of having to think and make decisions in much the same manner as a film composer would (Greher, 2002, 2003).

MUSICAL MOTIF

In this short scene from *Jaws*, several of the many links to the field of music that we would like our students to know and understand have been uncovered. On a macro level, we can explore and uncover the role of music in film, how it functions, how it can foreshadow the action, and how it helps the director tell the story.

The history of film music begins improbably enough with the burgeoning silent film era and is firmly rooted in the traditions of Western art music. Begin your class by asking your students what the original purpose of film music was. While music has become a major contributor to the film industry, the simple fact of the matter is that the original purpose of having live musicians in movie theatres during silent movie days was rather utilitarian. *Music was used to mask the sound of the projector and talkative audiences!* The decisions regarding who should perform the music and what music should be performed was left to the film exhibitor, rather than the film's director (Prendergast, 1992). Eventually commercialism took over, and music publishers began to create cue sheets of compositions in their catalogs that matched the moods and dramatic effects in the film.

Another practice was for music directors to "dismember the great masters, anything that wasn't protected from copyright" (Prendergast, 1992), essentially creating musical montages of excerpts collected from an assortment of works in the public domain by classical composers, saving money on rights fees. This is similar to today's practice of creating soundtracks from Top 40 and hip hop artists, though current songs do have to be negotiated with artists due to copyright protection.

There is an inherent emotional, expressive element to music. As Shore (Schelle, 1999) points out, much of music in film exists for its emotional value as opposed to commentary. The filmmaker can use music to support the visual or to play against the visual. As was done in the case of the film *Jaws*, the music not only fills in for some element that is absent from the visual, but also, through the use of a musical motif created for the shark, heightens the anxiety level of the audience. On a micro level, there exists a musical motif, which has become one of the most famous in modern times: a cultural icon. What happens when we hear that short ominous musical phrase? We know the shark can't be too far behind. We, as an audience, become conditioned to react. That is the power of music! Such a small musical gesture can lead to questions about how the composer and director accomplished this imprinting of the shark's image on our brains with just a few sounds. We can then put a name to this short musical gesture: *musical motif.* What other examples of musical motifs, be they rhythmic or melodic, exist so that the minute we hear one we know what it is? The opening phrase of Beethoven's Fifth Symphony or the *Addams Family* theme are two other examples that can be used in the classroom. Ask your students to think of other motifs from music and movies that they are familiar with and share them with the class. Because the *Jaws* motif is associated with a particular character and is played each time we see or are about to experience this character's presence in the movie, it is called a *leitmotif.* The leitmotif, a compositional device most often associated with Wagnerian operas, whereby the composer assigns a musical theme to a character or place, is often used as a structural element in film scoring (Kalinak, 1989). By using the *Jaws* motif the stage is set for a larger discussion of the origins of leitmotif. Begin with films, and perhaps cartoons, students already know and travel back in time to the roots of film music and musical theatre: opera. Like opera, film music exists to support the dramatic action and is often secondary to the action on the screen. Film composers do not have the luxury of creating music merely to express *their* feelings and show off *their* craft. Just as an opera composer must accommodate the libretto and the dramatic action, the film composer must accommodate the action on the screen, the dialogue, and sound effects. Unlike composing for opera, however, the film composer's role in a film was generally considered incidental to the film's creation (Kalinak, 1989), relegating the composer to involvement in postproduction, after the film has been shot and edited, as opposed to participating in the development stages of the film.

Leitmotif Activities

Middle school students can be engaged in critical and analytical thinking by being asked to think like the director or composer concerning the choices they need to make in regard to the leitmotif soundtrack. As an opening activity on leitmotif in film, *Star Wars* and *Harry Potter* come to mind as examples to model the following activities from. Then expand the lesson with examples shared by students:

1. Have your students create character studies, linking a character in the film to the character's musical theme.
   a. What are the personal traits/attributes of this character?
   b. What aspect of the music suggests those traits?
2. As an extension, have your students choose a character from a book that they are currently reading or a historical figure that they are learning about.
   a. Ask them to list the attributes of this character/person and list some musical qualities they could use to portray this character.

b. Using the musical resources you have available, have students create their own leitmotif for this character.

i. They can create an original leitmotif through acoustic instruments and found sounds from the classroom or through a looping program like GarageBand or Acid Studio if computers are available.

ii. They can find several pieces of existing music and through Audacity (http://audacity.sourceforge.net), a free, simple, audio editing software application, create a mix or mash-up to depict this character.

Follow up on these activities by listening to *The Overture to the Flying Dutchman*, by Richard Wagner, which is based on a folk legend about a ghost ship that can never go home and is doomed to sail the oceans forever.

1. Begin by playing the music without any explanation as to what your students are about to hear, other than to suggest there is a story behind the music and their mission is to figure out what that is.
2. Ask the students to describe what they are hearing and suggest possible scenarios for what is taking place.
3. Working in small groups ask the students to create their own stories based on the music, describing who the characters are, where they are, and what might be taking place.
4. Compare their stories to that of the *Flying Dutchman*.

Suggested Resources

Music

Harry Potter and the Sorcerer's Stone. Original Motion Picture Soundtrack. Warner Bros. (2001).

La Mer, by Claude Debussy, Vladimer Ashkenazy, and the Cleveland Orchestra. London Records.

Main Title from *Jaws* soundtrack by John Williams. MCA (1992).

Musically Speaking: Flying Dutchman, Das Rheingold, Gotterdammerung, Parsifal. Seattle Symphony. Commentary by Gerard Schwartz. www.musicallyspeaking.com/index.html

Star Wars: Episode IV—A New Hope (collector's edition). Sony (2004).

Video

Duck Amuck (1953). Directed by Chuck Jones. Warner Bros. cartoons part of the *Merrie Melodies* series.

Note: *Duck Amuck* is an interesting short Warner Bros. cartoon by Chuck Jones and is a fun example of what happens when picture and audio are at odds with each other, providing a good jumping-off point for discussion. *The Dot and the Line* is another Warner Bros. cartoon by Chuck Jones that demonstrates how music can create emotion in "characters" that are nothing more than drawings of a dot and a line.

Jaws (1975). Directed by Steven Spielberg. MCA/Universal Home Video. Universal Pictures (USA).

MUSICAL GENRES

As mentioned previously, music can be chosen to go with the action of the film or against the action. One of the most striking examples is the juxtaposition of Samuel Barber's Adagio for Strings against scenes of war and devastation in the film *Platoon.* If you were to play the film excerpt without sound for your students and then ask them to describe the type of music they would choose to accompany the action, most likely you will not hear suggestions of a soft, slow string composition. You could supply them with several choices of music chosen from a variety of genres, including the Barber composition, and ask them to choose which composition works best. Once you reveal the director's choice, be prepared for a lively discussion!

Another scene that would seem like an odd choice of music for a movie scene is in *Batman Forever*, where the director chose a waltz to accompany a fight scene. But the most improbable and perplexing musical decision for your students might be Spike Lee's decision to use Aaron Copland's music, and not Jay-Z's or a host of other hip hop artists' music, to underscore the film *He Got Game*. If you were to play the scene of the pick-up basketball game to your students without sound, the assumption would be that the director would choose an urban score based on hip hop or rap music. The following activity provides a good example for your students, reminding them not to box themselves into just one expected musical genre. This activity can be used as a prompt for a discussion about American music and its origins, the use of ballet music to score a basketball scene, the idea of choosing music that plays against a scene as well as the various ways one could treat a slow motion film sequence, and the use of rhythm.

Genre Listening and Creating Activities

Isolate the pick-up basketball scene from *He Got Game* as your film clip, which has the "Hoedown" movement from Aaron Copland's *Rodeo* as its musical soundtrack. At all times, play this scene *with the sound turned off.*

1. You will play the film once with no sound. Ask the students what type of music should accompany this scene in terms of pacing, mood, instrumentation, rhythm, and so forth.
2. You will then play the film clip four more times. Each time you will play it with a different piece of music either from a CD or MP3 file. It is important not to mention the names of the musical compositions—simply refer to them as A, B, C, or D.
   a. Play a recording of "Hoedown" (not the actual sound from the movie because the dialogue and sound effects from the movie track will give it away as the authentic music soundtrack) first or second to see how students react to the use of the original music with the film clip.
   b. Find three additional pieces of music that might work with the scene, making sure that at least one of the selections is a hip hop piece. In this instance, you may want to find an instrumental mix such as the instrumental version of "Holla Holla" by Ja Rule, to ensure its school appropriateness. Try to incorporate a diversity of genres.
3. After each playing, have a discussion about what elements of the music worked with the clip, what didn't work, and why.
4. When all selections have been played, ask for a vote as to which music track— A, B, C or D—worked best and why. When you play the actual track for your students, be prepared for some passionate discussion regarding the director's choice of music. This will most likely provide motivation for the next part of this activity, in which your students create their own music for this scene.
5. Divide your class into groups and ask them to create their version of what they think the soundtrack should be. This can be accomplished with classroom instruments, found sounds, a music looping program, vocal and body percussion, or any combination thereof.
   a. Keep the film clip playing in the background without sound so the students can figure out what type of music should accompany the various scenes. This will allow them to get some rough timings of how the music will align with the video.
6. Record their compositions to video playback, either on an MP3 player or with an inexpensive video camera.

Tip for a Low-Tech Way of Capturing Students' Performances

Once the students have created their soundtracks, consider having them perform their compositions with the video while you focus a video camera (any digital video device will work, such as camera phone, laptop, or digital camera) on the silent TV screen to record their performance along with the picture. This will also allow the students to compare their music with the original soundtrack and provide a basis for them to discuss the differences in their approaches as well as what worked and what they would do differently if they could do the project over.

Tips for Making R-Rated Films and Songs School Appropriate

Since showing a film in its entirety is not the point of this exercise, isolate short one- to five-minute segments. In this way, it is often easy to avoid showing those scenes where the dialogue may not be school appropriate. However, in the above-mentioned scene from *He Got Game*, there is some dialogue—a questionable word or two—that you may need to edit out, depending on which part of the film you choose to utilize. The easiest way to do this is to de-couple the audio from the video track and quickly dial down the track for that word or words. Or, as radio stations do, you can insert a beep in the appropriate spot. Similarly, when using a music track, it is important to find an instrumental mix of the song if that will serve your purpose, or work with the *non-explicit* version of the song.

Suggested Resources

Music

Adagio for Strings / 3 Essays for Orchestra by Samuel Barber. St. Louis Symphony Orchestra. EMI Classics (1989).
Main titles from *Waterworld* soundtrack by James Newton Howard. MCA.
"Holla Holla," by Ja Rule. Uni/Def Jam.
"Hoedown" movement from *Copland Conducts Copland*. Expanded Edition. Sony Classical/Legacy.
Las Vegas/End Credits from *Rainman* soundtrack by Hans Zimmer. Capitol.

Video

He Got Game (1998). Directed by Spike Lee. Touchstone Home Video. Buena Vista Distribution Company.
Platoon (1986). Directed by Oliver Stone. MGM (Video and DVD).

MUSIC AND MOTION

How might a composer create a piece of music to express motion? What are some of the compositional devices a composer might use? Certainly, rhythm is an obvious choice, changing tempo would be another, and playing with the directionality of the sound source could be another, to name a few. But is it possible to create a sense of music getting faster without changing the tempo? How might we play with rhythm and meter to give the illusion of changing speed? As Bamberger points out in her research (2011), students are intrigued by paradox. In kind, the following listening exercise and subsequent activity will no doubt pique the curiosity of your students.

The train has been the object of composers' attention for decades. In setting up this listening prompt, it is important not to give any information about what the students will be hearing beforehand. Let the music suggest what it is these composers are depicting. Choose four to five excerpts from the repertoire such as the following: *Pacific 231* by Arthur Honegger, which was originally written to accompany a film by the same name; *The Little Train of Caipira* by Hector Villa Lobos; "America Before the War," from *Different Trains* by Steve Reich; "Loco Madi," from the *ULWIS Suite* by Duke Ellington; or *Train Music* by Percy Grainger.

1. After playing one to two minutes of each selection, ask the students to describe what they might have noticed in each composition in terms of instrumentation, rhythm, texture, tempo, dynamics, and melodic material.
2. After all of the pieces have been played, determine the subject for each composition.
3. Once it is determined that the subject of each composition is a train, go into a discussion, comparing how each composer approached the subject of a train from a different perspective and compile a list of the aspect or aspects of the music that suggests a train.

Human Percussion Choir as Train Soundtrack Activity

The activity for this listening prompt will be the students' creation of their own "train" soundtracks, except the twist is that, rather than use traditional instruments or music technology, they are going to accomplish this by working either as a large class or group or in several small collaborative groups, to become a vocal/body percussion choir. To illustrate what can be done, view the British Honda commercial that is available on YouTube at www.youtube.com/watch?v=GuyaVcqTgic.

At this point, you could ask the students to create a train soundtrack in the abstract or you might find a short train video for the class to create the soundtrack for. Having an actual video to work from will give the students more of a structure to work with. There are many films with train sequences that could be used for this that are available on DVD, such as *Murder on the Orient Express*, or you may be able to find one on the following website, which is an excellent resource for films that are in the public domain: www

.archive.org/details/feature_films. Once they have created their soundtracks, have them perform their compositions to the video playback.

Suggested Resources

Music

The Ellington Suites. Fantasy Records (1990).
Honegger: Symphonies 1–5; Pacific 231; Rugby by Arthur Honegger, Charles Dutoit, and Bavarian Radio Symphony Orchestra. Warner Classics (Audio CD, 2006).
Percy Grainger: The Complete Piano Music. Nimbus Records (1997).
Reich: Different Trains, Electric Counterpoint. Kronos Quartet, Pat Metheny. Nonesuch (1990).
Villa-Lobos: The Little Train of the Caipira. Everest UK (2008).

Video

Murder on the Orient Express (1974). Directed by Sidney Lumet. Paramount Home Video. Paramount Pictures.

MUSIC AS STORYTELLING

Without Video

For this project start with any thematically based listening activity. In this case we will focus on music that portrays *space* or *space travel*. Choose four to five examples of music that depict one of these themes, such as a movement or two from *The Planets* by Gustav Holst, and a few examples from movie soundtracks, such as *Blade Runner*, *Aliens*, *Star Wars*, or *Star Trek* (avoiding the main themes, if possible). Try to choose selections that are varied in tempo and mood.

1. Before playing the excerpts, explain to the class they are going to hear several pieces of music, and if they listen very carefully, the music will tell them a story.
2. Play each piece twice. After the second listening of each piece, have students discuss what they hear while you write descriptive words on the blackboard. This discussion should lead to a variety of responses ranging from instruments and sounds the students heard to moods and descriptions of what may be taking place in the music.
3. Working in groups, ask them to create a story based on what they were able to pull out of the music.

4. Have each group read its story aloud and discuss the type of music or sounds that could be used to accompany the stories.
   a. What is the mood of this story? How might that mood be suggested in sound?
   b. Are there characters in the story that could have their own theme/leitmotif?
   c. Is there something in the story that requires a sense of motion or flight?
5. Once each group has a story, have them (with a minimal amount of narration) use music and sounds as a primary means to tell their story. Drawings or illustrations may also be created to accompany the stories.
6. Record their stories with an MP3 player or any digital video device to play back their work and possibly create a CD or DVD for each student to have.
7. After the students have their soundtrack ideas, and if the technology is available, expand upon their ideas by asking the students, if their story were going to be made into a movie, what would they imagine the "movie trailer" to look and sound like? The twist here is to ask them to create a sixty-second movie trailer or advertisement that will only run on the radio. They will need to conjure up images through the use of sound effects, music, and voices that will set the mood for their story and serve as a coming attraction for their hypothetical space movie.

While the students will enjoy this approach, it can also prompt a discussion on Gustav Holst and *The Planets* along with a comparison between music that was created to portray a scene or place without the support of any visuals and music that was created specifically to go along with film. One interesting issue arises when the "Mars" movement from *The Planets* is played: students will invariably attribute that composition to the movie *Star Wars*. At some point, have a back-to-back listening of "Mars" followed by the main *Star Wars* theme to discuss the similarities and differences. These activities can be accomplished with no technology other than a CD or MP3 player and whatever instruments are in your classroom. The most important resource will be your students' imaginations.

With Video

One-Minute Video Activity

This activity is one that, while it has strict parameters, it also encourages a great deal of creative thinking. Given the age group, it is important to set some ground rules regarding content, such as this: *Student videos should not contain violence or fight scenes or language that is not school appropriate.* In this video activity students will create the following:

1. A video story that has a beginning, middle, and end.
2. A video of no more and no less than sixty seconds.
3. A video with absolutely no sound: the viewer should be able to tell what is going on in the video without any dialogue, music, or sound effects.

Before beginning this project, students should work in pairs and prepare a one-page synopsis of their story to be turned in to the teacher. The students will need to preplan their video, taking care that the action is carefully sequenced and well thought out. Ideally, there should be no editing involved; the viewing of the video should be directly from the camera.

While it may seem counterintuitive to be creating a silent video in music class, the initial point of this is to not mask the communication of the story with any extraneous information.

1. After sharing their videos with their classmates, all the groups will create soundtracks for their videos as well as having the option of adding titles and transitions.
2. Upon completion, they will turn over a silent version of their video to another group, so that each group will eventually work on two different soundtracks: one for their original video and one for another group's video.
3. All groups will participate in a sharing session in which the different soundtracks are compared.
4. Students should keep a log of their decision-making with regard to both soundtracks.

Suggested Resources

Music

Main titles from the *Blade Runner* soundtrack by Vangelis. Atlantic/WEA Records (1994).
Star Wars: Episode IV—A New Hope (collector's edition). Sony (2004).
The Planets Op. 32, by Gustav Holst. Royal Philharmonic Orchestra. Telarc (1990).
Alien, by Jerry Goldsmith. Intrada (2007).
2001: A Space Odyssey. Original Motion Picture Soundtrack (1996 Reissue).

CONCLUSION

Ideally, this chapter will be a catalyst for devising relevant entry points for involving your students in processes of listening, creating, performing, analyzing, and learning more deeply about music. These activities are intended to both embrace the diversity of student preferences while also expanding their musical and sonic worlds to include music they may not be otherwise inclined to listen to. The proposed projects are "teen tested" and can be accomplished with a minimum of resources. All of the strategies place the students at the center of their learning by posing musical challenges that encourage creative and divergent solutions, whether approached individually or collaboratively. In this context they are given needed opportunities for self-expression. Through the proposed activities, it becomes apparent that many of the traditional boundaries between "high" and "low" art are indeed blurred. Perhaps the activities in this chapter will lessen the distinctions between students' perceptions of school music and *their* music, engaging them musically in creative and relevant ways.

REFERENCES

Allsup, R. E. (2003). Mutual learning and democratic action in instrumental music education. *Journal of Research in Music Education, 51*(1), 24–37.

Bamberger, J. (2003). The development of intuitive musical understanding: A natural experiment. *Psychology of Music, 31*(1), 7–36.

Bamberger, J. (2011). The collaborative invention of meaning: A short history of evolving ideas. *Psychology of Music, 39*(1), 82–101.

Copland, A. (1988). *What to listen for in music* (4th ed.). New York, NY: Penguin Books.

Duckworth, E. (1996). *"The having of wonderful ideas" and other essays on teaching and learning* (2nd ed.). New York, NY, and London: Teachers College Press.

Folkestad, G. (2006). Formal and informal learning situations or practices vs. formal and informal ways of learning. *British Journal of Music Education, 23*(2), 135–45.

Green, L. (2006). Popular music education in and for itself, and for "other" music: Current research in the classroom. *International Journal of Music Education, 24*(2), 101–18.

Greher, G. R. (2002). Picture this! © 1997: An interactive listening environment for middle school general music. Unpublished dissertation, Teachers College, Columbia University, New York.

Greher, G. R. (2003). Multimedia in the classroom: Tapping into an adolescent's cultural literacy. *Journal of Technology in Music Learning, 2*(2), 21–43.

Kalinak, K. (1989). Max Steiner and the classical Hollywood film score: An analysis of *The Informer*. In C. McCarty (Ed.), *Film music I* (pp. 123–42). New York, NY, and London: Garland.

North, A. C., & Hargreaves, D. J. (1999). Music and adolescent identity. *Music Education Research, 1*(1), 75–91.

Pogonowski, L. (2002). The role of context in teaching and learning music. In E. Boardman (Ed.), *Dimensions of musical learning and teaching: A different kind of classroom* (pp. 21–37). Reston, VA: MENC.

Prendergast, R. M. (1992). *Film music: A neglected art* (2nd ed.). New York, NY: W. W. Norton.

Resnick, L. B. (1987). The 1987 Presidential Address: Learning in school and out. *Educational Researcher, 16*(9), 13–20.

Schelle, M. (1999). *The score: Interviews with film composers.* Los Angeles, CA: Silman-James Press.

ADDITIONAL RESOURCES

Books

Bernstein, L. (2006). *Young people's concerts.* Montclair, NJ: Amadeus Press, 2006. (Reprinted with a new introduction by Michael Tilson Thomas and edited by Jack Gottlieb. Based on the original text by Leonard Bernstein.)

Dickinson, K. (2008). *Off key: When film and music won't work together.* New York, NY: Oxford University Press.

Hickman, R. (2006). *Reel music: Exploring 100 years of film music.* New York, NY: W. W. Norton.

Kalinak, K. (2010). *Film music: A very short introduction.* New York, NY: Oxford University Press.

Kassabian, A. (2001). *Hearing film: Tracking identifications in contemporary Hollywood film music.* New York, NY: Routledge.

Prendergast, R. M. (1992). *Film music: A neglected art* (2nd ed.). New York, NY. W. W. Norton.

Ross, A. (2001). *The rest is noise; Listening to the 20th century.* New York, NY: Farrar, Strauss, & Giroux.

Internet Resources

www.archive.org/details/feature_films
www.moviesfoundonline.com/

Suggestions for Inexpensive Multimedia Software Solutions

Audio and Video Editing Software/Freeware

Audacity (freeware): http://audacity.sourceforge.net/download/
iMovie (part of iLife Suite by Apple)
Windows Movie Maker (comes with Windows operating systems)
Camtasia and Snagit (video capture software): www.techsmith.com/camtasia.html
www.techsmith.com/snagit.html

Looping Programs

GarageBand (part of the iLife Suite by Apple)
Wavosaur Audio Editor: www.filesland.com/companies/Wavosaur-free-audio-editor/
  Wavosaur-audio-editor.html
Zulu Professional DJ Software: http://www.filesland.com/companies/NCH-Software/
  Zulu-Professional-DJ-Software.html

MP3 Devices for Capturing and Recording Audio

Low-cost digital video camera, cell phone video, iPad video, or laptop video

Chapter Nine

World Music

Janet Welby

Multicultural lessons in the middle school general music classroom have come a long way from the occasional song "from a distant land" or the annual "International Fair." Students are exposed to far-reaching cultures through the Internet, rich social studies curriculums, and often, classmates who hail from different countries. The National Standards for Music Education require interdisciplinary teaching, and music teachers are increasingly encouraged to work with teachers of other disciplines. Therefore, lessons that incorporate elements of other cultures enrich middle school students' view of the world. The activities, dance, and music that emerge from other cultures are interesting and allow for the creation of diverse experiences for students. The task of presenting materials from a number of other cultures may seem daunting when you have most likely devoted your lifetime to the music of your own, for example, Western music. Yet how can you gain the expertise necessary to successfully teach *other* music with authenticity and respect? How do you create interest in and attention to different types of music with middle school students? World music may be taught creatively, efficiently, and successfully through imitation, dramatization, stories, rituals, cultural understanding, mnemonics, movement, play, and social learning; such are the basic techniques for leading your students to the music of different cultures.

YOUR LEVEL OF EXPERTISE

The term *general* found in the professional title *general music teacher* is significant. In the sense of multicultural music, general knowledge of world music has great potential as a basis for many significant musical experiences.

Yet the greatest challenge for many music teachers is a reluctance to teach something they have not personally experienced. With an open mind and a spirit of exploration, you will find that it does not take long to learn enough about a culture to engage musically in its practices with your students.

Fortunately, there are many helpful resources available that focus on specific areas of the world, written specifically for music educators. These authors have done the major work, which is to glean the important and memorable aspects of a country's cultural music, and provide musical examples that will be interesting to your students (see the extensive list of resources at the end of this chapter). Often you will have to select and adapt these resources, choosing difficult activities for some classes, while simplifying them for others, such as with *Ancient Traditions* (Montfort, 1985), a rich resource of Indian, African, and Balinese rhythmic patterns. You will find that you can differentiate your instruction to challenge students who have prior ensemble instruction and to accommodate those students who do not have the same level of musical skill, providing all students with a meaningful multicultural experience.

Authenticity is a must in global music lessons. For instance, examples of singing don't always have to come from the teacher. A recording of a foreign singer conveys the authentic style and accent of the music. Recordings of instruments from a Japanese Gagaku ensemble are as fascinating and genuine as our traditional use of symphony recordings. The Internet is also a valuable source of visual examples of a culture's dances and instruments. With some background knowledge about the culture, you will be able to recognize what is authentic and what is not. Also, look to your students and culture bearers in the community. Some of your students may be from a culture that you wish to teach about and can provide you with insights and information that you will not find in a book, recording, or on the Internet.

Although authenticity is important when designing lessons for students to experience a culture and its music, remember that all music comes from something that came before it. Through the migration of people, music and its traditions have also traveled to different places, melding with other musical styles. Do not be reluctant to re-create something from the different styles of world music and allow your students to improvise and create using the rhythms, melodies, and sounds of the music they are studying.

APPEALING TO MIDDLE SCHOOL STUDENTS

Finding materials that are relevant and interesting to middle school students is paramount to obtaining and maintaining their interest. Middle school students often respond well to music that is extreme in its style. Music that is "cool" and upbeat, with a recognizable rhythm (such as Caribbean and South American music), or challenging and intricate (such as an African drum ensemble), or exquisitely beautiful (as are some of the songs from Eastern Europe) are all appealing to adolescents. Teachers who share their passion for music create an infectious learning environment (Wolk, 2001); thus, to expose and teach your students unfamiliar genres of music you must love it yourself and share your passion for it. This is more easily accomplished if you have established a relationship of trust and respect with your students. When presenting music from other cultures, let your students know that the music is important, commands respect within its culture, and because it is different, it should be approached with an open mind. Acknowledge that the music might seem strange at first, then give your students an immediate experience with the music using the world music methods discussed later in this chapter. By providing your students with an activity that is fun, slightly challenging but accessible, and a thrilling experience—such as when you perform intricate polyrhythms or gorgeous harmonies—you will pique their curiosity and capture their attention.

WORLD MUSIC TEACHING METHODS

People have taught or *passed down* music to their youth since the beginning of human history—and in every part of the world. The following methods and techniques are based on the research of many fine educators, some who developed the resources at the end of this chapter. These methods create success for all students, not just those who are exceptionally talented. Musically educating all students is the goal of general music in public education, and these methods will work with middle school students as well.

Aural-Oral Transmission

Campbell (2004) and a number of other world music researchers articulate the powerful role of imitation in learning: "Aural and oral means [of musical transmission] remain central to the essential discovery of essential features of a song or instrument piece. . . . The teacher utilizing the modeling-and-imitation strategy becomes an artist-in-residence within the classroom" (Campbell, 2004, p. 10). If the music teacher displays a high level of musicianship and a passion for music, the students have an ideal role model. Use of imitation is also extremely efficient in today's time-strapped school day. Explanation is minimal, lecturing is unnecessary, and the class can delve right into the music at hand. Imitation may be used to teach songs, drum patterns, and dances.

Students who learn through imitation in the way other cultures learn music will be part of a rich, global tradition. Campbell (1991) articulates the role of imitation in a variety of societies. She calls it a shared "first step" for the process of learning music. Some cultural examples of learning by imitation are found in Balinese children who attend Gamelan rehearsals with their parents, the Venda children of the Northern Transvaal, and the Maori of New Zealand who participate in community ceremonies of dance and song. In similar fashion, there are the drummers of Ghana, traditional Irish fiddlers who learn to whistle and sing nonsense syllables, and the Chope xylophone players who watch and listen for years to the complex layers of patterns played by their elders before playing on their own.

Global Songs

Global songs for the middle school level should be thoughtfully chosen, and the students should hear and sing the song immediately through imitation. Play a recording of the song or sing it with the style and energy required for an authentic performance. Quickly involve the students with the song by using call-and-response techniques. Challenge your students to sing foreign lyrics accurately, requiring them to listen carefully to the singer. The following are some examples:

- "Ho Taru Koi" ("Firefly") from Japan: This song has a fascinating sound when sung as a three-part round; a choral version is also available.
- "Sunshine Reggae" and "Sun Is Shining" from Jamaica: Reggae-style songs can be taught along with Reggae dance moves; an introduction to some Patois language can also be included.
- "Mbube" ("The Lion Sleeps Tonight") from South Africa: The history behind this popular song is very rich, and there are many interesting arrangements and recordings of "Mbube," both in Zulu and English.
- "A Sprengisandi" from Iceland: This song has a haunting melody with vivid imagery in the lyrics.

Choral arrangements of global songs are also useful and can be adapted to classroom teaching.

Playing Instruments and Movement

Students enjoy playing all types of instruments, ranging from recorders, keyboards, and percussion to instruments fashioned out of everyday objects, such as kitchen utensils. Use the call-and-response technique with rhythmic mnemonics, play with authority, and the students will do the same. The same is true for dance patterns and movement. Avoid too much explanation and just "do" the dance! Break down the movement into easily learned patterns, stand in front of the class and demonstrate the various dance moves. Create words or phrases that help them remember the moves and have them say these words with you as they dance, taking care to have students begin moving right away. If the choice of a dance is interesting for this age group, and it is not too simple, but energetic and fun, such as an Italian tarantella, the students will learn it in a short amount of time. The important thing is to be the master, by knowing the material well and performing it with passion.

DRAMATIZATION AND TELLING THE STORY OF THE MUSIC

Children at any age are drawn to music when they learn the "story" of the music. Page (1995) stresses the power of a song's story, such as when children learn who wrote it, and find out what cultural traditions give a song its meaning, and why. Consider those themes that relate to what is important to a middle school age student such as popularity, communication, life changes, peer pressure, and authority. These themes are found in songs from all cultures.

Drama enables students to explore their world of feelings. Through drama, middle school students can make connections among the stories of their own cultures and those of broader world cultures. Creating a classroom environment in which students want to act may take patience, but middle school students love drama as a means for expression. Through the presentation of their own cultural stories, underscored with music, students can be someone or something other than themselves. This type of an activity will allow them to feel safer emotionally than if they are asked to expose their own feelings.

The story of the music should be introduced right from the start of a lesson, as a way to engage the students personally with the song or instrumental piece, as in the following examples:

- Japan: Present samples of haiku poetry and have students create accompaniments for the reading of the poems. Then have students write their own haiku poetry, presenting it with instrumental accompaniment.
- Africa: Tell some of the Anansi spider stories and have students choose African rhythms that represent the themes behind the stories. Use the African rhythm patterns to accompany a telling of an Anansi story, or perform the rhythms together as an African drum ensemble.

- Europe: Learn songs that are based on folk tales and ask the students to choose one to which they relate. Have them create a modern dramatization of the tale.
- New Zealand: Show a YouTube video of the *haka*, an appealing dance of the Maori people. It has a fascinating history, such as its use as intimidation in battle, and its current use by rugby teams prior to playing a game. Teach your students the *haka* dance and its corresponding words.
- China: Present character roles from Chinese opera. Watch a YouTube video of Chinese opera so that students can see how the characters interact and hear the accompanying music. Then, have students choose one character to study: its personality, makeup, movements, and sounds. Form groups of students who will then create a story with their characters. The story can be acted out in a simple manner, using the gestures and personality of the character, or it can be elaborate, with costumes, makeup, or puppets made by the students.

MUSIC, CULTURE, AND RITUAL

"Life in culture is . . . an interplay between the versions of the world that people form under its institutional sway and the versions of it that are products of their individual histories" (Bruner, 1996, p. 14). "Culture" is a complicated term, for it is the characterization of a social group, but what defines a social group? In the case of world music, it refers to nations or various groups within nations. Culture can also refer to the groups formed among the students. World music lessons make connections between world traditions and the traditions the students have among their peers and in their families. With this connection, you have a strong teaching tool. Some examples of traditions include rituals, family relationships, social gatherings, clothing, food, unique or colloquial words in conversations, and music preferences.

Respect for Differing Cultures

Central to cultural appreciation is respect. Respect and equality is extremely important to middle school students, no matter what you see in their behavior. They want to be respected and treated fairly by their peers, families, teachers, and society. Respect for music—and musicians and their instruments—is crucial if you are going to teach global music. Just as you need to show your passion, you also must demonstrate a deep respect for the music. To demonstrate such concepts, discuss the Indian tabla drummers who do not allow anyone to touch their drums. Show your students a video clip of the reverent manner in which a Gagaku Hichiriki player puts together his or her instrument. I have found that no matter what my students show outwardly, if I insist on respect for the culture, its music, and its culture-bearers, they eventually feel and show respect for the music as well.

Connecting to Rituals of Different Cultures

Some ways to connect ritual and music include the following:

- Native American pow wows: The pow wow is a ritual of many dimensions, including the opportunity to gather and socialize. Students can find similarities between the pow wow and a middle school dance, a Fourth of July picnic complete with food and performing groups from the community, or an award ceremony with instrumental fanfare. Ask students to compare and contrast the differences among such rituals and the types of music used within them.
- Indian instrumentalists: The master musicians of India are revered and respected. Have students explore the similarities between their "stardom" to that of Western pop stars. What differences exist? Explore the importance of *ragas* (melodic patterns) and *tabla* (drum patterns) to Indian people. Teach your students *ragas* and *tabla* so that they can try them on their own instruments.
- Irish fiddlers: Irish musicians and singers often sit in on a music-making session in their community. Your students can learn Irish tunes, playing a melody on a keyboard, recorder, or an instrument they know. Teach them a drum pattern or drum together, and have them join in the music at will. Encourage them to improvise!
- Spanish Flamenco music and dance: Show examples of singing and dancing from regions in India, the Middle East, and Europe. Follow the migration of the Roma people on a map and through music. Teach dances from these regions and explore how Indian dance evolved into Flamenco.

MNEMONICS AS A MEANS TO ASSIST LEARNING AND MEMORIZATION

In lieu of written, symbolic notation, how might students retain or memorize the music they learn? How is this memorization used to improve musical skills? One aid to memorization is through the use of mnemonics. Mnemonics is a device found in many cultures that helps organize information through a recoding process (Campbell, 1991). Examples of mnemonic teaching include European-based *solfège*; the duration and strokes of South American, Northern Indian, and sub-Saharan African drumming; and syllables used to teach jazz patterns.

Mnemonics for Learning Global Music

Authenticity is important in a global music lesson. If the lesson is about a particular style of music, use the mnemonics of the culture. Resources at the end of this chapter contain examples of rhythm patterns and the mnemonics that will assist you in teaching them. Because the use of mnemonics as a means to aid skill and memorization is so powerful, I sometimes use my own choices of words or syllables to teach a rhythm or melodic pattern. To facilitate the learning process, I will create chants or nonsense words that sound like the rhythm pattern I intend to teach. Some examples include the following:

- African additive rhythm combinations: Say "cher-ry" for two beats of equal duration, and "straw-ber-ry" for three beats of equal duration, such as "cherry, cherry, cherry, strawberry, strawberry" or "cherry, cherry, strawberry, cherry, strawberry."
- Latin clave rhythms: Chant the phrase "Give that dog a treat."
- Syncopated rhythms from many cultures: Use jazz-style syllables such as "du wop" or "shoo-be-du bop."

MNEMONICS AND THE DRUM ENSEMBLE

Mnemonics allow students to readily perform layers of rhythms in a drum ensemble. World drumming ensembles are very popular and exciting among middle school students. My students of all ages, kindergarten through college, tell me that they love drumming, and I witness a collective joy and engagement when they are drumming together. Mnemonics are a quick and effective method to facilitate these students to begin drumming immediately. Do not explain anything. Simply hand the students drums or other percussion instruments and begin teaching your chosen chant through imitation. Use rhythm syllables, word combinations, or your own system of mnemonics to teach drumming patterns. Have students recite each chant, and then play it on their instrument. If any group of students is not playing correctly, demonstrate how to do it using imitation, and continue the chant. Play the chants in a variety of combinations. Have a student play a call with the class collectively improvising a response. Group students into sections, each creating its own chant to play. Conduct the various patterns to create a unique drum composition. Layer two or more chants so that students experience differing textures. Adapt your instruction to include easier or more difficult patterns as necessary.

Mnemonics and Melody

Mnemonics aid melodies as well, such as those found in Chinese pentatonic songs or Gamelan ensembles:

- Chinese melodies: Examine Chinese art and traditional songs. Discuss the importance of nature in Chinese music. Sing words such as "cherry blossoms" or "moonlit water" for a pentatonic accompaniment to a song. Then create accompaniments on a xylophone or glockenspiel.
- Gamelan ensembles: Sing melodies in Gamelan music using the names of the pentatonic tones *ding*, *dong*, *dèng*, *dung*, and *dang*. The resource *Ancient Traditions* (Montfort, 1985) explains these tones and how they are used in more detail.

USE OF MOVEMENT

"The music plays, the body moves" (McClary & Walser, 1990, p. 278). A good deal of movement in world music is through a culture's authentic dance, or folk dance. Use careful and thoughtful research to choose folk dances for your self-conscious middle school students. An emotionally safe environment, humor, trust, and respectful attitude will help them to be comfortable with participating in folk dance. World dances teach musical skills and style, as well as the traditions of different cultures. Some suggestions for dances include the following:

- Circle dances with interesting movements, without a partner, as in the dances from Greece and Israel.
- Fast-paced dances with optional instrument playing, such as Italian tarantellas or Irish jigs and reels.
- Dances that depict strong emotions, such as the competitive New Zealand dances performed before rugby games.
- Brazilian samba dance moves performed to the accompaniment of samba drumming, either by students, recordings, or both.

LEARNING THROUGH PLAY

The misconception that if something is fun, it is not work, often prevails in education. Play has been a subject of serious study, and research shows that students often learn through play. My experience with students of all ages convinces me that an atmosphere of play and fun serves as a foundation for the imparting of knowledge as well as a means to develop students' musical skills. Motivation to learn comes when the personal interests, cultures, life experiences, opinions, ideas, questions, and the curiosities of students are taken into account in the music classroom (Wolk, 2001). The possibilities for playful activities are limitless. Below are a few suggestions to add an element of play to your world music lessons:

- Have students research the types of instruments used in Gamelan, Caribbean, African, or Indian ensembles and make their own representations. Be resourceful and create them from as many materials as you can provide.
- Create Indonesian *wayang*, also known as shadow puppet theatre. Show a video clip of *wayang*. Determine a subject or theme and have small groups of students create shadow plays. Have students make shadow puppets with cardboard, fasteners, and sticks. Then bring a large sheet to school and a strong flashlight for students to present their shadow plays. Accompany the plays with Gamelan music played by your students.
- Participate in stick-passing or African stone-passing games. Choose a song from one of the West African countries such as Mali or Ghana. Just as African children pass a stone to the rhythm of the song, your students can create their own passing games, using a variety of objects. Challenge them to find new, creative, and challenging ways to pass the objects while they sing the song.

THE SOCIAL NATURE OF LEARNING

Middle school students learn by interacting, creating, and performing with their peers: "Learners inevitably participate in communities of practitioners and the mastery of knowledge and skill requires newcomers to move toward full participation in the sociocultural practices of a community" (Lave & Wenger, 1991, p. 29). Walk into the hallway of a school and you might see students performing complicated hand-clapping rhythms with each other. Others watch and learn. I have found that social interaction adds a dimension to music lessons that extend my students' learning. The teacher-student relationship is one approach that is enriched by learning that happens from another point of view, the student-student relationship. Social interaction allows students to learn on their own terms, in their own language, and in the safety of their peers. Instead of passive observers, they are active in their learning. A socially comfortable environment creates conditions for individual students' potential to emerge.

Peer Collaboration

Many of the activities suggested in this chapter can become collaborative group projects by having your students

- re-create a ritual from another culture;
- create game variations like the African stone-passing game;
- develop dramas and stories for the culture that is being studied;
- accompany dramas and stories with sound effects, rhythm patterns on percussion instruments, or melodies on melodic instruments;
- learn drum patterns and have them teach the patterns to other students;
- create drum or melody patterns that work together in an ensemble; and
- create a new dance from the movements of familiar folk dances.

The suggestions in this chapter provide a point of departure for the exploration of the rich and limitless subject of world music. Your classroom will reflect the spirit, joy, playfulness, honor, and skill of world musicians as you teach global music lessons.

Music for All

Most cultures encourage all their people to participate in music, not simply the talented ones. Kreutzer (2001), who spent time observing music acquisition in the African Nharira people, suggests that although developmental progress for music acquisition is parallel across cultures, the level of achievement is accomplished by community factors. The Nharira children have the opportunity to participate fully in music from birth. Music participation is expected, learned informally among peers, and no concept of being "musical" or "nonmusical" exists. Kreutzer's research indicates that cultural differences may not affect an individual's cognitive learning process but may have an influence on whether an individual achieves to his or her full musical potential.

Your classroom can also be a source of encouragement for all students to be musicians. You, the master teacher, will infuse your classroom with passion, musical skill, and mutual respect among the students. Although not an expert in every detail of all world musics, you can choose resources that will bring authenticity to your teaching and allow your students to experience the best music of other cultures. The way world musicians teach is often the best way to teach the music of their culture. Through imitation, dramatization, stories, ritual, mnemonics, movement, play, and cultural and social experiences, you will successfully transmit musical concepts and skills to your middle school students. These methods, along with the many excellent resources of music collections, are powerful teaching tools for your general music class.

REFERENCES

Bruner, J. (1996). *The culture of education.* Cambridge, MA: Harvard University Press.
Campbell, P. S. (1991). *Lessons from the world: A cross-cultural guide to music teaching and learning.* Toronto: Schirmer Books.
Campbell, P. S. (2004). *Teaching music globally.* New York, NY: Oxford University Press.
Kreutzer, N. J. (2001). Song acquisition among rural Shona-speaking Zimbabwean children from birth to seven years. *Journal of Research in Music Education, 49*(3), 198–211.
Lave, J., & Wenger, E. (1991). *Situated learning: Legitimate peripheral participation.* Cambridge: Cambridge University Press.
McClary, S., & Walser, R. (Eds). (1990). *Start making sense! Musicology wrestles with rock.* New York, NY: Pantheon.
Montfort, M. (1985). *Ancient traditions—future possibilities: Rhythmic training through the traditions of Africa, Bali, and India.* Mill Valley, CA: Panoramic Press.
Page, N. (1995). *Sing and shine on! The teacher's guide to multicultural song leading.* Portsmouth, NH: Heinemann.
Wolk, S. (2001). The benefits of exploratory time. *Educational Leadership, 59*(2), 56–59.

ADDITIONAL RESOURCES

Alves, W. (2008). *Music of the peoples of the world* (2nd ed.). Boston, MA: Schirmer Cengage Learning.
Anderson, W., & Campbell, P. S. (2010). *Multicultural perspectives in music education.* Lanham, MD: MENC/Rowman & Littlefield Education.
Barz, G. (2004). *Music in East Africa: Experiencing music, expressing culture.* New York, NY: Oxford University Press.
Bates, E. (2010). *Music in Turkey: Experiencing music, expressing culture.* New York, NY: Oxford University Press.
Belli, R. D. (2001). Drumming: The future is in your hands. *Teaching Music, 9*(3), 48–51.
Brinner, B. (2007). *Music in Central Java: Experiencing music, expressing culture.* New York, NY: Oxford University Press.
Campbell, P. S. (1991). *Lessons from the world: A cross-cultural guide to music teaching and learning.* Toronto: Schirmer Books.
Campbell, P. S. (2004). *Teaching music globally: Experiencing music, expressing culture.* New York, NY: Oxford University Press.

Cohen, N. (2005). *Folk music: A regional exploration.* Westport, CT: Greenwood Press.

Diamond, B. (2007). *Native American music in eastern North America: Experiencing music, expressing culture.* New York, NY: Oxford University Press.

Douglas, G. (2009). *Music in mainland Southeast Asia: Experiencing music, expressing culture.* New York, NY: Oxford University Press.

Dudley, S. (2003). *Carnival music in Trinidad: Experiencing music, expressing culture.* New York, NY: Oxford University Press.

Eduardo, C., & Kumor, F. (2001). *Drum circle: A guide to world percussion.* Van Nuys, CA: Alfred Publishing.

Gold, L. (2004). *Music in Bali: Experiencing music, expressing culture.* New York, NY: Oxford University Press.

Haas, K., & Edwards, G. (2000). *Flamenco!* London: Thames and Hudson.

Hart, M., & Lieberman, F. (1991). *Planet drum* (2nd ed.). Novato, CA: Grateful Dead Books.

Hast, D. E., & Scott, S. (2004). *Music in Ireland: Experiencing music, expressing culture.* New York, NY: Oxford University Press.

Havighurst, J. (1998). *Making musical instruments by hand.* Gloucester, MA: Rockport Publishers.

Lau, F. (2007). *Music in China: Experiencing music, expressing culture.* New York, NY: Oxford University Press.

Marcus, S. L. (2006). *Music in Egypt: Experiencing music, expressing culture.* New York, NY: Oxford University Press.

Marshall, J. (2000). *Hand drums for beginners.* Van Nuys, CA: Alfred Publishing.

Montfort, M. (1985). *Ancient traditions—future possibilities: Rhythmic training through the traditions of Africa, Bali, and India.* Mill Valley, CA: Panoramic Press.

Moore, M. C. (2010). *Kaleidoscope of cultures: A celebration of multicultural research and practice.* Proceedings of the MENC/University of Tennessee National Symposium on Multicultural Music. Lanham, MD: MENC/Rowman & Littlefield Education.

Moore, R. (2009). *Music in the Hispanic Caribbean: Experiencing music, expressing culture.* New York, NY: Oxford University Press.

Murphy, J. P. (2006). *Music in Brazil: Experiencing music, expressing culture.* New York, NY: Oxford University Press.

Nettl, B., Capwell, C., Bohlman, P. V., Wong, I. K. F., Turino, T., & Rommen, T. (2007). *Excursions in world music* (5th ed.). Upper Saddle River, NJ: Prentice Hall.

Page, N. (2001). *Sing and shine on! An innovative guide to leading multicultural song.* Wauwatosa, WI: World Music Press.

Rice, T. (2003). *Music in Bulgaria: Experiencing music, expressing culture.* New York, NY: Oxford University Press.

Roberts, J. S. (1998). *Latin tinge: The impact of Latin American music on the United States.* New York, NY: Oxford University Press.

Ruckert, G. E. (2003). *Music in North India: Experiencing music, expressing culture.* New York, NY: Oxford University Press.

Sheehy, D. (2005). *Mariachi music in America: Experiencing music, expressing culture.* New York, NY: Oxford University Press.

Stone, R. M. (2004). *Music in West Africa: Experiencing music, expressing culture.* New York, NY: Oxford University Press.

Turino, T. (2007). *Music in the Andes: Experiencing music, expressing culture.* New York, NY: Oxford University Press.

Viswanathan, T., & Allen, M. H. (2003). *Music in South India: The Karnatak concert tradition and beyond: Experiencing music, expressing culture.* New York, NY: Oxford University Press.

Volk, T. M. (1997). *Music, education, and multiculturalism: Foundations and principles.* New York, NY: Oxford University Press.

Wade, B. C. (2004). *Music in Japan: Experiencing music, expressing culture.* New York, NY: Oxford University Press.

Wade, B. C. (2008). *Thinking musically: Experiencing music, expressing culture.* New York, NY: Oxford University Press.

Chapter Ten

Engaging Adolescents with Music and Technology

Alex Ruthmann

Music and technology are inseparable within the lives of today's adolescents. It seems like our students spend all of their time with their cell phones—tucked under their pillows texting at night and stealing time in between (and during!) class to text their friends and update their Facebook statuses. With the advent of portable digital music players, their music is always nearby providing a soundtrack to their lives. This soundtrack accompanies the profound changes—physical, mental, and social—occurring at home, with friends, and at school. Our students' lives revolve around their relationships with each other. They are simultaneously exploring and hiding from the world, testing the waters of friendships and their own self expression, while negotiating their changing identities. Music, mediated by all kinds of technologies, performs a key role in this process.

This chapter presents an emerging picture of promising practices with digital media and technology and advocates for a relational pedagogy (Ruthmann & Dillon, in press) where teachers actively design musical experiences informed by their students' musical and technological lives. Practical strategies for easing into initial creative experiences with music and technology are shared, followed by projects that explore the affordances of new mobile and online music technologies in the classroom and community. This chapter concludes with two digital remix projects—one for student-created video games and another that explores music videos as source material for original creative works. All of the projects are united by the common theme of active, social music making with technology.

FIRST STEPS: CONNECTING WITH YOUR STUDENTS

When integrating technology into the classroom, it is all too easy to be drawn in by the flash and quick spark of technology. In my own practice, I have found that when planning for the music learning experience begins with technology as the starting point, it's not as successful and often does not sustain the students' interest beyond a class or two. Even when introducing technologies like the iPad to students, with all of the possibilities afforded by that tool, it helps to have musical and educational goals in mind first. Rather than integrate technology for the sake of technology, we need to understand how we might develop relationships among our musical goals and experiences as teachers, the affordances and constraints of the technology, our broader curricular and community contexts, and our students' interests and needs (Ruthmann & Dillon, in press).

Getting to Know Your Students' Musical and Technological Lives

As teachers, it is a never-ending challenge to stay connected to and knowledgeable about our students' ever-changing interests and tastes in music, let alone adolescent culture in general. We know what we see in our classrooms and in the hallways between classes, but this is only a small window into our students' musical world. When working with adolescents, I begin by asking my students a set of questions as a way to get to know them and the place of music and technology in their everyday lives. My first step is to take a stab at answering the questions myself, making predictions of how they might answer. This helps me, as a teacher, document and push my own assumptions about who my students are and where music and technology might be in their lives out of my head and onto paper or the computer screen. After I have done this preparatory work, I distribute the following questions to my students:

1. Where do you experience music in your life?
2. How do you use technology in your everyday life? What technologies do you use?
3. What does music mean to you?
4. What music do you listen to?
5. Do you ever make music?
6. Are you a musician? Why/Why not?
7. If you could learn anything about music, what would it be?
8. What do you like about music in school?
9. What do you not like about music in school?

After reading through my students' answers, I compare them to my own predictions. This process no doubt surprises me each time I do this activity. I always gain new insights into what music is currently popular, which technologies my students are using, and the ways in which music is meaningful in their lives. Starting with their answers, I make time to explore the Internet and sites like YouTube listening to and getting to know *their* music. Much of what I have discovered from this activity is then used in future lessons and discussions.

Building Community in and around Our Classrooms

To best support our students' music learning, our classrooms need to be safe spaces for exploring, creating, learning, and expressing ourselves through music. Technology can be leveraged to support these goals both in and outside of school. While many schools prohibit personal technologies—such as cell phones and iPods—to be used by students in school, these technologies present multiple possibilities for music learning and making inside and outside of school. In addition, many schools also prohibit access to social media sites such as YouTube and other online media providers. It is important to know the policies that exist in your school so that you can be an advocate for the music learning and expressive possibilities for your students.

Part of establishing a community is building relationships with building administrators, your colleague teachers, and the technology staff. A good place to start is to collaborate on a project with other teachers in your building. Your students can begin to use technology to create their own music for projects in other classes and compose school songs. Once you have small projects like these up and running, and relationships formed with other teachers and staff, it can be easier to pursue larger technology integration projects within your classroom and throughout your school.

A Focus on *Doing* Music, Not Just Learning *about* Music

Many middle school general music courses can be classified as either advanced versions of elementary general music classes or diluted versions of introductory college music history or music appreciation classes. Courses that take these forms neglect to consider the unique nature and needs of adolescent students. Middle school students are neither advanced primary students nor are they premature college students. They are experiencing a unique developmental phase—a period of rapid maturation and growth—physically, mentally, and socially. As such, the nature and scope of musical experiences for adolescents in schools should support and reflect these realities.

Nothing bores a middle school student more than another worksheet or quiz about a dead composer or doing a report on musical instruments. Even Internet-based research and Webquests lose their appeal quickly among students. More importantly, these technologically mediated tasks are really information technology tasks applied in the context of learning *about* music, rather than engaging students directly in making, creating, and responding to sound and music. These approaches to using web technologies keep students occupied with online busy work, but we as teachers must leverage technology in support of active, social music *making* that emphasizes the *doing* of music, rather than solely focusing on the learning *about* music. The curricular ideas shared throughout this chapter are specifically designed to share musical experiences where students are active music makers with and through technology.

Promoting and Sharing Student Work

When a technology-integrated music curriculum is organized around active music making, the sharing and celebration of students' music becomes essential. Technology can play an important role in the creation and making of music and in the documentation, reflection on, and sharing of their musical works. One easy way to set this in motion is to establish an online site where student work is posted and published. This website can serve many purposes beyond an online public exhibition space; it also can be a highly visible vehicle to advocate for your music program. Your website becomes a forum for sharing the creativity and music learning happening in your classes with parents, administrators, and your community. Public advocacy work such as this serves to raise awareness and build support for your programs.

A step beyond a music program website is to set up a curated blog where students have input in what gets shared and posted online. All content to be posted to the site can and should remain moderated by the teacher. However, by sharing responsibility for content, your students can engage in learning about professional presentation, copyright and permission issues, and awareness of an audience for their works; additionally, you can reinforce broader school-wide goals such as "writing across the curriculum" through creating new opportunities for student-authored blog posts and commentaries on their music.

A further step is to create a school-wide online radio station and music label (Ruthmann, 2007) where students are responsible for the production, selection, and promotion of their music online. In this model, student compositions can be published online through services like iTunes where their music resides next to all of the music they listen to. This can be an extremely motivating proposition for students. They begin to see their music as valued and view themselves as musicians. The music shared online not only helps create community within the class that created the music, but it also extends throughout the school and community, including future students who can listen to that music in years to come.

EASING INTO CREATIVE MUSIC PROJECTS

Many traditional music and non-music software programs (e.g., notation, sequencing, looping, audio editing, word processing) are based on the metaphor of a blank canvas or void. When the program is launched, the user is presented with a blank slate upon which to place notes, audio waveforms, images, or words. For many students, it can be intimidating to start from scratch. In my own teaching I have seen many students who have been reluctant to add their first notes to the page, sometimes wondering if they have anything of value to "say." Of course, they do have something valuable to say, but starting from scratch is not always the best place for them to begin What follows are examples of how to use a variety of technologies to ease students into creating music for the first time.

Improvising with Generative Media Software

A new class of generative music software is emerging for both desktop computers and portable, hand-held computers. For example, jam2jam (www .jam2jam.com) is a new family of collaborative media performance software in which users interact together and network online to improvise and perform with preexisting sets of music, images, and video (Brown & Dillon, 2007; Dillon & Hirche, 2010). The software is designed for children and adolescents. Users manipulate broad musical and visual parameters such as balance, filter, frame-rate, tempo, texture, and density in a live, interactive setting. If a user does not interact with the software, the preexisting sound and images stay in a repetitive state, which gets boring quickly. This "feature" motivates users to interact with the software to change its state and move the composition forward. Through exploration, users begin to discern finer details about the music and gain more control of the performance environment. This software can also be used with acoustic instruments as part of a multimedia c-Jay performance.

Legendary music producer Brian Eno's Bloom and Trope applications for the iPhone and iPad are similar generative applications in that the user interacts with the software through touch to perform an improvised composition. Based on preprogrammed musical algorithms or sets of computational instructions, the software becomes an improvisational duet partner with the user, providing both visual and aural feedback. For students who are more hesitant to start creating their own music, these applications can be a great way to begin teaching critical listening and improvisation skills, leading toward future work with more advanced applications.

Subtractive Processes: Learning from Sculpture

Another way of easing students into creating is to begin with experiences where students start by listening critically and making adjustments to pre-existing musical material. Working with loop software (e.g., Mixcraft or GarageBand), I assign a musical sculpture project where students begin by crafting a solid "block" of musical sound. Students explore and select ten to fifteen preexisting loops and paint each of them into a separate track from time zero to two minutes. After saving the file, students switch seats with another class member and adopt a new sound block from which to work.

Before moving on to the next step, I search Google and share examples of bas-relief sculptures and discuss the artist's processes for revealing the final work through a subtractive process of slowly removing bits and pieces of material from a solid block over time, revealing a final artwork. In bas-relief, the artist can only transform or remove material; she cannot add it back. Following this model, students transfer that process to their newly found sound block in the loop software, exploring transformative functions like panning, balance, silence, and sound effects along with subtractive elements such as slicing and removing portions of tracks, creating variations in texture and a final form. This process attunes students to listen for subtle differences in the music when a small piece is removed or transformed. This focusing of critical listening, in turn, helps students better understand the building blocks of music they listen to.

Decoding and Remixing Musicians' Multitrack Audio Files

Another great place to begin with adolescents is to provide them opportunities to work directly with the music they listen to and hear on the radio. The adolescents I work with want nothing more than to be able to remix and work directly with their favorite music. Until recently, educators have only had access to the basic stereo audio files released on CD or online. A new culture has emerged where artists are beginning to release multitrack recordings of their works for fans to remix and make their own. Though a variety of unauthorized multitracks float around the Internet, artists such as Lily Allen, David Bowie, Nine Inch Nails, and Radiohead have all released their music this way and are actively being used in music classrooms across the country. Freely available multitracks can be found on iTunes, Acid Planet, and Indaba

Music, as well as by searching on the Internet for "music multitracks" or "music stems."

Once these files are loaded into software such as GarageBand, Logic, or Mixcraft, a good starting place is to listen and compare the original CD release to the multitrack recording. Encourage students to solo and mute various tracks as they listen to the multitrack. Using the preexisting material, students can then remove, rearrange, or add tracks to the song. Students can also record their own singing or rapping and mix it with, or replace, the original.

Beat-Boxing with Google Translate and Audacity

It is amazing what can be done with an inexpensive microphone, simple audio editing software, and Google's online translation tools (http://translate .google.com). Beat-boxing is a favorite activity among a number of adolescents I work with. Sometimes, however, students are hesitant to try beat-boxing in front of their peers and friends. Google's translate tools provide a safe, private way of exploring the techniques of beat-boxing without having to practice and share it aloud.

Google recently added computer-generated speech capabilities sonifying the text input of the translation box (see figure 10.1). In the United States, the default setting is to translate from English. Changing the "From" and "To" languages to German results in consonant groupings being "spoken" similarly to beat-box sounds.

Once the sample text is input into the box, the user can click on the "Listen" button to hear the faux computer generated beat-boxing. The audio files generated by Google Translate can then be recorded into music software like GarageBand or an audio editor like Audacity, which is free and

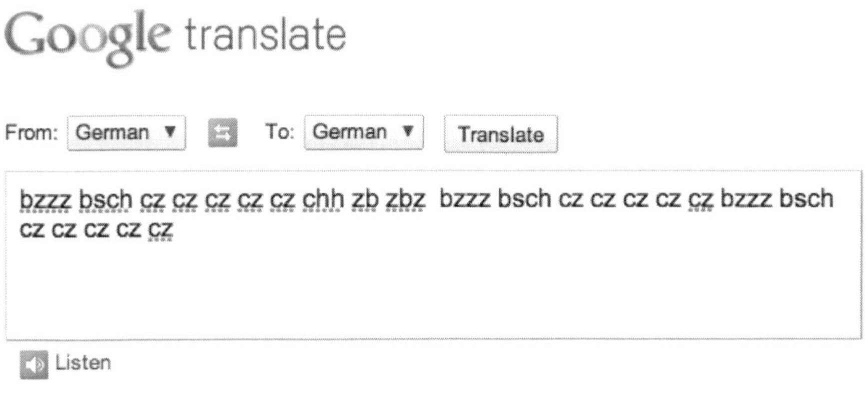

Google translate

From: [German ▼] [⇄] To: [German ▼] [Translate]

bzzz bsch cz cz cz cz cz chh zb zbz bzzz bsch cz cz cz cz cz bzzz bsch cz cz cz cz cz

🔊 Listen

Figure 10.1.   Google Translate

available for download to all common computing platforms. The computer-spoken files can then be cut up and arranged and integrated into larger compositions as a creative effect. Students who choose to begin beat-boxing projects this way often rehearse with and open up to sharing and recording their own voices in later projects. Beat-boxing and hip hop culture become an engaging context for sampling, musical expression, and working with the music of others (see Thibeault, 2010).

These sample introductory projects help create a safe community for musical exploration and sharing. Providing adolescent students with the option to explore their voices and music privately behind headphones before sharing with a group, or having the option to begin with critical listening and arranging projects, rather than being presented with a blank canvas, can decrease students' anxiety about creating their own music. As experienced musicians, it is often hard to remember what it was like to make music or explore a piece of music software for the first time, particularly during the turbulent adolescent years. Creating safe introductory experiences to creative musical work can set the stage for more social music making and exploration in later projects.

MOBILE AND ONLINE MUSICIANSHIP

New mobile technologies such as iPads, iPhones, and iPod Touches are powerful portable music production tools. Unchained from the tether of power cables and computer mice, these devices can go anywhere, and by design promote collaboration through their multi-touch interfaces. Since their launch, a wide variety of music making and production applications have been developed for this platform. Everything from digital emulations of harmonicas, xylophones, synthesizers and pianos to multitrack audio recording software, to generative music composition tools, and beyond have been invented. Whereas the traditional computer is designed for one person to use at a time, many of the application designers have created programs that rely on social interactions to make and experience music.

Innovations in online social media have also influenced online music making and sharing technologies, building on and extending social relationships in real life to virtual and online spaces. While there is legitimate reason to be cautious in bringing these technologies into school settings, the reality is that social media is an available and integral part of our students' lives. Students use it to communicate and collaborate outside school. These same affordances can be leveraged in safe and beneficial ways inside music classrooms.

iPad and iPhone Ensembles

One of the most promising areas of exploration for adolescent music classes is in using iPads, iPhones, and iPod Touches as instruments in small ensembles. Recent pilot projects with middle school students have involved using iPads and iPods in like- and mixed-instrument ensembles for both covering songs and creating original compositions. Modeled after the first iBand power trio from Austria (http://iband.at), students begin by finding tunes they know on acoustic instrument emulation applications (e.g., Virtuoso Piano or GarageBand). Once they've found a tune they like, they teach it to the other members of the group. From there, students work together to create, rehearse, and perform an original arrangement of the tune using only iPod or iPad applications. Follow-up projects include integrating instruments the students play and other classroom instruments as desired into either another cover tune or an original composition. After a basic experience covering a song, students are encouraged to explore other musical applications and submit ideas for future projects.

One of the challenges of this project is how to amplify the sound of each iPod or iPad so that the other students can hear. One solution is to have each iPod and iPad connected to headphones and a series of headphone splitters. Another solution is to plug the inputs of each device into an audio mixer, which mixes and amplifies the audio to an external set of speakers. The mixer/speaker solution is particularly useful when students want to perform using their own or the classroom instruments.

iPads, iPhones, and other smartphones often come equipped with audio and image recording capabilities. These can be leveraged in the music classroom as tools for conducting portable field recordings; capturing images, videos, and sounds to be used in multimedia projects; and conducting composer interviews and commentaries on their music (Ruthmann, 2007).

Social Music Notation: Composing Music Together Using Noteflight

Innovations in online Internet technologies have led to the launch of the social music creation and collaboration platforms Indaba Music and Noteflight. com. Noteflight is a free, fully featured online platform for social music notation. Students and teachers can create free accounts and notate and share music they create alone or together. What differentiates Noteflight from other music notation programs is that it is a software-as-service delivered to the user through an Internet browser, similar to Google Documents. Users can share their scores and enable others to view and even contribute to them. Noteflight also periodically saves your progress and keeps track of different versions of your compositions, which can be helpful for tracking individual contributions to collaborative notation projects.

A recent research project documented adolescent students' initial explorations of Noteflight in a classroom setting (Ruthmann & Dillon, in press). This project was conducted with students who had not been formally introduced to music notation in class. The goal of the project was to see what students knew and were able to express in music through notation, supported by a social, online environment. The project began by the teacher sharing a contemporary piece of art such as *Geostructure VI* by Franklin Jonas (see figure 10.2) and asking students to work in groups to create an original composition in Noteflight that expressed the artwork.

The student compositions that emerged showed a much greater depth of musical understanding among the students than the teacher had expected. By starting with an open-ended compositional experience of translating a piece of art to a notated composition, the students had the opportunity to bring their musical ideas to the project, rather than work within a fixed set of parameters. As a result, each of the group compositions showed a complex understanding of form, melodic structure, and tension and release. The complexity of the students' compositions caused the teacher to develop more advanced follow-up projects building on the strengths and weaknesses demonstrated in part by the composing project. Sample compositions from the project can be viewed online at http://web.me.com/prhsfapa/Site/Art-Infused_Composing.html.

The Music of Lowell: A Digital Ethnomusicology Project

Inspired by a found music composition posted to Noteflight and the ethnomusicological processes of Australian composer Percy Grainger (see Ruthmann & Hebert, in press), middle school general music students and a class of college music education majors are applying digital ethnomusicology to the documentation of the traditional music of immigrant families in Lowell, Massachusetts. This current, ongoing project integrates iPads, Noteflight, and Audacity as part of a community-based digital ethnomusicology project. Using the audio recording and portability features of iPads, middle school students working side by side with college students are digitally recording the songs and stories of students' parents and grandparents in the community. These recordings are downloaded to computers, edited in Audacity, and translated into English by the middle school students and community members. Transcriptions of the songs are then notated in Noteflight and are posted to a community website, along with the edited audio recordings and translated stories.

After gathering all of this material, the middle school students digitally remix the recorded and transcribed songs and stories as musical source material for

Figure 10.2.   *Geostructure VI* by Franklin Jonas. Used with permission. (Photo courtesy of Anne Ruthmann, www.anneruthmann.com)

original compositions and remixes. This process enables students to integrate aspects of their musical culture with that of their parents and grandparents. When the project is complete, the student remixes are posted back to the community website, to be shared alongside the originally recorded source material.

Increasingly powerful and portable mobile computers, and an emerging sophistication of online social music software are affording new and exciting possibilities for technology-infused music experiences in schools. Though mobile technologies such as iPhones and iPads are currently quite expensive, the possibilities afforded by only one or two iPads or iPod Touches in a music classroom are worth exploration. Over time, these costs will come down and students will have greater access to these tools at school and at home.

REMIXING GAMES, MUSIC, AND VIDEO

Creating and Remixing Music and Games

A tool that many middle school technology and media specialists are beginning to use in their work with adolescent students is the Scratch visual programming environment (http://scratch.mit.edu). Originally designed to adapt
the metaphor of "scratching" and remixing of samples of sound in hip hop
music to teaching computer programming and math, Scratch enables students
to remix, share, and create original interactive games, stories, and other programs. A quick visit to the Scratch website will reveal a number of existing
games and musical applications programmed by middle school students from
around the world. A key feature of this site and software is that all programs
can be downloaded and portions remixed and adapted into new games. A
companion site for teachers (http://scratched.media.mit.edu) presents free
lesson plans and support for beginning projects in Scratch, including the integration of music (see figure 10.3).

Scratch has nearly unlimited potential for music projects, especially in
the realm of composing music for games. Students can embed digital audio
files that they record or edit in Audacity, or code original MIDI music using
algorithms similar to those underpinning jam2jam, Bloom, and Trope. Current work with middle school students and Scratch focuses on creating music
that responds to video game play. Learning experiences include creating
algorithms for mapping musical tempo and dynamics to character movement
through a game level. If you ask around, you might find that students and
teachers are already using this software at your school.

Found and Recorded Video Remixes

With the advent of social media sites like YouTube, entire new worlds of musical practice and musicianship emerge every day. The video/musical artist
Kutiman's Thru-You project (http://thru-you.org) is a sophisticated example
of the new social media musicianship that is emerging online. Music videos
uploaded to YouTube serve as Kutiman's sonic and video palette. As a musician, he scours YouTube for musical snippets, which he then orchestrates into
entirely new compositions using video editing software. Rather than working
exclusively with audio, clips from videos serve as the musical material.

A Norwegian "amateur" musician, Lasse Gjertsen, takes a related approach to creating his own music. Self-professing to not being able to play a
traditional musical instrument, he sets up a video camera and records himself
playing sounds on a drum set and individual keys on the piano. He then edits

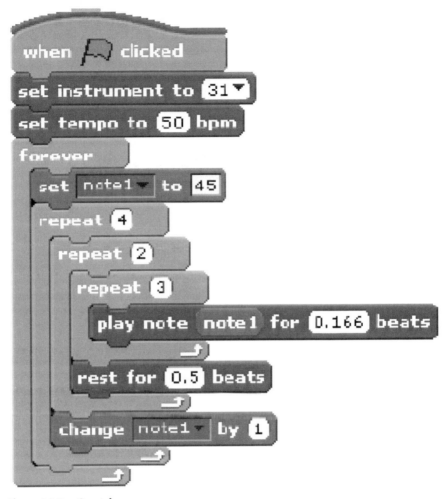

Figure 10.3. Scratch

these videos and isolates each pitch and drum sound (see www.youtube.com/
watch?v=JzqumbhfxRo). Again, using video editing software, he arranges his
edited clips into complex musical compositions and arrangements.

   Middle school students using a computer with a webcam or a portable
video camera can accomplish projects such as these. One way to proceed is
to ask students to record pitched and non-pitched sounds found around the
music classroom or school via video camera. Students can then split up the
recorded video file in video editing software (e.g., iMovie or Windows Movie
Maker), isolating each recorded sound. From there, students can create or

cover a melody, rhythmic pattern, or entire composition. By switching the composing environment from audio software to video software, students have to rely on and develop their aural and visual skills to accurately realize rhythms and melodies.

CONCLUSION

Music is no longer just an aural experience, if it ever was. This is especially so for today's students. Music, image, video, and technology are insepara- bly linked together in the lived experiences of our middle school students. Technology defines their music as much as they perceive their music to de- fine them. As such, projects that connect to and draw upon students' youth culture have the potential to be engaging and relevant in schools. The start- ing place for engaging music technology projects begins with the building of relationships among ourselves as teachers, our students, their culture, and our schools and community.

Because policy often lags behind possibility, teachers may initially run into barriers using technologies as suggested in this chapter, particularly those that call upon the open use of the Internet to gather musical resources or the use of iPods in the classroom. However, I encourage you to first adopt some of these technologies personally, and figure out how to best integrate them with your students in your school and community contexts. Each school and set of students is different, and music technologies should be selected based on the needs of your students and curriculum.

Technology is more than just a tool; it's a platform for creating, sharing, interacting, performing, assessing, and reflecting on the music we and our students make together. By taking the time to get to know and understand our students' musical and technological lives, we can better design music learn- ing experiences that are culturally relevant to them. When technologies are chosen and learning experiences are designed within this framework, tech- nology can be used in support of meaningful musical engagement in middle school music classrooms.

REFERENCES

Brown, A., & Dillon, S. (2007). Networked improvisational musical environ- ments: Learning through online collaborative music making. In J. Finney & P. Burnard (Eds.), *Music education with digital technology* (pp. 96–106). London: Continuum.

Dillon, S., & Hirche, K. (2010). Navigating technological contexts and experience design in music education. In J. Ballantyne (Ed.), *Navigating music and sound education* (pp. 173–90). Newcastle upon Tyne: Cambridge Scholars.

Ruthmann, A. (2007). The composers' workshop: An emergent approach to composing in the classroom. *Music Educators Journal, 93*(4), 38–44.

Ruthmann, A., & Dillon, S. (in press). Technology in the lives and schools of adolescents. In G. McPherson & G. Welch (Eds.), *Oxford handbook of music education*. New York, NY: Oxford University Press.

Ruthmann, A., & Hebert, D. (in press). Music learning and new media in virtual and online environments. In G. McPherson & G. Welch (Eds.), *Oxford handbook of music education*. New York, NY: Oxford University Press.

Thibeault, M. (2010). Hip-hop, digital media, and the changing face of music education. *General Music Today, 24*, 46–49.

ADDITIONAL RESOURCES

Selected Music and Media Applications for iPad/iPhone/iPod Touch

Bebot—Theremin-like touch-based synthesizer.

Bloom—An interactive, generative music environment composed by Brian Eno.

GarageBand—Enhanced version of Apple's GarageBand music software for iPad.

GraphMusic—An interactive music drawing program.

Magic Fiddle—A virtual, interactive string performance instrument.

Reactable—Easy to use, but feature-rich touch-based audio exploration environment.

Singing Fingers—Records sounds to drawings, which can be performed via touch.

Sound Cloud—Application for audio playback and recording directly from/to an online file.

SoundDrop—A music and physics composition environment driven by falling orbs.

Sound Thingie—Drawing based loop software.

Space Oddity—Interactive multitrack remix recording of David Bowie's song "Space Oddity."

Talking Carl—Interactive robot that parrots back audio input and plays sound effects.

Trope—An interactive, generative music environment composed by Brian Eno.

Virtuoso Piano—A social piano application for multiple performers.

Recommended Online Resources

MusicPLN (Professional Learning Network for Music Educators): www.musicpln .org. (The MusicPLN is a network of music teachers from around the world [but primarily from the United States] sharing best practices for learning and teaching music with technology.)

Phil Kirkman's Blog: www.kirki.co.uk. (Phil's blog presents a perspective on music education and technology from the United Kingdom.)

jam2Jam: Collaborative Media Performance Software: www.jam2jam.com. (jam-2Jam is free software for improvising and performing collaboratively with images, video, and sound.)

Scratch: http://scratch.mit.edu; ScratchEd: http://scratched.media.mit.edu. (Scratch is free software for programming original video games, interactive software, and composing music. ScratchEd is an online space for collaboratively sharing educational resources around Scratch.)

Music Resources for Scratch: www.scratchmusic.org. (This website is a collection of music-specific resources for working in and with Scratch.)

SoundCloud: www.soundcloud.com. (This website is a free audio storage, sharing, and social commenting website.)

Audacity: http://audacity.sourceforge.net. (Audacity is free audio editing, analysis, and production software.)

Recommended Further Reading

Brown, A. (2007). *Computers in music education: Amplifying musicality*. New York, NY: Routledge.

Finney, J., & Burnard, P. (Eds.). (2007). *Music education with digital technology*. London: Continuum Press.

Ruthmann, A. (2007). The composers' workshop: An emergent approach to composing in the classroom. *Music Educators Journal, 93*(4), 38–44.

Thibeault, M. (2010). Hip-hop, digital media, and the changing face of music education. *General Music Today, 24*, 46–49.

Watson, S. (2011). *Using technology to unlock musical creativity*. New York, NY: Oxford University Press.

Chapter Eleven

Experiencing Composition: A Creative Journey for Middle School Students

Michele Kaschub and Janice P. Smith

The study of music provides students with a means for understanding and communicating human experience in and through all its feeling dimensions. Composition provides unique access to this manner of knowing and being when students are invited to create and manipulate sounds in ways that are meaningful to them. To ensure that students derive maximum benefit from compositional engagement, composing activities must include attention to purposeful intent and expressivity in partnership with the development of supporting technical skills and knowledge.

The idea of leading composition activities can be daunting. However, the task often seems overly involved because teacher and students hold several important misconceptions about composition:

1. Composers must be able to notate their work using traditional notation.
2. Composers must be able to sing or play an instrument with exceptional proficiency.
3. Composers must have access to computers.
4. Composition must follow the "rules" derived from the study of music theory.

None of these assumptions need to hold hostage composition's place in the music curriculum. Notation is not always necessary. Novice composers typically hold their early compositional efforts in memory while composers of more complex ideas may choose to record or otherwise preserve their ideas. This positions notation as a skill that can be learned in support of composition rather than as a prerequisite to composing.

Similarly, while students may sing or play instruments as they create, composition is about the inward imagination and the manipulation of sound for expressive purposes. As long as composers can externalize the sounds they wish to share—and here it is important to note that some composition may be fully internal, highly personal, and not for sharing—then the ability to play an instrument or sing is not an absolutely necessary skill. As with notation, the ability to sing or play an instrument will provide composers with an additional layer of musical understanding and compositional resources; yet, ultimately, the key issue is that composers should be able to share their musical ideas in a manner that can be acknowledged as the product of composition.

Computers and the ever-emerging array of newer and increasingly portable technologies for personalizing, producing, and preserving sound comprise a powerful collection of tools for the composer. While composers have created music for centuries without such aids, these emerging technologies represent an increasingly common way for middle school students to engage the world of music. As these tools are often readily available in backpacks and hip pockets of most middle school students, teachers would be wise to capitalize on their powerful potential for deeply engaging students in the study of music. (See chapter 10 in this book for a detailed examination of technology.)

Finally, most music teachers have experienced a preparation for their field that included a significant study of music theory. Indeed, music theory classes may have been the only courses in which preservice teachers were asked to create original music. These experiences often lead teachers to assume that knowledge of theory must precede composition. This is simply not true. Music theory and its study provide an understanding of what composers have done in the past. The summation of compositional practices from various times and cultures can often seem "rule-like" and can be presented in that fashion. However, this leads to very dull and often expressionless pieces. It is important for teachers to remember that while an understanding of past practices and theoretical constructs may become advantageous as composers mature musically, composition is about the origination of new music and represents students' emerging understanding of both music and human experience. There are no formulas or "rules," as each composer's journey will be unique.

Having addressed some of the fundamental misconceptions about composition, we will now present some of the truly wonderful realities. In the remainder of this chapter, we will address the qualities of middle school composers that make them unique. We will discuss several specific composition projects that have been used in middle school general music classes along with specific suggestions for including songwriting and film scoring in working with this age group. Finally, the chapter will conclude with ideas for teachers to consider as they further their own capacity to present composition opportunities to their students.

CAPITALIZING ON COMPOSITION

Musical Interaction and Inquiry

Composition activities undertaken in middle school must foster students' abilities to understand their world in new ways. The sounds that people experience in the world are meaningful, and those meanings are often grasped and found poignant by middle school learners. As students invent, structure, and produce their own music and its inherent meanings, both their musical and personal autonomy must be accessed. In this way, students exercise their generative potential and their ability to make meaning through the artistry of composition. Creating one's own music is a powerful act of self.

Students at all levels of musical skill and ability can benefit from composing. The students draw upon all prior musical learnings to construct works that uniquely represent their perspectives. For some, this may include many years of instrumental or vocal study; for others, it may include highly developed listening skills. Still others may be relatively inexperienced, musically speaking. Regardless of the level of experience, any generative interaction with musical materials will challenge young composers to draw upon previous experiences and very likely develop new skills. As they explore their own experiences, what they understand of the perspectives of others, and how these two viewpoints can be expressed artistically, they often become quite excited as they discover and shape new musical meanings.

Composition can be considered a form of research as it leads to the generation of new knowledge that very often surpasses the limitations of verbal knowledge by tapping into the feeling of experience. Like research, the processes of composing involve defining a problem, testing various hypotheses, formulating an original response, and sharing the experience with others. As a medium for intellectual inquiry, composition can explore historical and cultural contexts from new perspectives. Composition affords the composer, performer, and audience an opportunity to chart explorations of the inner, subjective facets of human experience in order to make sense of the world. The potential for combined intellectual and expressive growth at this age level is scarcely matched by any other area of the academic or music curriculum.

Traits of Middle School Composers

Composition is a particularly appropriate curricular focus for middle school students because they possess qualities that match the requirements for being composers. They are guardedly curious and eager to manipulate sounds that intrigue them—especially the sounds of electronic instruments and computers. Middle school students can be quite intuitive about the use of musical gestures and can draw upon different gestures to achieve varied effect. They are able to project feeling—they can imagine what feelings might be experienced in a particular situation. They usually create music that is deeply reflective of their own experience. Most importantly, middle school students often feel a deep ownership of their work: it is often highly personal and important to them. Consequently, they can be either very eager or quite hesitant to share their musical products.

Another trait that makes young adolescents comparable to composers is their need for a balance of rules and freedoms. Composition implies a certain adherence to rules in order for the piece to be perceived as music. Yet there needs to be great freedom within those boundaries, or the young composer will not view the piece as his or her own work. Too many teacher prescriptions usually result in inexpressive exercises, not evocative compositions. Often these challenges can be overcome by exposing students to multiple composition models and pieces created by more experienced peers.

Social Learning

Conveniently, middle school students are masters of social learning. When one student or group of students needs a particular technique or skill, peers will be sought out for advice and guidance long before the question or concern reaches the teacher. This is not a glimpse of their commentary on the teacher's ability; they simply prefer each other and are accustomed to seeking peer advice through their myriad social networks. These natural tendencies to congregate and interact provide the foundation for establishing a community of learners where helping each other can be a routine matter. Establishing the music classroom as a community of learners is a process. Some students may find it difficult to learn to trust and value each individual in a middle school general music classroom. Peer approval is very important to these students, and some will be reluctant to try to compose if they feel they cannot succeed at it. Even those who do create pieces may be reluctant to share them if the setting is not psychologically safe. Yet most composers benefit from the peer interaction and feedback that a community of peer composers can provide. For advice on creating a community of composers, please see chapter 6, "Designing and Working in a Composing Community," in *Minds on Music: Composition for Creative and Critical Thinking* (Kaschub & Smith, 2009).

Finally, it is the composition teacher's challenge to help middle school students find the balance between *thinking in music* (the naturalistic finding and making of meaning in sounds) and *thinking about music* (using knowledge of tools and techniques to enhance the artistic craftsmanship that can shape sounds into meaningful organization). It is a worthy instructional goal to assist these students in exercising their understanding of musical meaning through the process of original creation. This is best accomplished with a combination of asking questions to encourage reflection, encouragement in the process, and praise for what composer, peers, and teacher all recognize as productive musical efforts and achievements.

GETTING STARTED: PROJECTS THAT WORK

There is a wide range of composition activities that are attractive to and appropriate for middle level composers, partly because there is such a wide range of interests among these students. All of the composition projects that follow have been successfully used in our own classrooms as well as in the classrooms of the students who have graduated from our college music education programs. The first few examples are short introductory projects that work well in introducing students to composition. These are followed by two more teaching projects that appeal to a very wide range of students: songwriting and film scoring. It is not necessary for the introductory activities to precede the longer projects. They may be undertaken in any order.

LEITMOTIFS FOR FAVORITE OBJECTS

The purpose of this lesson is to develop students' awareness of feelingful human experience; in this case, the feelings relate to a particular object and sound (see table 11.1).

VARIATIONS ON A THEME

Listening to music fulfills several important functions for adolescent composers. First, it allows them to develop their personal definitions of music. Through exposure to music, students discover universal, cultural, and individual ways of thinking about and within music. Second, they develop analytical and critical listening skills that are important components of self-assessment. (Young composers need to learn to objectively evaluate their own compositions.) Finally, it is through listening that young composers develop their aural palettes—the bank of sounds and sound gestures that are available for manipulation within their own work. Every direct engagement with music fosters another way of knowing and understanding music that can inform compositional practice (see table 11.1).

INVENTING NOTATION FOR FOUND SOUNDS

The activity also outlined in table 11.1 is designed to help students discover why standardized notational practices have evolved and how composers use notation to communicate their compositional intentions to performers.

While these activities are good introductory exercises, the real power of composition at the middle school level comes through two longer projects that often have broad appeal among these students: songwriting and film scoring. The next two sections of this chapter provide guidelines and suggestions for implementing these compositional projects.

SONGWRITING

Songs are omnipresent within our culture. They are used to celebrate cultural holidays, enhance religious observances, and reflect on important historical and political events. Songs can be used to portray and reflect upon conditions and events that are analogous to both real and imagined human experiences. By allowing us to experience a range of feelings and emotions, songs can be important tools for developing an understanding of ourselves, of others, and of the cultural context of the world. When songs are used to mark memorable events, they make such events special by drawing people into a unified experience. For example, when people gather at birthday parties and sing "Happy Birthday" (Hill & Hill, 1893), all attendees are drawn into a common experience for the duration of the song. In this way, songs build community and a sense of belonging. Similarly, middle school students often share musical tastes as a way of connecting with peers and defining inclusive and exclusive peer groups.

Perhaps at no other time are humans so thoroughly engaged in the exploration and definition of self than during the middle school years. Songwriting is well matched to this developmental stage because it allows for personal exploration and expression with a safe context. Middle school students are walking contradictions. They want rules and freedom, autonomy and guidelines, independence and acceptance. Teachers can capitalize on these natural tendencies by balancing freedom and boundaries. Students are generally most comfortable, productive, and successful when those freedoms are framed with a few imposed constraints.

Table 11.1. Leitmotifs, Variations, and Found Sounds

Leitmotifs for Favorite Objects

Teacher modeling	Bring an object to class that has particular meaning for you. This might be a memento of a vacation, a favorite item of clothing, an item from your own adolescence or anything you think might interest your classes. Bring several objects if you wish. Discuss the significance of the object and have the students identify the emotional tone color of the items.
Student preparation for composition	For next time, invite students to bring a single object that has meaning for them. At the start of the next class, discuss the objects and the type of emotional tone color.
Defining concept and related activity	Explain what a leitmotif is and have the students try to create a leitmotif for their objects. These can be created on instruments, computers, or vocally on a neutral syllable. Encourage them to keep the motifs short enough that they can remember them until the next class. If possible, record their motifs.
Reflective compositional analysis	During the next class, play the recordings or have students perform for the class while the class tries to identify the feeling or possibly guess the object. Discuss similarities and differences among the various thematic fragments. Why do these similarities and differences exist?
Extensions	Partner composers of contrasting leitmotifs together to join their work to create a longer piece, or ask individual composers to create a second leitmotif reflecting the original object in an unusual setting (e.g., teacup in a pool; baby rattle in a locker; sports trophy in a bathroom, etc). Combine the original and new leitmotifs into a longer work Alternatively, ask the composer to use the leitmotif as the melodic basis for a short, composition. Offer a variety of options, as different students might prefer different tasks.

Variations on a Theme

Teacher model/ collaborative listening analysis	Work with students to either create or follow a listening map for Charles Ives' *Variations on America* or Morton Gould's *American Salute* or another theme and variations work.
Defining key concepts	Discuss how the variations identified were created (including appropriate vocabulary such as augmentation and diminution). Create a list of variation techniques.
Compositional activity	Divide students into small groups and allow them to select one or two variation techniques to apply to a familiar song or simple tune (*This Land is Your Land* or the first section of *Yankee Doodle* work well). Each group will need a least one melodic instrument or confident singer.
Performance/ listening analysis	Invite each group to share their variation while listeners try to determine which variation techniques the composers used.

Inventing Notation for Found Sounds

Student preparation	Ask students to find something at home that can make at least two different sounds and to bring it to class.
Exploring materials	In class, have the students demonstrate their sounds and classify them in similar timbre groups.
Composition activity	Have students form groups of mixed timbres (three or five per group) and make up a short piece.
Notation	Instruct students to create a score for their piece without using traditional notation. Once pieces are scored, have groups trade scores and instruments.
Performance/creating need-to-know	Each group is to prepare a performance from the score they were given. Have the composers comment on the accuracy of the performance. Note: these performances tend to be quite inaccurate!
Discussion	After all performances and commentary, discuss why composers use notation and what traditional and nontraditional notation can and cannot convey.

Songwriting can capitalize on the preferred learning styles of the students. Many middle school students like to work with peers. They gain new knowledge and perspectives as they draw upon what others say and do in their own work. Their reactions to the music of others often informs their own choices and can lead to supportive learning environments when encouraged and reinforced by the teacher. Other students may prefer to work alone and find solo songwriting to best suit their individual working processes.

Songwriting can capitalize on a wide range of student interests. Popular music is, by its very nature, interdisciplinary. It can provide opportunities for students to deeply engage themselves in a wide range of topics. Such study can lead to accessible and highly desirable connections to other areas of learning. Growing up, love, politics, social justice, current events, and historical events are just a few of the more common topics middle school students can explore through songwriting.

The Building Blocks of Popular Song

A common language often facilitates peer feedback and discussion among groups of songwriters. For teachers who need a refresher on the typical parts of a popular song, here are some terms and definitions useful for discussing songwriting with students.

Intro   An abbreviation of *introduction*. The intro is often instrumental and sets up the song. It may outline an underlying chord progression or establish a unifying motive.

Hook   The part of the song that catches the listener's ear. This is often an ironic lyric or musically interesting motive.

Lyrics   The words to the song. They provide information about situations, stories, emotions, and characters within the song.

Verse   The organization of lyrics into multi-line units. The verse typically tells the story or presents information within the song. Verses feature the same music, but have different lyrics.

Pre-chorus The lines of the song leading to the chorus or refrain. Often the same each time they occur, they may vary slightly to reflect an unfolding story. The pre-chorus is often included to create a sense of anticipation that heightens the emotional impact of the chorus.

Chorus	The lines or lines of the song that are repeated between verses. These lines often contrast musically with verses. The chorus is usually heard three or four times. The lyrics and music of the chorus are the same or almost the same for each repetition. The chorus is often the most memorable part of the song and requires special attention. The song's title is usually included in the chorus.
Refrain	A chorus consisting of a single line or musical phrase, which may be repeated once each time it recurs. However, the word *refrain* is often used as a synonym for the word *chorus*, and teachers may choose not to distinguish them.
Bridge	A contrasting section that establishes anticipation prior to the return of either verse or refrain. The bridge can also connect verse and chorus with lyrics, melody, and chord progressions that differ from previously heard material.
Beat	Often refers to the nonvocal layers of a hip hop or rap song. The beat is typically composed of looped recordings of drum rhythms, which underpin the song.
Collision	Requires that two or more different parts of a song are brought together and overlapped. This is usually done to create tension.
Breakdown	Takes a fully developed section of the music and introduces it again beginning with a single part (perhaps the beat) and then adding other parts until the whole is again present.
Instrumental solo	Features a single instrument, often the guitar, but other instruments as well. The solo is often called the instrumental verse as it typically precedes a repetition of the chorus.
Outro	The conclusion of the piece, which is often achieved through *repeat and fade*. The outro is the equivalent of a *coda* in classical music.

While the formal organization of songs can take many shapes, the most common form for the lyrics of popular songs is verse 1/chorus/verse 2/chorus/bridge/chorus. Audiences find this form appealing because it provides both repetition and contrast (we hear two verses that are identical melodically but with different words and three choruses identical in both text and melody). Another similar form includes the instrumental verse, which usually goes verse 1/chorus/verse 2/chorus/instrumental solo/chorus. Most often, these forms are preceded by an intro and end with an outro. Examples of popular standards where the verse contrasts highly with the chorus are "Penny Lane" by the Beatles (1967) and "California Girls" by the Beach Boys (1965).

Occasionally songs follow a simple verse-chorus form in which the music is the same or very similar for both the verses and the chorus. Examples of this include "Umbrella" by Rihanna featuring Jay-Z (2007) and "La Bamba" by Ritchie Valens (1959). Even these sometimes have a contrasting bridge section as in "Purple Haze" by Jimi Hendrix (1967) or "New Divide" by Linkin Park (2009).

Another form often used by teachers of middle school students is the twelve bar blues with its distinctive chord progression and AAB lyrical form. This can be appealing to many students if they are already familiar with the form. If not, this type of activity will need careful preparation using a variety of co-compositional activities, including listening, singing, playing, and improvisation, so that the young composers have the sound and feel of the twelve bar blues in their ears. Without this aural palette, these compositions can be somewhat less than satisfactory.

Planning for Songwriting Activities

Every songwriter finds an approach to writing that fits his particular creative process, but it is important for teachers to consider the overarching elements of the experience before beginning work with students (see table 11.2). Careful consideration of these guiding questions will help ensure that the activities are successful for students and the teacher.

Approaches to Songwriting

Songwriting, like all composition, is a process. One idea eventually will lead to the unfolding or discovery of the next. Some ideas will be discarded and others will be reworked. Experienced songwriters usually know a good idea when they have it, but it can take a long time to critically and objectively reflect on a song to refine and polish their initial ideas into musically effective moments. Still, sometimes magic happens and things intuitively fall into place. A specific approach to songwriting does not exist. Middle school students need the time to try out various ways of working so that they can find and develop a method that reliably works a majority of the time for themselves.

Table 11.2. Planning for Songwriting Activities

1. What are students to learn as they compose?

2. What is your goal as a teacher for this assignment? Is it a goal that students will understand and adopt?

3. What do students already know, both formally and informally, at the outset of the activity?

4. What foundational knowledge or skills will students need to be successful? How will they acquire this knowledge/skill/understanding?

5. Why will the students be interested in this project? If not, rethink. How can the teacher create "buy-in" for this activity? How will the teacher keep students engaged and moving forward until internal motivation is established?

6. Can students access song models to inform their work? How will they do this?

7. Will students work alone, in pairs, in small groups, as a whole class or in some combination?

8. What tools (instruments, recording devices, computers, etc.) are available for students to use? Is there any way to increase the tools available? Can students provide any?

9. How much instructional time will be devoted to this project? Will students have work to complete outside of school?

10. Will the resulting products be shared or performed? At what points? (For example: Sharing beginning ideas? Sharing for feedback as the work progresses? Sharing only with teacher? Public performance?)

11. Will the work be formally assessed? How will this be done and to what end? Will there be a rubric, checklist or some other set of guidelines? If so, when will these be shared with the students?

Often teachers decide which should come first—the text or music—based on their own ideas of how songwriting should proceed. This may or may not be compatible with the way young songwriters begin. It may be better to present an assignment and step back to see what happens as the students begin to work. The text or lyrics question is not the only way of proceeding. Many singer-songwriters (people who are very comfortable and familiar with singing melodies) often imagine "lyrics and melody" as one unit and do not create them separately. Students who are comfortable with their singing voices may also work things out in this manner.

Conversely, songwriters who are principally instrumentalists may begin with a melody without text, or create a chord progression, before finding suitable lyrics to join to their musical ideas. Students required to create either lyrics or melody first may view such guidance as a roadblock to their natural creative processes. Therefore, teachers must think carefully before prescribing an approach to songwriting. While teacher modeling of music-first or lyric-first approaches can be helpful to inexperienced songwriters, some students will have their own effective ways of approaching the task and should be allowed to flourish in this capacity.

Working with Lyrics

Regardless of whether students begin with music, words, or a combination of the two, at some point every songwriter must consider lyrics. What is the song really about? Is there an underlying theme? Is the song a story, commentary, or some other type of work?

Multiple vantage points and statements can be made about any topic. Suppose the students plan to write about parents. What is it they wish to express about that relationship? Can they think of a good metaphor? How many related words can they list? These words can be turned into phrases and spun into lyrics. Lyrics may rhyme or not, but sometimes rhyming is the easiest approach for novice songwriters. As songwriters generate lyrics, they should consider perspective. Will the song be delivered in first or third person? Is the songwriter the narrator or is the song being sung for someone else to sing? Lastly, who is the intended audience for the song? If students are using a lyric-first approach, it is now time to develop music.

Song-Getting

Lyrics often have inherent melody and rhythm. These natural tendencies are good starting places for creating a song melody, but it is also interesting for students to expand or play with these initial ideas to create something more poignant and interesting for the listener. While students are often firmly wedded to their own first ideas, it is possible to get them to think more creatively about their work if they see many models of techniques for expanding an idea.

One approach to deriving a melody from the lyrics is to read them aloud multiple times while listening for the natural rhythm of the words. Inspiration may be found through practicing the lyrics of other songs while attending to how the words have been crafted. Students can play with different ways of saying a line and should be encouraged to read the lyrics expressively, but differently each time. With each repetition, they can notice where things seem to naturally lift higher or drop lower. They may choose to elongate some words, or make other changes that enhance the natural flow of the line. (Note that good ideas have feet and brilliant ideas can quickly run away!) Record ideas whenever possible to make sure that students don't lose their best ideas in the process of finding others.

Memorable melodies exhibit several key characteristics. They often have internal repetition. Composers use repetition to provide a sense of unification. Another tool used to boost memory power is varied phrase lengths that unfold in some sort of pattern. The combination of repetition, phrase patterning, and rhyme schemes within lyrics helps the listener remember the song. Additionally, songs that stick in one's memory often have a hook. This important little idea plays a big role in helping people recall tunes and may figure prominently in the selection of a song title. While hooks are often critical to the success of a song and the evolution of a song title, titles typically emerge in the mid-to-late stages of songwriting as the song matures and begins to assume its nearly finished form.

Rap and Hip Hop for Beginners

Some songs are lyric driven but de-emphasize melody in favor of more complex rhythmic elements delivered through speech. Rap and hip hop songs fit this category and are very appealing to middle school composers. Lyrics, often with complex internal rhyme schemes, are coupled with fast-moving rhythms to create a sense of urgency and forward motion. Rap and hip hop songs are usually created over a rhythm track. To create these songs, artists typically begin by laying down a beat.

The beat is the background rhythm track that provides a foundation for the lyrics of the rap. There are many Internet-based or freeware programs that students can use at a computer (in addition to commercially available products such as GarageBand, Acid, or Reason), plus a rapidly expanding collection of similar products intended for use on cell phones. Creation of beats through looping and sequencing programs is usually the first step in writing this type of music.

Rap and hip hop songs typically have a verse/chorus form. While rap may feature spoken word throughout, hip hop songs typically include verses spoken over the rhythm track with a sung chorus. Vocals may also occur during verses but typically are set in the background and contribute to the overall mood of the song rather than being the focus of attention.

Chord-driven Songs

The chordal accompaniment of a song often precedes lyrics for some students. For students just beginning to play guitar or piano on their own or in music exploratory classes, simple tonic–dominant (I–V) chord songs can provide entry to working with harmony in songwriting. (For more information, see Kaschub & Smith, 2009, chapter 11.) In these types of projects, young songwriters begin with common C–G, D–A, or G–D chords and expand to C–am–F–G⁷ or G–em–C–D⁷ (I–vi–IV–V7) progressions as technical skills are acquired. Students may gain further understanding of how these progressions work by following the chord progression used in another song and creating original melodies and lyrics to go over the progression (melodies and lyrics are copyright protected; chord progressions are not).

For students with limited or no access to acoustic instruments, there are computer programs and cell phone applications that allow students to play chords and record chord patterns. Once the foundation of musical accompaniment is established, students can play the progressions repeatedly, trying different combinations of words, phrases, and rhyme schemes until a lyric emerges.

Providing for Performance

Beginning songwriters benefit from opportunities to share and receive feedback. When carefully planned, modeled, and monitored for psychological safety by teachers, a composers' workshop can be an invaluable resource. Although workshops may involve an entire classroom of students, small groups of five or less work best for this type of activity. These workshops can be places to share works-in-progress, ask questions, seek and provide advice, or gauge audience reaction.

The main goal of the workshop is to assist the songwriter in getting his or her own ideas into play. It is not for the teacher or a classmate to reject the composer's efforts or hijack the piece with superimposed ideas. Ownership must be respected at all times. Ideally, these small groups of students help each other grow by sharing and performing their works in an intimate and supportive setting.

As learning to offer and accept constructive commentary is critical within the composers' workshop, students must be taught to ask questions that address songwriting issues rather than performance issues. Students should be encouraged to think about how audiences hear their songs by listening to the reactions of other members of their workshop group. Similarly, they learn to offer comments to their peers that reveal their understanding of the music being shared. Learning to offer constructive criticism that is useful to other composers can be an important step on the path to evaluating one's own ideas.

As students become fluent in the critical analysis of their own works, they begin to consider and experiment with revision. Unless critique is held in balance, it can be difficult for young composers to stop reworking their materials. For this and other reasons, it is good to have deadlines such as opportunities to share their songs with a wider audience. Polishing a song to the point where it is ready for a public presentation is an important and worthwhile endeavor that not all songwriters will be willing to undertake. Sometimes, songwriters are willing to have songs performed, but seek to have others fill the role of performer. Regardless of presentation format, young songwriters should be encouraged to share their songs in places where it is safe and appealing for them to do so. In-class performances can be one option, but public performances where family and friends can attend can also be beneficial. Applause and appreciation can be great motivators to continue creating songs.

FILM SCORING

No longer is scoring an exotic process done in some faraway place. . . . Directors everywhere can hear their synth mockups instantly, and the composer can be the kid down the street.

Sonny Kompanek, 2004

Film scores provide a means for unifying the experience of a film-going audience. This practice began with pianists and organists improvising at theatres showing silent films. Later, "fake books" emerged with pieces titled "Magic: Apparition" or "Heroic Combat." Musical directors often sent notes to theatre musicians suggesting which fake book excerpts to use at different points in the film (Zamecnik, 1913). Finally, these evolutions led to the current practice, in which original music is created for nearly every new film intended for commercial marketing.

Experience in film scoring requires students to explore and develop empathy and awareness of the experience of others. Adolescence is marked by an increased awareness of "I" as students grow toward their adult selves. It is also a time when tweens and teens become increasingly aware of the perceptions and experiences of others. Film scoring draws on this emerging awareness and allows—even requires—young composers to seek artistic ways to explore this new terrain.

Film scoring is appealing to middle school students because it immerses them in multiple facets of technology. It presents a robust, creative, electronic canvas on which they control innumerable variables. Film scoring is an opportunity to both reveal creative potential and exercise control and is perfectly matched to the developmental world that many middle school students inhabit. Moreover, it presents a unique balance of freedom and constraint by the very nature of the task. More importantly, middle school students get to shape and tailor a range of ideas to their own unique needs and interests as they work on these tasks.

Building Blocks of Film Scoring

Without music, the emotional content of films would not be nearly as apparent. Music makes movies come alive and sometimes provides a counterpoint to the actual action. Music provides the emotional lifeblood of each scene, even though it usually is in the background. Music can also provide an emotional frame of reference that enlivens characters and settings in ways that challenge the viewer to recall or project feelings in relation to contexts and experiences. Music helps the movie seem real by awakening feelingful response.

As mentioned in the songwriting section above, a common language often facilitates feedback and discussion. Teachers need to become familiar with these terms and use them with young film score composers.

Score	Sometimes called the *underscore*, the score is the background music for the entire movie.
Source music	Music that comes from a source on-screen such as radios or live performance. It is something that the characters can hear (as opposed to the underscore, which exists for the audience).
Spotting session	A session between director and composer to discuss what kind of music should occur at various points in the film.
Temp track	Existing music inserted under rough cut of film to facilitate communication between director and composer. A temp track is an aural model of what the director wishes the composer to create.
Sequence	A piece of music that is created digitally and played along with a movie clip to test the general appropriateness of the musical idea.
Cue	One specific piece of a musical score for a film. It can range from two seconds to several minutes.
Mock up	A synthesized or digital version of a cue created for a director to preview/approve before live musicians are hired to record.
Rough mix	A recording played along with movie excerpts to determine if the composer's ideas are matching the director's auditory goals.

Sync point or *hit*   A place where the music has to line up exactly with a specific frame in the film. It may require adjustments in the music at the duration of eighth or sixteenth note. Any change in the film also requires a change in the music or the music and picture will not hit.

Planning for Film Scoring Activities

Music interacts with film in the form of "partnership." Film scoring, then, is a collaborative endeavor undertaken by the director and the composer. Film directors want music that will reflect and emotionally enhance the story they are sharing. Composers serve an extension of the director by using their unique talents and skills to carry forward a comprehensive artistic vision.

Often the first task for the composer is to determine the theme of the film and to ascertain that this is the theme the director has in mind. This is not a musical theme, but an overarching musical vision of what the screenwriter, producer, and director are trying to say about the subject or story. The theme is not always obvious. The director and the composer need to make sure they share an understanding of what the theme is and how it is to be conveyed in the film. This ensures that the story's theme will be reinforced through the music.

Each type of film genre is accompanied by certain musical expectations. These expectations are culturally determined. For example, repeated exposure to certain sound and image pairings makes many Americans expect the driving rhythms of hoof beats and expansive brass melodies as the camera sweeps the plains in cowboy/western films. Similar expectations could be defined for other genres of film. A class discussion exploring what type of music students expect to hear for action, adventure, comedy, crime, drama, documentary, historical/period, horror, musicals, sci-fi, or war/antiwar films would establish a foundation for viewing and analyzing how music is used within a particular genre.

All music within a movie is usually related in some fashion. This can easily be heard in many of the scores of John Williams (*Jaws*, *ET*, or *Harry Potter*) or Michael Giacchino (*The Incredibles*, *Ratatouille*, *Up*, or *Star Trek*). Western film scores, like much of Western art music, have both vertical (timbre and tone) and horizontal (melodic and harmonic) elements. While horizontal impressions are the tunes we most readily recognize, the vertical elements capture the essential mood and character of a film. Composers create a unique aural landscape, what we refer to as soundscape, by the choices that they make. These choices include the instruments used, the style of the music, and the relationships between the themes of the movie and of the music. All are important aspects of the sonic/visual palette.

Establishing and Activating a Sonic-Visual Palette

When music for movies is well done, people often pay little attention to it as they watch the film. Movie music is meant to unobtrusively support the visual action. Novice film scorers must establish a sonic-visual palette that they can draw upon as composers. Watching, listening, and discussing short film clips can help build a sense of how film scoring works.

It is helpful for students to watch a film without sound and imagine what sounds they might compose. They should then watch the clip with sound and discuss what choices were similar and different and why. It is not that one composer is "right" and another "wrong" in their choices, but that different approaches may yield a different feeling that envelops a scene. A reverse approach to this activity would be to play only the film music and try to describe what action might be taking place. These activities can then lead seamlessly into short scoring activities.

Scoring

Imagine

Before going on to specific projects, there are common tasks to be considered for film scoring work. First, composers should begin each project by watching the video or reading through the script or book to imagine how the music might sound. Suggest that they take notes about each scene. They should consider what they understand about each scene and what questions they have about it. They should also note any general impressions and sound ideas they have for the work. Can they then discuss how these ideas relate to the director's vision?

Create a Draft

Composers need to be aware of the use of *set-up* music. This is a small motif, or theme, heard many times across a film and blossoms at just the right moment to create an intense emotional impact. It may help to first identify where this impact should occur and what that sound should be like. Next, they can create that theme. Other themes can follow that relate to or contrast with the set-up theme. Sometimes the set-up moment is composed first and then earlier moments are created by stripping away some of the material from the set-up.

In addition to the set-up, film composers often use leitmotif (offered earlier in this chapter as an entry-level project) to capture the emotional overtones of characters or important objects within character-driven stories. Perhaps one of the most widely recognized leitmotifs from the world of film is that associated with the shark in *Jaws*. The very simple two-pitch, half-step exchange set at a very low register has caused millions of people to look down into the deep, even if they are just in their swimming pools! Other excellent examples of leitmotif include Klaus Badelt's theme for the pirate ship the *Black Pearl* in *Pirates of the Caribbean* as well as John Williams's themes for Darth Vader and Princess Leia in *Star Wars*.

Score

Creating a full score can be an exciting as well as a daunting task. Regardless of the size of the project, students need to analyze the film to identify its major scenes. Next, they need to create title and credit sequences as well as smaller episodes of music that simply fill or support transitions between scenes. Once a thorough listing of all these musical episodes has been created, composers can begin to organize their musical ideas with a meta-vision of how the music will unfold across the entirety of the film. After the musical outline is completed, composers can work at major sections and smaller sections in any order as long as they remain aware of how they are using set-up moments and meeting sync points.

Before students begin to fully score movies, it may be beneficial for them to hear from other composers and movie directors about the processes and approaches that they have found to be highly successful. The following is a list of video interviews with some of the most sought-after composers of film scores:

1. Interview with Hans Zimmer—*Pirates of the Caribbean*: www.youtube .com/watch?v=Mikd1erXdJw
2. Interview with John Williams—*ET*: www.youtube.com/watch?v=noGnO_ glDek
3. Interview with Michael Giacchino—*Up*: www.filmscoreclicktrack .com/2009/06/composing-for-characters
4. Sampling of some of the best film scores for 2009: www.filmscoreclicktrack .com/2009/12/top-10-film-scores-of-2009

Getting Started: Pre-Film

One of the easiest places to begin with middle school students is to score picture books. Halloween picture books are particularly good for this. *The*

House That Drac Built by Judy Sierra, with illustration by Will Hillen-brand (1995), is a particular graphic book that lends itself well to imaginative scoring. Another book for this project is *Shake Dem Halloween Bones* by W. Nikola-Lisa and Mike Reed (1992). A children's librarian can help locate other picture books that can work well with this type of assignment. The key factors to consider when choosing books are engaging stories, evocative settings, interesting characters, and implied or stated sounds. The music that composers create for books follows the same guidelines as those indicated for creating leitmotif or background music for film. Their completed projects could be shared with younger classes, siblings, or the local children's library.

Longer picture books and shorter chapter books with many pictures can also be used. One that we like especially well for this assignment is *Louise, the Adventures of a Chicken* by Kate Dicamillo, illustrated by Henry Bliss (2008). This book can be divided among the members of a class with each group responsible for one of the four sections of the text. Having a copy of the book for each group when working on this project is very helpful for facilitating the work of the composers. A unifying theme for the main character, Louise, can be created by the class, with various other ideas representing her adventures created in small groups.

Working with Shorts, Cartoons, and Films

One possible place to start working with actual films is with clips from old silent movies. Charlie Chaplin is particularly appealing, and clips of his work are often quite short. Teachers can *scrub* any sounds out of the movies using GarageBand or other similar software, or simply turn the sound off when playing a movie for the class. Students then create a soundtrack for the film using looping software, classroom instruments, or whatever tools are available.

A similarly organized project might draw on a segment from a recent popular movie. Even scoring a teaser or a trailer from a film that is currently showing in theatres can be intriguing and instructive. Students can select their own segments and justify their choices, or teachers could present a variety of segments from which the students choose one to score. Here, the element of choice is an important one: students need to feel a sense of ownership and identity. When possible, avoid having everyone do the same assignment on the same segment.

Cartoons can be another powerful entry into the world of film scoring and can help students develop an understanding of what makes for humorous sounds. Analyzing old *Looney Tunes* clips for effective use of sound and then creating new soundtracks for them is often entertaining. Some students will be drawn to adventure cartoons and may enjoy creating a soundtrack for an imaginary video game or for a video game they enjoy playing. (A broad array of cartoons, movies, and short films for these projects can be found at www.archive.org.)

While creating music for existing films is rewarding, it will not take long for students to suggest that they could create their own videos. Storyboarding becomes an important element when at first approaching this project. The video usually precedes the creation of the score. In fact, creating a radio ad where there is only sound that complements a script is advisable before attempting a video project. Fake political ads work well, as will political ads for peers who are running for class offices. Often it is helpful to study real political ads—both positive and negative—and then have students try to create similar ones. These audio projects must also be storyboarded before they are recorded. The process for creating audio that accompanies video becomes clearer when the students create video shorts.

Video shorts can be related to other curricular areas. Time-lapse videography enhances science and science fair presentations. Videos created in the style commonly associated with Ken Burns can augment history and history fair exhibits (for examples, see www.pbs.org/kenburns). Even a book report comes to life with a video segment acted and scored by classmates. These longer projects can often work well when team-taught with the other curriculum area teachers. There are many ways to learn more about video production and editing using whatever video software is available on the platform used at your school. On Apple computers use iMovie, iDVD, and GarageBand. On computers using Windows consider using Acid Music Studio and Windows Movie Maker 2. Tutorials are available for all of these programs. In fact, older students may already be familiar with them.

Showings (Popcorn and Movie Nights)

Once projects have been completed, they should be shared. The first sharing may be held before the product is finished so that the composers can obtain feedback from their fellow composers about what seems to be working well and what might need to be reconsidered in their work. This initially can be in the form of a composers' workshop, and as things near completion, a whole class viewing, complete with popcorn, provides a celebratory context.

Eventually, there should be a public showing for parents, friends, and other interested people to attend. This "movie night" can be advertised and accompanied by popcorn and other refreshments. Here, brief presentations by the composers and filmmakers, either before or after the viewing, where they describe what to listen for and notice about the music and the film, might be included.

CONCLUSION

Once students begin to compose, it is helpful to encourage them by expanding their opportunities. Bringing a professional composer into the classroom can be an interesting experience and often expands what the students consider to be *real* composition. When a local composer is not available, Internet conferencing is a possibility. In this situation, a composer at a local university may be interested in fulfilling this role.

Encourage students to submit their compositions to regional and statewide composition activities, especially those that provide comments and feedback to all participants. Additionally, set up composition concerts to display students' compositions for those who wish to perform them. Encourage all composers to participate or to have their pieces performed.

Students learn to compose by composing. No number of class discussions about music, analyses of listening or video examples, or exercises in applying rules extracted from historical or cultural practices will, in and of themselves, teach students to compose. Songwriting and film scoring appeal to different types of students. Once introduced to the basics of these musical activities, middle school students often use the techniques on their own and for their own purposes. Many find it a source of strength and self-expression to be able to communicate using these media.

Composition can be taught. Teachers who provide opportunity, inspiration, guidance, feedback, and support through all stages of the process allow students to develop and exercise their musical autonomy. In so doing, they will watch their students blossom musically and become self-motivated, engaged, focused, and artistically empowered. Well-taught composition classes are powerful gifts, a gift of time and of artistic power that all middle school students deserve.

REFERENCES

Kaschub, M., & Smith, J. (2009). *Minds on music: Composition for creative and critical thinking.* Lanham, MD: MENC/Rowman & Littlefield Education.
Kompanek, S. (2004). *From score to screen: Sequencers, scores and second thoughts— the new film scoring process.* New York, NY: Omnibus Press, Schirmer Trade Books.
Sam Fox Moving Picture Music. S. Zamecnik, 1913.

ADDITIONAL RESOURCES

Deutsch, D. (2010). Mentoring young composers: The small group, individualized approach. *School Music News, 73*(5), 24–28.

Wiggins, J. (1990). *Composition in the classroom: A tool for teaching.* Reston, VA: MENC.

Chapter Twelve

Making Music Mine!
A Centers-Based Approach
for Middle School General Music

Suzanne L. Burton

Middle school students are naturally drawn to music. For most adolescents, music serves as an outgrowth for self-expression and creativity. Because middle school students learn best through interaction with their environment and active participation (Knowles & Brown, 2000), the use of a music-based learning center in general music is an optimal way to structure and extend their musical learning. The idea of learning centers in education is not a new concept. Many teachers use them, but they are typically found in early childhood and elementary education (Burton, 2004). The principles for using learning centers in middle school general music are similar to those found in the early years; a music center approach offers educational autonomy to the learner while providing a means for extending and differentiating instruction (Reyes, 2010). Moreover, a music center approach caters to adolescents' needs for socialization and the social construction of knowledge (Bruner, 1986; Myers, 1993). Learning through a music center approach provides middle school students with opportunities for engaging in musical inquiry and developing musical independence, while nurturing artistic and creative processes that build musical skills to last a lifetime.

WHAT IS A MUSIC CENTER?

There are no set rules that govern how a music center is implemented in middle school general music. In basic terms, a music center is an area within a classroom that is created to help students fulfill curricular goals through hands-on activities. The arrangement of the center depends on students' needs, curricular priorities, space limitations, and scheduling considerations.

A music center may be a single station within the middle school music class-room, designed to focus on a particular aspect of music—a place where students work independently on a specific project, such as a listening center or a composition center. At the other end of the continuum, a music center may be the conversion of an entire classroom into a number of stations. In this paradigm, students are charged with being self-starters, rather than being taught solely through direct instruction from the teacher. Stations may be designed for students to work independently, collaboratively in small groups, peer to peer, or through a combination of these approaches. In this type of center, a variety of musical and learning options are provided to students, and each student is able to work in ways that complement his or her musical ability.

MANAGING THE VARIABLES

Your Students

Depending on where you teach, students may be legally required to have some type of music class throughout their middle school education. This means that those students who are not in band, chorus, or orchestra are automatically enrolled in general music. In other states, students may be required to have an arts credit, creating a situation in which some students will choose general music over other visual and performing arts. Still, for other states, there are no requirements and students may choose general music from a host of other elective options. In all of these circumstances, determining the musical backgrounds of your students may take some investigation on your part.

Middle school students in general music will typically have heterogeneous musical backgrounds, spanning from high achievement on an instrument or voice to little or no musical experience beyond elementary general music classes. Moreover, many elementary schools within a district do not coordinate their curriculums so that all students leave their music programs having achieved similar musical skills and knowledge. This creates a scenario in which students arrive at middle school having had diverse educational experiences and encounters with a range of musical methodologies and materials.

To ameliorate this situation, develop an informal assessment to define the extent of your students' prior musical experiences and their musical knowledge. A student musical experience inventory, administered during the first class meeting, will help you to determine your students' abilities, provide information on what your students would find personally meaningful to learn and achieve musically, and help inform you of the types of activities or stations you might include to meet individual students' musical needs (see table 12.1).

Table 12.1. *My Musical Self* Inventory

My Musical Self Name:			Block:
1. *If your life were a movie, what would be your "intro" song?*			
2. *Who is your favorite artist, musician, band?*			
3. *Circle the genres of music you like.*			
Hip Hop	R&B	Rap	Country
Rock	Classic Rock	Punk	Classical
Electronic/Techno	Musical Theatre	Jazz	Other (Describe)
4. *Are you in band, orchestra, or choir?*			
5. *What is your musical background?*			

Do you play an instrument? Yes No
If yes, what do you play?
How long have you been playing the instrument?
Do you take lessons?

Do you sing? Yes No
If yes, do you sing in a choir, band, or solo?
Do you take lessons?

Does anyone in your family play an instrument? Yes No
If yes, what do they play?

6. *If you had a choice, what instrument(s) would you like to play?*

7. *What do you remember about music class from elementary school?*

Class Size

Another variable to consider is the number of students enrolled in your class. Implementing a multi-station learning center may be more difficult for larger groups of students. However, if the number of students participating in any one station is kept between five or six, you can create the appropriate amount of stations for students to participate in simultaneously, keeping everyone involved musically. For classes with large enrollments, a single station may be sufficient to enhance your curriculum by providing a space for small groups of students to rotate through to work on independent musical projects.

Scheduling

No two middle schools share the same scheduling format for general music. For some schools middle school general music is scheduled for an academic year, for others it is scheduled on a semester basis, and some schools treat the class as a six-week exploratory module. Classes may meet daily or within some type of rotation. Instructional periods range from blocked scheduling with longer class periods nearing ninety minutes to shorter class periods of an hour or less. When designing your music learning center, it is necessary to keep the scheduling of the course and your allotted instructional time in mind in order to design a practical number of stations for your class and set realistic achievement expectations for your students.

Resources

Like students' musical achievement, class size, and scheduling, resources also vary widely from one school to another; you may have access to a full keyboard and technology lab, or you may have a sparse number of Orff and percussion instruments at your disposal. A lack of resources shouldn't stop you from developing a music center, as there are a variety of ways to create viable stations that will be musically engaging for your students. Aside from the model described in this chapter, other chapters in this book provide many useful ideas for the creation of stations such as those based upon technology, composition, songwriting, arranging, and listening.

Using the Space

A number of options exist for the formal design of a learning center. How the center is ultimately developed and used will depend on the size of your classroom, how that space is laid out, the number of stations to be included, and student accessibility to each station. One way to create spaces within your classroom is to section off areas with office partitions, large pieces of cardboard, curtains, throw rugs, or a portable chalkboard/whiteboard. A shower curtain on a tension rod also works well as a partition. Boundaries between stations can likewise be structured from classroom items such as bookshelves, tables, chairs, and/or desks. Sections can also be made with the use of large bins that hold materials for particular stations. Students pick up the bins and take them to designated places within the classroom. As you design the center, be sure to take time to think through traffic patterns for student movement between stations, the flow of activities, and how best to structure the space for students' full engagement with the materials.

USING BACKWARD DESIGN FOR AUTHENTIC ENGAGEMENT

When designing the music center, the desired learning goals for your students should be identified and provide the overall framework for the various stations that you choose to include. You may have curricular guidelines that have been set in place by the state, school district, or school that you teach in. The National Standards for Music (www.nafme.org/resources/view/national-standards-for-music-education) provide guidance on what middle school students should know and be able to do musically. The performance standards work well as overarching learning goals, while the achievement standards are helpful for defining objectives, or expectations related to the students' achievement level, and guiding the creation of appropriate assessments (www.nafme .org/resources/view/performance-standards-for-music-grades-5-8).

As suggested by Wiggins and McTighe (2005), working backward in planning the stations of your center will help to ensure that learning is student focused and as authentic or *real-world* as possible. Start by determining the learning goals or outcomes that you desire your students to achieve. Next, create the performance task and rubrics that will be used to measure and evaluate what your students have learned. The performance task should ensure transfer of learning so that students are engaged musically in ways that will facilitate their musical participation outside of the classroom. The rubrics that you develop should also be shared with your students so that they have full understanding of what is expected of them. Consider creating self-assessments with your students as well. Your students will be challenged and more motivated to work diligently toward the performance task when they take part in the assessment process (Rohlheiser & Ross, n.d.). Once you have determined the outcomes for your center, the authentic performance task, and the rubrics you will use to assess student learning, you are ready to develop your music learning center and stations.

A MODEL MUSIC LEARNING CENTER

The Stations

Due to the varied levels of music achievement of middle school students, you should plan for the *process* of music learning *to take precedence over the product* when creating the stations of the center. The model described here was implemented with seventh-grade students. In this school, the general music classes, each with approximately twenty-five students, were on a rotating block schedule, meeting two or three times (depending on the rotation) per week for seventy-two minutes for the duration of a semester. The learning goals of the center were standards based with the highest consideration for engaging students in practical ways with music. Stations were designed to involve students with (a) playing guitar, keyboard, percussion instruments, and drum set; (b) improvising and composing; (c) listening to musical selections and learning about musical concepts and terminology; and (d) writing or creating responses to journal prompts or articles about musicians and genres, as might be found in the magazine *In Tune* (www.intunemonthly.com). Singing was emphasized as a whole group activity and was often used as the basis for learning how to play the guitar and keyboard. Rhythmic development was also an aspect of group instruction and was further enhanced in the percussion station.

Classroom Design

The use of a centers approach to middle school general music will result in a productive, yet noisy, classroom. Therefore, the design of the classroom and consideration of noise level guided the layout of the stations I desired to include. There were permanent risers, which were a natural fit for the guitar station. Because students could use headphones for the keyboard, listening, and electronic drum set stations, these stations were placed near walls with electric outlets. The composition and read-and-write stations were assigned to one end of the classroom so that students could have as much quiet as needed to concentrate on their work (see figure 12.1).

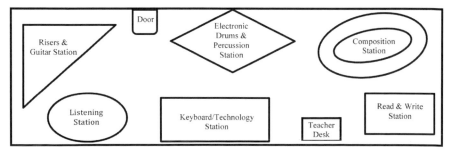

Figure 12.1.   Classroom Layout

Typical Class Format

Class normally began with whole group instruction. During this time, students would learn to sing popular or multicultural songs along with chord root accompaniments that were based on the song's harmonic progression. After whole group instruction, students were sent to the different stations. They worked on learning the tunes and accompaniments that had been taught at the beginning of class in the guitar, keyboard, and percussion stations. In these stations they also learned how to follow a lead sheet and read basic music notation—all based upon the familiar music they had learned aurally in whole group instruction.

In the listening station, students tracked and created listening maps to music from a wide variety of musical genres ranging from classical to pop and rock. They read about musicians and the music industry and completed creative writing projects (such as developing interview questions for the artist whose music they were learning to play) in the read-and-write station, and made instruments from recyclable materials students brought in to class to be used in compositions that they had created in the composition station. The students rotated in clockwise fashion in small groups among three different stations per class period. That way, all students had ample time in each station in a given week. An appointed timekeeper, who used a kitchen timer to track the amount of time students spent in each station, would signal students to move from one station to the next.

Station Materials

Materials were carefully prepared for students to begin working on without my immediate help so that I could move among the students and provide them with small group and individual instruction. Peer-to-peer learning was also implemented, and students often used the *show me how to play* method of shared instruction. Instructional worksheets, YouTube videos converted on Zamzar (www.zamzar.com) and downloaded for playback in QuickTime, GarageBand loops and tutorials, and other Internet materials also functioned as teaching assistants. In addition, each station had a station master, a student who acted as a peer facilitator. Station masters were selected according to their level of musical achievement and/or ability to take on a leadership role and were responsible for making sure that each station had the necessary materials (music, instruments, equipment), and for overseeing that all materials were in order for the next group to use. Station masters changed with each station.

BIG JAM UNIT

One goal of the middle school general music curriculum was to provide an ensemble experience for students to use and develop their singing voices and play instruments that they would be likely to play outside of school (such as guitar, keyboard, and percussion instruments). This musical experience was created to emulate informally based ensembles that occur outside of the classroom. The performance goal became the basis for the culminating experience, or performance task, of the general music class, with the hope that students would, in turn, be inspired to seek out these experiences. In association with backward design, the performance task was the creation of a final performance of a song in which students would use the musical skills and knowledge that they had obtained from participating in whole group instruction and in each station of the learning center. For this unit, the performance task was referred to as the *Big Jam*, and the refrain to Bob Marley's song "One Love" was at the foundation of the music center and its corresponding stations. Implementation of this unit took place during the last ten class periods of the semester with a *Big Jam* performance of "One Love" given at the final class.

Assessment of the *Big Jam* Performance Task

Myers (1994) suggests, "Assessment should reflect the nature of music learning and not be reduced to easily graded tests of information" (p. 67). Assessments that address students' individual musical growth and the extent that they incorporate active music making into their everyday lives should serve as the measuring stick for musical achievement in your class (Myers, 1994). When considering the type of assessment that will be used to measure and evaluate your students' performance, bear in mind that the assessment should relate to the knowledge and skills that students have learned and practiced (Duke, 2011). While assessing students' musical engagement outside of class may be a difficult task, you should address students as musical individuals as well as how they compare with their peers (Gordon, 2007). Both types of information are valuable when teaching a class that caters to the development of individual musicality and music making with others. The performance task of the *Big Jam* provided an opportunity for individual student assessment as well as for surveying musical achievement across students within a class.

After determining the outcomes for the *Big Jam*, the assessments were developed. By creating the assessments prior to instruction, the focus of instruction became centered on the evidence that would demonstrate if students had met the outcomes of the unit (Wiggins & McTighe, 2005). Table 12.2 presents a rubric that addresses the performance and achievement standards for singing, playing instruments, and reading music from the National Standards for Music Education. The achievement standards and performance task of the *Big Jam* have been meshed together to create an authentic assessment that denotes students' musical achievement from basic to advanced levels.

The Foundation of the Center: A Song

To prepare students for the *Big Jam*, they first learned to sing the refrain of "One Love" by rote, in the key of C major. The key of C was chosen due to its sing-able range for most middle school students, the general ease of playing the I, IV, and V chords on the guitar, and the ease of locating and maintaining a C major hand position on the keyboard. Through this process, students heard the song performed with solfège, learned how to keep macrobeats and microbeats, and how to identify the tonality and meter of the song. They were then taught to sing a root melody based on the harmonic progression, and eventually sang the song in two parts—the melody with an accompaniment of chord roots; then in five parts—and the melody with an accompaniment of chord tones (for more information on teaching a rote song through this method, see www.giml.org/mlt_classroom.php). I then projected a lead sheet with the melody and chord symbols and modeled how to read (chanting the rhythm with syllables and singing the melody with solfège) the music for the students: first the rhythm, then the melody and the chord roots. We then read the music together. Teaching the song and chordal accompaniment was spread out over four class periods.

After group instruction on the song, students moved to the different stations in the classroom to continue their work on previous projects and begin a transition into stations relating to the *Big Jam* performance task. In the new stations, students researched the history of the reggae genre, listened to a variety of reggae music, and learned about its style and form. They learned about Bob Marley and the Wailers, who made the song famous, as well as other notable reggae artists.

Instrumental Accompaniment

As the class continued to learn "One Love," I modeled how to sing and play the chord progression on the guitar on the macrobeat while the students sang the song. Next, the students followed my model by singing the roots of the I, IV, and V chords while I continued to demonstrate how to play the chords on the guitar while singing the song. We repeated this sequence with students playing "air guitars," gaining kinesthetic practice before actually playing the guitars. I then projected the music and modeled how to read what I had played from the lead sheet. Next, we "played" it together, again with students pantomiming how to play the chords on air guitars. I also taught simple strumming patterns on macro- and microbeats for students to play. After this, the lead sheet for "One Love," a worksheet for students to fill out the fingering for

Table 12.2.   Rubric for Assessing *Big Jam* Performance Task

Performance Standards			
1. Singing, alone and with others, a varied repertoire of music. *2. Performing on instruments, alone and with others, a varied repertoire of music.* *5. Reading and notating music.*			
Achievement Standards	**Basic**	**Proficient**	**Advanced**
1d. Students sing music written in two and three parts.	Student is able to sing the melody of the song.	Student is able to a) sing the song with a small group and b) sing the root melody within a small group performance of the song.	Student is able to a) sing the song with a small group, b) sing the root melody for the harmonic progression, within a small group performance of the song, and sing pitches of the chords from the harmonic progression within a small group performance of the song.
2d. [Guitar; Modified] Students play by ear simple melodies on a melodic instrument and simple accompaniments on a harmonic instrument.	Student is able to pluck the root of chords on the macrobeat during a small group performance of the song.	Student is able to strum full chords on the macrobeat during a small group performance of the song.	Student is able to play full I, IV, and V chords on a down-up strumming pattern on the microbeat during a small group performance of the song.

2d. [Keyboard; Modified] Students play by ear simple melodies on a melodic instrument and simple accompaniments on a harmonic instrument.	Student is able to play the chord roots in 5-finger position hands alone or together on the macrobeat during a small group performance of the song.	Student is able to play open 5th for the I chord, extended 6th for the V chord, and open 4th for the IV chord hands alone or together on the macrobeat during a small group performance of the song.	Student is able to play the dotted 8th-16th reggae rhythm alternating hands with the left hand playing the chord root or chord outlines and right hand playing the outlines of the chords during a small group performance of the song.
2a. [Drum set; Modified] Students perform on at least one instrument accurately and independently, alone and in small and large ensembles, with good stick control.	Student is able to play bass drum with quarter notes on beats 1 and 3 and quarter notes on the snare drum or cymbal on beats 2 and 4 during a small group performance of the song.	Student is able to play bass drum with quarter notes on beats 1 and 3 and two 8th notes on the snare drum or cymbal on beats 2 and 4 during a small group performance of the song.	Student is able to play bass drum with two 8th notes on beats 1 and 3 and a quarter note on the snare drum or cymbal on beats 2 and 4 during a small group performance of the song.
5b. [Modified] Students read familiar melodies, rhythms and lead sheets in the treble clef.	Student reads the vocal or instrumental part from a treble score or lead sheet with many errors; identifies a minimum of musical symbols.	Student reads the vocal or instrumental part from a treble score or lead sheet with some errors; identifies most musical symbols.	Student reads the vocal or instrumental part from a treble score or lead sheet with few errors; identifies all musical symbols.

the "One Love" guitar chords, and a YouTube video that demonstrated how to form and play the chords on the guitar were incorporated into the guitar station for students to begin learning the accompaniment.

The following class I modeled the C major five-finger position on a keyboard and taught students how to sing and play the melody with the right hand. Students sang on solfège while playing imagined keyboards on their thighs. By playing imagined keyboards before using paper or actual keyboards, students were able to gain experience controlling their fine motor muscles without being encumbered with playing the correct keys. I then projected the notation and modeled the process of playing the melody line while singing with solfège; we then played it together, this time with students playing paper keyboards. The lead sheet and a GarageBand loop of the guitar accompaniment were incorporated into the keyboard station for students to practice with. Having headphones for the keyboards and the guitar loop was critical for students to practice and learn how to coordinate their timing of playing the melody with an accompaniment.

For the next class I demonstrated how to play an open accompaniment on the macrobeat using a fifth (C–G) for the I chord, an extended sixth (B–G) for the V chord, and a fourth (C–F) for the IV chord with the left hand. After singing the root melody and playing the left-hand accompaniment on imagined keyboards, I projected a lead sheet with the lyrics and symbols for the chords. A GarageBand loop of the "One Love" melody was added to the keyboard station for students to coordinate the playing of the accompaniment with the melody. In the following class I taught the students how to play the melody with the accompaniment, hands together, again showing them how to associate the notation of the music to what they had just experienced. This was an essential step for students who were ready to play hands together.

During the sixth class, I demonstrated how to play a simple drum set accompaniment that consisted of playing beats one and three on the bass drum, with beats two and four played on the snare drum or hi-hat. Students chanted the rhythm and pantomimed playing the drum set as I played a recording of the song. The technique of modeling and giving students an opportunity for kinesthetic practice—without the complication of coordinating their movement with an instrument—was once again a critical step toward successful transfer to the electronic drum sets. I then showed them how to read the drum chart and incorporated the notation into the percussion station along with the instrumental recording of the song that I had created on GarageBand. Students were then able to hear the drum set and the song through headphones, allowing for student autonomy when practicing.

For the next class, I began instruction with everyone singing "One Love" with the lyrics and root melody on a neutral syllable. Students then moved to the various stations and continued learning the instrumental parts for the song in preparation for the *Big Jam*. During this class period, students also filled out a questionnaire regarding their choice of instrument to play for the *Big Jam*. They were asked to rank their preference for singing, playing guitar, keyboard, or drum set. After class, I made a list of five ensembles based on the students' first or second choice of instrument preference. I also asked the students if they wanted to invite the head and associate principals to the *Big Jam*. The students were very enthusiastic about having the administration come to their performance—so much so that two students created and hand delivered invitations to both principals and their office staff!

Differentiating Instruction

As students practiced their parts in the guitar, keyboard, and drum set stations, I moved among them to facilitate their progress. Because students who are in middle school general music possess widely varying musical skills, I found it necessary to differentiate my instruction to help each student achieve to the best of his or her ability. Table 12.3 indicates the instrumentation and several ways that instruction was differentiated to meet students' needs for playing the guitar, keyboard, and drum set. Notice that the first three skill levels correspond with the performance task rubric found in table 12.2. Students who are able to perform beyond skill level three should be guided toward achieving at skill level four or be challenged according to his or her ability.

Incorporating Self-Assessment

We began class eight by singing and harmonizing "One Love." I then announced the members for the five ensembles. After the ensembles met briefly, they had an opportunity to practice "One Love" while I coached them. (During this time, the other students continued to work at the various stations.) Students were allowed to create their own arrangements based upon their level of ability to play their chosen instruments and their imaginations! Class nine was similar to class eight, with the exception of my sharing a self-assessment rubric with the students so that when they practiced with their ensembles they had criteria to guide and focus their work (see table 12.3). Students completed the rubric and turned it in at the end of the period. The self-assessments provided me with information to further guide students' final practice on the day of the *Big Jam*.

The *Big Jam*

The students were ready to perform "One Love" in their ensembles by the tenth day of instruction. Each group had seven minutes to warm up and practice. I gave the ensembles tips, based on the information I had gleaned from their self-assessments. After each ensemble had practiced "One Love," about forty minutes of class time remained. During the *Big Jam*, each ensemble performed for the class and the school administration, with a final performance of the refrain by everyone in the class. The event was videotaped so that students could watch and evaluate their performances with the *Big Jam* rubric during the next class. At the very end of the performance, everyone enjoyed a reception of cookies and punch to celebrate the musical achievements of the class.

Table 12.3. *Big Jam*: Differentiated Instruction

Instrument	Skill Level 1	Skill Level 2	Skill Level 3	Skill Level 4
Guitar	Pluck chord roots	Strum chords on the beat	Strum chords with a down-up strumming pattern on the microbeat	Play a dotted 8th-16th reggae strumming pattern over chord changes
Keyboard	Play chord root in 5-finger position hands alone or together on the macrobeat	Play open 5th for the I chord, extended 6th for the V chord, and open 4th for the IV chord hands alone or together on the macrobeat	Play the dotted 8th-16th reggae rhythm alternating hands with the left hand playing the chord root or chord outlines and right hand playing the outlines of the chords	Play the melody with the right hand and the outlines of the chords on the macrobeat
Drum Set	Play bass drum with quarter notes on beats 1 and 3 and quarter notes on the snare drum or cymbal on beats 2 and 4	Play bass drum with quarter notes on beats 1 and 3 and two 8th notes on the snare drum or cymbal on beats 2 and 4	Play bass drum with two 8th notes on beats 1 and 3 and a quarter note on the snare drum or cymbal on beats 2 and 4	Play bass drum with a dotted quarter-quarter rhythm and a quarter note on the snare drum or cymbal on beats 2 and 4

Practice and Performance Self-Assessment

Big Jam	Rubric	Name:		Block:
My Group	4-All of the time	3-Most of the time	2-Some of the time	1-None of the time
1) Started the song together				
2) Finished the song together				
3) Stayed together throughout the performance				
4) Played with correct rhythm				
5) Played correct notes				
6) Played with good balance and blend				

I can help to improve the performance of my group by: _____

My group can help to improve our performance by: _____

Reflection

The *Big Jam* unit brought students together in the type of musical ensembles that resembled *out of school* music, creating possibilities for music making that students may have not previously considered. Students learned basic competencies of playing guitar, keyboard, and drum set, as well as how to function in a peer-based ensemble. While this mode of making music was, at times, messy, and did not provide the pristine sound of typical school ensembles, it gave a sense of musical ownership to those students who may not have otherwise had an opportunity to engage in authentic music making.

PRACTICAL CONSIDERATIONS FOR IMPLEMENTING A LEARNING CENTER

Teacher's Role

Your participation in the learning center will take different forms as determined by your students' needs and musical skill levels. You may function as the lead teacher, or as facilitator, guide, active participant, or observer of your students' learning. Participating within the center's activities will help you to view the function of each station from the students' vantage point. As an involved observer, you can watch for ways to extend your students' learning and monitor the usefulness of the activities within each station. Through your involvement you can better time the introduction of specific stations to the center, while determining when stations or activities within them have lost their appeal. Thinking ahead about provisions for differentiation within station activities will be important to enable your students to work independently, thus being overseers of their own learning.

Use of the Center

Once the center has been planned, materials developed and gathered, and everything is ready for use, take time to introduce the stations to your students before they interact with the materials. Provide brief explanations of each station, demonstrating how to use the instruments and equipment as well as how to clean up and store materials. Care should be taken to ensure that students understand whether they are to approach station activities independently, in pairs, or in small groups. Establish guidelines for using each station by cooperatively determining a behavior code to ensure smooth operation of the center. Set specific time limits for working in the stations. Assign the duty of timekeeper to one student, and give leadership roles to students by assigning them to the role of station master to facilitate smooth transitions between stations. Finally, involve your students in the evaluation of the center: ask them for their opinions and their ideas for activities. At this age, they often know the tools they need for learning music and have great ideas to share.

CONCLUSION

Music-based learning centers are ideal for middle school students who come to the general music classroom with varied skills and abilities. Through their use, both independent and collaborative music learning is fostered. Moreover, the social, inquisitive, active, and involved nature of adolescent learners may be capitalized upon. A music-based learning center has much to offer your students, whether it is a springboard for musical creativity or a way to develop or strengthen musical skills. Whatever your learning goals, a music-based learning center just might be what you need in your classroom for your students to learn in a fresh and novel way.

REFERENCES

Bruner, J. (1986). *Actual minds, possible worlds*. Cambridge, MA: Harvard University Press.

Burton, S. L. (2004). *Making connections through music-based learning centers*. Retrieved from www.teach-nology.com/tutorials/teaching/music

Duke, R. A. (2011). *Intelligent music teaching*. Austin, TX: Learning and Behavior Resources.

Gordon, E. E. (2007). *Learning sequences in music: A contemporary music learning theory*. Chicago, IL: GIA.

Knowles, T., & Brown, D. (2000). *What every middle school teacher should know*. Westport, CT: Heinemann.

Myers, D. (1994). General music: Present and future. In J. Hinckley (Ed.), *Music at the middle level: Building strong programs* (pp. 63–68). Reston, VA: MENC.

Myers, J. (1993). Curricular designs that resonate with adolescents' ways of knowing. In R. Lerner (Ed.), *Early adolescence: Perspectives on research, policy, and intervention*. Hillsdale, NJ: Lawrence Erlbaum, 191–206.

Reyes, C. L. (2010). A teacher's case for learning center extensions in kindergarten. *Young Children, 65*(5), 94–98.

Rohlheiser, C., & Ross, J. A. (n.d.). *Student self-evaluation: What research says and what practice shows*. Retrieved from www.cdl.org/resource-library/articles/self_eval.php

Wiggins, G., & McTighe, J. (2005). *Understanding by design* (2nd ed.). Alexandria, VA: Association for Supervision and Curriculum Development.

ADDITIONAL RESOURCES

Books

Bennett, M. D. (1978). *Surviving in general music II*. Memphis, TN: Pop Hits.

Hinckley, J. (Ed.). (1994). *Music at the middle level: Building strong programs.* Reston, VA: MENC.

Regelski, T. (2004). *Teaching general music in grades 4–8.* New York, NY: Oxford University Press.

Schafer, R. M. (1976). *Creative music education: A handbook for the modern music teacher.* New York, NY: Schirmer Books.

Spanko, J. (1985). *Taming the anthill: Zany alternatives for general music.* Memphis, TN: Memphis Musicraft.

Websites

National Association for Music Education: www.nafme.org/s/general_music
Musical Futures: www.musicalfutures.org.uk
Music Education Madness: www.musiceducationmadness.com/beginning.shtml
Noteflight: www.noteflight.com/login
(The) Radio Music Hour: www.theradiohour.net/g01basiclessons.htm
Show Me How to Play: www.showmehowtoplay.com
Vermont Midi Project: www.vtmidi.org